WHY DIE

V. MISLJENOVIC

Cover art by Maria Offin, Kingston, Ontario.

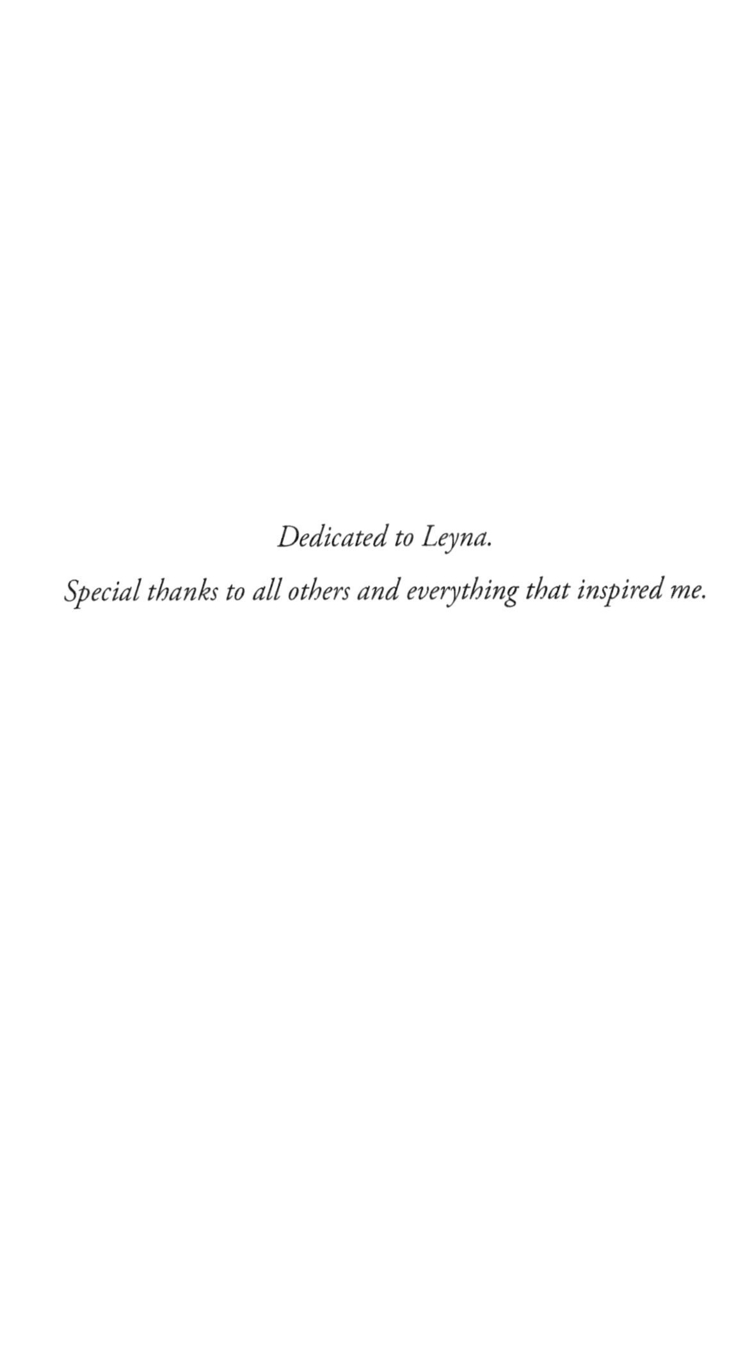

Dedicated to Leyna.

Special thanks to all others and everything that inspired me.

CHAPTER 1

BUSINESS AS USUAL

5:50 AM, I have to visit the bathroom before I damage my internal organs. I couldn't last until 6:30 AM when the alarm usually goes off so I might as well just get up. I shouldn't have had that second beer last night while watching *Vikings*. But it always feels like a good idea at the time, and it will again tonight, and tomorrow night, etc... It's not as bad as it used to be, the drinking, at least I don't get juiced something fierce and spend the next day in a hangover induced fever. Literally fever. These days 2-3 beers tops and I'm hungover the next day. So 1-2 max. to get a little buzzed, and that's it. It's almost as if I'm not living life to the fullest unless I have at least one beer a night. Oh, I'm sure the experts will call this borderline alcoholism. But I disagree. It's just enough liquid to make me feel that I'm not a complete drone slave Monday to Friday. But nowhere near enough to have me classified as an alcoholic. And they love to diagnose everything in this society. Everything needs a label, a drawer and a cabinet to be put inside. I'll do my own thing regardless. So I'm sticking to my diagnosis. Anyways I digress...

I'm slated to do nightly bridge inspections in Ottawa. Starting 9 PM tonight, till 5 AM. Bureau of Transportation doesn't allow inspections of their main expressway arteries during the day, too much traffic, and since Ontario only has a couple of major expressway to begin with blocking traffic to any capacity would pretty much cause the entire economy to self implode. I'll be hanging out over the 417 in a metal boom bucket. The weather is supposed to suck, to be cold and snowy, however Bureau insisted on having the inspections completed now, they probably have to use up their yearly fiscal budget for 2018 before the year-end. So come hell or high water, or in our lucky Canadian's case, come -20C and snow these bridges must get inspected now. So why am I up so early considering I don't have to be hanging under a bridge until 9 PM?! Well I have to get ready, check my emails and make sure I have everything for the inspection including sub-Arctic clothing. I'm training new people from our Ottawa office too so I'm guessing and hoping I won't have to go back next week as I figure one of the young engineers could handle inspecting an entire bridge by himself after only a couple of days shadowing me. He'll get more training than I did when I started out and now I'm a regular champion when it comes to inspecting steel fatigue on our fine and salted Ontario highways. God bless the salt....otherwise I would be out of work...as would be the entire Civil Engineering profession in Canada.

The morning started on a good note. Wife and I spent a significant amount of quality time performing Olympic worthy acrobatics underneath the sheets. Although it was mainly and technically above the sheets. Otherwise, I pretty much feel all morning like I was just given birth to, with eyes opening and closing like those of a newborn. Afterwards I proceeded with warming up the toilet, grooming my body hair (with special attention to plucking my nostrils, if only I could make wishes off of nose hairs like with eyelashes, several would come true already), I showered, shaved, clipped my toe and fingernails, ate breakfast and mucked around on the computer researching the latest obsession that peaked my interest. Now it was firearms, I got my firearms license and everything. I figured it was about damn time to embrace the warmth and love of the killing machines we are so talented at producing. Although my sole intention was to kill small sheets of paper at the shooting range.

Then I decided that I don't need to go to the office, check my emails, talk to my boss, etc...I'll just go grab the rental car, load it up with the equipment crap I have currently in my car and then book it to Ottawa. I'll check my email after I set up my laptop there. See I'm full of great ideas like these which I explain to myself are such clever ways of saving time, staying organized and thorough while at the same time not at all losing on productivity, all the while ensuring not to stress out too much and be short on time. In reality, it's patting myself on the back while coming up with amazing new ways to fulfill my enduring destiny of being a lazy sack of crap.

Finally, 1:30 PM rolled around. I put all my change of clothes, toiletries, equipment, construction winter jacket, long johns (for fucks sakes, it's November 12th...), gloves, winter hat, balaclava (Jesus....), heat packets for hands and feet and God knows whatever else I grabbed and I set off for the car rental place. While I was getting ready political party representatives rang our doorbell twice asking us to vote for whatever mayoral candidate was running for office in our city. I must say I surprised myself at how I was blissfully clueless as to who any of the candidates were as I was equally incredibly surprised that anyone votes worth a shit these days. I used to vote. I got engrossed in politics. From an early age.

And once you stretch that elastic band past its elastic tolerance into the plastic realm and find out shit you probably shouldn't have then good luck voting ever again. And don't tell me the movie *The Matrix* isn't an analogy of our real life. Oh who am I kidding I still read politics only to see to what degree we are being pimped, screwed over and lied to, while at the same time observing who still out there believes in the system. It's fascinating. Witnessing the impending downturn in human civilization. And what a fine, sarcastic cynic I've become. One of the best. It's quite the protective shield. It used to be anger for me, but that became too risky and dangerous, these days sarcastic cynicism does just fine. We are governed by a highly inefficient but ardently hypocritical system of politics. Attention to detail and endless nit-picking is focused on things that matter none while matters of importance go by unnoticed like black energy of the Universe, biggest in volume, strength and magnitude but seldom to be seen, noticed or understood.

I'm finally off with all my equipment, some snacks and a whole lot of dread in my head at the thought that I have to hang out under a bridge all night in -12C. I'm also thinking of my administrative assistant's choice of hotel. Beds Inn. Cheap and effective. Good for the company, bad for the individual person's propensity for rashes. First two nights won't be as cold, ONLY -5C, the middle and end of the inspection tenure is going to be rough. As I was driving I realized I should give my brother a call, haven't had the chance to speak with him earlier, but now being on the road and having 2 hours to kill until my destination I figured what a perfect time to....kill some more time. Now he'll say I only call him during time slots where I'm bored out of my mind and not having anything else important to do, usually to pass time until the next relevant thing I have on the agenda. And I tell him if ever there was an example of the pot calling the kettle black. But unintentional hypocrisy has always been one of my family's trademark traits. My family's tradition actually. We couldn't escape it if you surgically removed it from us. Oh well, everyone carries their crosses. It's Sunday, so still technically the weekend (although Sundays were usually spent by me feeling persistent dread in my stomach due to the fact that the next day was working Monday), so overall still a good time to call him as we usually chat on weekends. The fact that I had to start working Sunday night because I was doing night inspections was a convenient trick actually, it will make me feel Monday that it's Tuesday so that much closer to next weekend.

I dialed Stan's phone number.

"Hey, where are you at?" Our classic start to every conversation.

"I'm here (as if that defined anything), driving to Ottawa for those nightly bridge inspections."

"Uh huh, ok what's new?"

I could have pretty much told him that I just discovered an Alien race living in my basement and his reaction would have been the same. Not quite sure if he registered a single word I said.

"Oh, not much, same old, working away, I have to wrap up some construction projects for the year then focus on designing a couple of bridges during winter while the construction season is down."

"Uh huh, I see..."

"So, what's up with you?"

Dreaded question on my behalf as I know it will lead to the inevitable rambling on about his job.

"Oh, same old, I'm here at my cottage, fiddling around with some design software on my computer. Friday and Saturday night I was up till 3 AM designing away, I feel like my eyes are about to pop out. I didn't get enough done at work, so I had no choice but to continue at home. Plus, people have been getting continually laid off. Who knows what will become of this?! I mean I guess most of the engineering department is still safe but...anything can happen. Fuck my life, every company I work for it's the same thing, when am I ever going to be in safer waters? I'm 43 and still constantly feeling like there is a gun at my head. Like I'm at the beginning, having to prove myself. My eyes are bloodshot, but I just want to get a better handle on working this software, it's super interesting but challenging. I have to pick our lead designer's brain, just in case, he might quit one of these days as he is sick and tired of the bullshit."

Often when we talk, the conversation is frequently steered away from any topic towards the theme of his work. Whether meteor shower or World War 3, Stan tends to steer the discussion towards perpetual fear of losing his job, and how amazingly interesting design work is. During the process he manages to repeat sentences, phrases, words, about 10 times repeatedly like a perpetuum mobile Singer sewing machine. Also, and unfortunately for me Ontario countryside from the 401 was about as interesting as staring at a washing machine so I couldn't exactly get distracted by my surroundings either.

Let me tell you, this was no Slovenia. Luckily for me I have a rather decently ingrained case of ADHD so for a while there I was successfully zoned right the fuck out just staring at the boring ass road in front of me while daydreaming about...weird things I'd rather not disclose. 50 km must have gone by easily in such a manner. However, a danger lied in that approach, I was starting to get sleepy and nod off. Highway hypnosis I believe they called it (back in Driver's Ed class). So I needed to think of something fast to prevent me from flying off the road or from me throwing the phone out the window. Since I couldn't utilize music or the Internet my brain was shutting off quick and I needed a distraction. Alas, I figured it out! The gun course! Of course!! Wife and I recently passed our firearms courses, non-restricted and restricted and if there was one thing Stan would want to talk about would be guns. So that was my perfect way out of this topic that Stan would surely not mind switching over to. He was a great guy really, deep down as good as bread, I just always needed a spare topic at hand to lift him out of his perpetually worried mind. "So yeah Alicia and I completed those firearms courses last weekend. Non-restricted all day Saturday, Restricted all day Sunday. The whole weekend went to that but it was worth it, we got it done."

"Oh, right on! It's about time you got something done right, hehe, we can finally go target shooting together. So, what are you thinking about getting? Rifle wise? Handgun wise?"

"Well I don't want to spend an exorbitant amount of money, but at the same time I want to buy something quality, you know durable, reliable, dependable, that will last."

"Get a Sauer 202 for a rifle and a Sig Sauer P226 for a handgun, in .40 S&W."

"Well like I said I don't want to spend an exorbitant amount of money. I'm not an avid hunter nor am I a secret agent so I don't need the best rifle and best handgun in the world. Sauer 202 is $3,000 and Sig P226 is $1,200, I'm sure I can find quality for less. I'm thinking of getting a Tikka t3x Stainless Varmint, it runs for about $1,200 and a Walther Creed, or Sig P250, they both run for about $500."

"What?! Get the Sauer and the P226, listen to me! They are the best. Go for flagship quality don't cheap out, you got tons of money." Stan always thought I had tons of money and not a worry in the world, for some odd reason. "First of all I nowhere near have 'tons' of money as you say. Especially now that Alicia and I are expecting a baby. And again, there is no need. I will end up paying less than half of what you paid and I'll have the same quality which will last me a lifetime. It's not like I am going to shoot 500 rounds a day, I'll hit the range maybe three times a year at best."

"Whatever, you do what you want!"

Yup, I should have thrown the phone out the window. Well, at least the conversation became stimulating enough to ensure I didn't fall asleep while driving. Nothing like a nice epileptic inducing discussion with my brother to get me wide awake and alert. This conversation was by no means unique to Stan and me. All of my family talked like this; tense and high strung as a fully cocked single-action semi-automatic Colt 1911 (since we are all into gun lingo I might as well continue with gun analogies. Really we are not gun nuts at all, we just liked to target shoot....and occasionally stroke our weapons at night.....but with no live ammo in the house...that's it). I was surprised that only my mother had hypertension and the rest of us had low blood pressures considering how perpetually agitated we all were.

We were all doing well all things considered. War in ex-Yugoslavia, immigration. Stan got dealt with some rough cards early on. At the age of 28 he got diagnosed with Stage I melanoma. The survival rates of this type of cancer were around 95% percent but our family was, initially at least, inconsolable. Especially my mother. The stigma of the word 'cancer' was too heavy, too over-consuming, overwhelming, too suffocating. For days we were going to sleep and waking up in a daze. Kept hoping the whole diagnosis was a dream, however nightmarish as long as we eventually woke up from it. Only after Stan got out of the surgery, came home with us, simply had to take one radiation pill in case cancer had spread (which was very rare for this type of cancer and in Stan's case it didn't) with no other chemotherapy needed did we start to calm down. And it was reassuring to see how quickly he started coming around, recuperating and looking and acting like nothing ever happened. Finally, we began appreciating the doctor's good news and realizing that indeed, everything will probably be alright. And it was, and it still is, fifteen years on. He was a seemingly perfectly healthy 43 year old.

I finally arrived in Ottawa.

CHAPTER 2

NOT MUCH

Beds Inn, my castle for the next four nights. The room looks decent, can't complain. King size bed, tidy and clean. A nice working desk with a TV stand next to it. Good setup for my laptop. I unpacked my things. First thing I checked the forecast. -5C, dipping down to -8C during the night. I immediately went over by the window to assess the heating unit situation. As I thought, it was ancient and I had no clue how to work it while at the same time praying that it would work at all. It had a bunch of random knobs and buttons that looked like they will fall off if I touched them. So I decided to call room service and had them bring in their hotel maintenance guy to come and take a look at it. Sure enough, the maintenance dude came up within five minutes, turned the heat on and said he thinks everything is functioning properly. I thanked him. I was impressed. Impressed that the heating unit didn't explode in our faces while at the same time wondering when and if I will ever move out of Ontario. Now that he got it working, and just at the right temperature and setting I was positive I wasn't going to touch it or turn it off for the next four days. The comfort of the basic things was never to be taken for granted. I'm amazed in what a good mood a functioning heating unit just put me into. The most important thing here in Canada whenever I stay at any motel or hotel is that I ensure there is no cold air blasting from somewhere, AC or otherwise. And that the heating unit works. Ironically air conditioning in winter famous Canada seemed more of an essential part of living than running water, while heating units went completely neglected, and people couldn't seem to get enough of it, summer or winter apparently. One would think in this land where winters are no shrinking violets that the population would be allergic to air conditioning like the Devil to Holy water. It was the exact opposite. Air conditioning galore everywhere, lobbies, hotel rooms, bars, toilets, offices, elevators, etc....I'm surprised they don't have jobs where like those squeegee kids they also don't engage teenagers with portable air conditioning units running after you and cooling you off while you're walking down the street, or awaiting a bus. And the continuation and staying power of air conditioning units throughout the winter no matter where I go is uncanny and fascinating, if not idiotic to the extreme. Or at least of some cold air blasting somewhere. So everywhere I go first thing I do, both my wife and me, is we look for that source of cool air so we can either avoid it (restaurants, bars, etc...) or turn it off such as in hotel rooms. So now that I knew no cold air source or vent was covertly placed and functioning somewhere beneath the bed, or out of the sink tap or the toilet bowl strategically positioned to cool off my ass from overheating as its firing off projectiles into the mini pool of water beneath, I was a happy camper. The mini pool of water in the bowl alone does that job just fine, whether I like it or not, splish-splashing my underside like a car wash. Also, since most public places have toilets with stalls that barely shield a person from view, the drafts and blasts of air whizzing in and around the raggedy stall walls are enough to make you feel like you're taking a shit in an open farm field in Saskatchewan. And the gases of my own making from within that stall are ever so efficiently dissipated and carried away from me....to a person's face washing their hands at the sink 1 m away.

So with the heat comfortably soaking in the room air I started changing for the nightly inspection. Long johns, thick wool socks, three T-shirts and a hoodie, combined with a thick winter construction coat, hat, gloves and face balaclava. I'm as ready as I was ever going to be. Off I went.

2:00 AM - We got shut down by the Bureau of Transportation (Bureau) because wet snow started falling. Although the accumulation and the amount was not as heavy per se, the visibility reduction was significant enough to jeopardize oncoming traffic safety and us hanging in a boom bucket from a crane arm of a Bridgemaster truck essentially behaving like a roadblock in the middle of 417. So we packed up and were done for the night. We barely inspected a third of one bridge. Three bridges to do, all similar details and geometry, to be inspected for fatigue deformations and defects in steel and welds in three nights. One night down, three to go, at the rate we were going this was not going to happen. Comfort-wise, this was a Godsend. By 1 AM my fingers and toes started freezing and going numb. I made the mistake of not utilizing Little Hotties (hahaha) hand and feet warmers. The new guy I was training who joined us in the bucket had his and kept raving about how his hands and toes were nice and toasty as all I kept thinking about was distracting him and stealing his, as if he wouldn't notice. Oh well, I swore I wouldn't make that mistake again tomorrow, as the temperature was supposed to go down to -12C.

The next day was rough. And slow. And again inefficient. The weather was cold and brutal, but we encountered no precipitation or wind so once operational we did our inspections stoically and as effectively as we could. My Magnetic Particle Tester was a smart man. Singh. Had a metallurgical engineering degree back in India, couldn't get an engineering job here except as an inspector. He worked efficiently with the equipment, had a lot of heavy tools to carry too. He had been doing this job for years. Told me many times before that his hands are getting ruined with arthritis and carpal tunnel syndrome due to all the repetitive motions endured by his fingers and wrists in all sorts of weather conditions handling awkward and heavy metal equipment. He is one of the many smart minds that could do so much more in this country with his intelligence and credentials but instead he is working a job well below his capabilities and qualifications. It makes me wonder what it all means when they say this country is short of highly educated labor. And then we import all this highly educated labour only for them to be working jobs well beneath their skill set since our highly 'tolerant' country doesn't recognize educational institutions of most other countries?! And when I say 'it makes me wonder' really I know exactly what's going on but I'm being hypocritically coy in my rhetorical question approach. Labor is like any other commodity, priced based upon its availability. Presuming one gets 'lucky' and is allowed to work in their field of study, meanwhile hundreds of thousands of other well-educated immigrants have to settle to work driving cabs and serving fast food. No wonder it takes years to find a family doctor in this society.

The third day was identical to the second, and the Little Hotties helped. Hahahahaha, ah yes, the name is brilliant and it keeps bringing a smile to my face. Cheesy but literally and metaphorically made me feel warm and fuzzy inside. Or maybe I'm also smiling as I found out that the fourth day of inspections was canceled due to the fact that a blizzard and 15-20cm of snow was coming Thursday night. I came back to Beds Inn and went straight to bed. I couldn't wait to head back home tomorrow. I'll tell you who wasn't going to leave this place anytime soon. The prostitutes living and working out of this hotel with the full awareness and consent of the management. This one in particular was hilarious, she kept staying in a different room on a different floor every night. I caught her trying desperately to get a pop can out of a vending machine in the front lobby for a good 5 minutes. Eventually, I helped her out....only with the pop can. She, of course, started to strike up a conversation which was hard to understand due to both her missing and remaining uneven and ruined teeth but what I finally made out to be along the lines that if I felt like I wanted to 'party' she would give me a sweet deal for $100 per half an hour. Even if I wasn't married I can't quite estimate the amount of liquor that would have been necessary for me to go for this...'tempting' opportunity.

The next morning I packed up my shit, had breakfast at Cora's then headed on home back to Kingston.

CHAPTER 3

TEDIOUSLY OBSESSING DEEPER

Driving back home and listening to music all rejoicing at the fact that the torture of polar inspections was over and that as far as I knew it in the given moment I did not yet contract pneumonia, my thoughts drifted back to Stan. Specifically to cancer he had. Out of all the things I could be thinking of right? Often times I drift into random dwellings about random subjects. And it's often about something dark and depressing. I love to zone out, at times with no thoughts in my head whatsoever. Most times however something is usually on my mind. If my computer was with me I would be searching for all related things pertaining to whatever topic was momentarily on my mind. Since no computer was with me and I was driving I could only formulate broad thoughts but with very specific questions that I couldn't answer due to the inability to look up any existing documentation. I could only hope to remember all the things I'll want to look up once I'm again close to a computer. I was being unsafe too. I was putting keywords into my phone under 'Reminders' as I was driving, and swerving the road as I was doing it. In short, I started wondering about the mechanics of any disease or illness in general, but then I quickly zeroed it in specifically towards cancer. I am surprised most times that I function at all in life considering how much I zone out about nonspecific matters. That I don't get into more accidents, fall off the cliff more or end up in some random little shithole town in Northern Ontario like Leslie Nielsen in Naked Gun ending my conversations with myself with the line 'And where the hell was I.....' So many times I find myself at home, in a particular room of our house, completely unaware of when or how I got there and not actually remembering leaving work or the trip from work to home. Not because I had an early onset of Alzheimer's, I was simply that spaced out. Luckily the house....is always the right house, the wife inside is mine and the time is correct too for when to arrive home from work. Plus I still wasn't fired, so I must have been doing it right. Some angel is most definitely watching over this hollow-headed lunatic.

As I was saying my thoughts gradually focused on cancer. Pretty soon I stopped feeling sorry for my brother and all I could think about solely was cancer itself. The disease of our time. The plague of the 21st century. The entire drive back that's all I thought about. How it worked, how it begins, why it's so lethal, why no permanent cure.

When I came home I hugged my wife (my attempt at getting laid failed, apparently according to her we do it too much, according to me nowhere near enough, plus it greatly reduces my anxiety). I unpacked my things, told her about my useless frostbite inducing bridge inspection expedition, went over other routine topics of conversation all the while antsy to get to my computer and start searching everything under the Sun about...cancer. Sick I know right? But I couldn't help it, it was on my mind. I read this shit before when Stan got sick but I wanted to remind myself again. The mechanics of it. The synthesis of it, the growth, the mechanism of action, what makes it grow, tick…die…not a whole lot makes it die. I at least waited until Alicia went to bed before I jumped into research, so she wouldn't tell me that I'm having a love affair with my computer and that I cared more about it than her.

So I started reading. According to the Internet (Wikipedia specifically what else) cancers are a large family of diseases that involve abnormal cell growth with the potential to invade or spread to other parts of the body. They form a subset of neoplasms.

A neoplasm is a type of abnormal and excessive growth, called neoplasia, of tissue. The growth of a neoplasm is uncoordinated with that of the normal surrounding tissue, and it persists growing abnormally, even if the original trigger is removed. This abnormal growth usually (but not always) forms a mass. When it forms a mass, it may be called a tumor.

The 10th revision of the International Statistical Classification of Diseases and Related Health Problems (ICD) classifies neoplasms into four main groups: benign neoplasms, in situ neoplasms, malignant neoplasms, and neoplasms of uncertain or unknown behavior. Malignant neoplasms are also simply known as cancers and are the focus of oncology. Prior to the abnormal growth of tissue, as neoplasia, cells often undergo an abnormal pattern of growth, such as metaplasia or dysplasia. However, metaplasia or dysplasia does not always progress to neoplasia.

Reading further; all tumor cells show the six hallmarks of cancer. These characteristics are required to produce a malignant tumor. They include the following:

i) Cell growth and division absent the proper signals

ii) Continuous growth and division even given contrary signals

iii) Avoidance of programmed cell death

iv) Limitless number of cell divisions

v) Promoting blood vessel construction

vi) Invasion of tissue and formation of metastases

vii) The progression from normal cells to cells that can form a detectable mass to outright cancer involves multiple steps known as malignant progression. Causes can be numerous, tobacco smoking, radiation, alcohol, chemicals, genetics, etc... And the prognosis is extremely varying. Although the incidence of cancer is rising due to people living longer and other diseases being eradicated, many forms of the disease are now able to be treated, with 5-year survival rates being 70, 80, 90, 99%. As was the case of Stan's stage I melanoma, thank God. However, at the same time certain forms of it, like esophageal cancer, pancreatic cancer, lung cancer, brain cancer, etc....were still extremely deadly with five-year survival rates only being between about 5-18%.

The biggest mechanism of....the deadliness of cancer if you will is the so-called metastasis. Metastasis is a pathogenic agent's (cancerous cell or mass) spread from an initial or primary site to a different or secondary site within the host's body; such spread is common by a cancerous tumor. The newly pathological sites, then, are metastases (mets). It is generally distinguished from cancer invasion, which is the direct extension and penetration by cancer cells into neighboring tissues.

Needless to say the mechanics of this disease I found fascinating. It was almost as if....it had a mind of its own. Like it was an entity, evil of course, a sinister demon spirit invading our otherwise healthy bodies and meticulously destroying us. I spent hours reading. Afterward, I started to hone in on two particular points of cancer characteristics which I found the most unbelievable. It's avoidance of programmed cell death and a limitless number of cell divisions. I read those two attributes over and over again. Avoidance of programmed cell death and a limitless number of cell divisions, avoidance of programmed...

Programmed (?!?!) cell death. I couldn't help but be overwhelmed by an unmistakable sensation of machinations of some sort of intelligent design. And I'm not religious by any means. Spiritual yes, in the sense that I firmly believe that there is a higher power than us, not sure if in the form of a spiritual deity or a far superior and older extraterrestrial alien race or just self-aware energy of some sorts. And when I hear the word 'programmed' that usually doesn't go together with 'random', so engineering seems to be at play..... The literal description on the Internet is that programmed cell death (or PCD) is the death of a cell in any form, mediated, get this, *by an intracellular program*. If I didn't know I was reading Wikipedia I could have sworn I was reading science fiction.

So now I switched over from cancer straight to reading about what specifically causes cells to die, and insatiably reading on I found out that programmed cell death (PCD) or apoptosis is a form of cell death that occurs in all multicellular organisms. Biochemical events lead to characteristic cell changes (morphology) and death. These changes include blebbing, cell shrinkage, nuclear fragmentation, chromatin condensation, chromosomal DNA fragmentation, and global mRNA decay. The average adult human loses between 50 and 70 billion cells each day due to apoptosis. For an average human child between the ages of 8 to 14 years old approximately 20 to 30 billion cells die a day.

The following information caught my eye and sparked endless wonder in my head. Apoptosis progresses quickly and *its products are quickly removed, making it difficult to detect or visualize* on classical histology sections.

In contrast to necrosis, which is a form of traumatic cell death that results from acute cellular injury, apoptosis is apparently a highly *regulated* and *controlled* process that confers advantages during an organism's life-cycle. For example, the separation of fingers and toes in a developing human embryo occurs because cells between the digits undergo apoptosis and die. Unlike necrosis, apoptosis produces cell fragments called apoptotic bodies that phagocytic cells are able to engulf and remove before the contents of the cell can spill out onto surrounding cells and cause damage to them. Because apoptosis cannot stop once it has begun, it is a highly regulated process. Apoptosis can be initiated through one of two pathways. In the intrinsic pathway the cell kills itself because it senses cell stress, while in the extrinsic pathway the cell kills itself because of signals from other cells. Weak external signals may also activate the intrinsic pathway of apoptosis. Both pathways induce cell death by activating caspases, which are proteases, or enzymes that degrade proteins. The two pathways both activate initiator caspases, which then activate executioner caspases, which then kill the cell by degrading proteins indiscriminately. Research on apoptosis has increased substantially since the early 1990s. In addition to its importance as a biological phenomenon, defective apoptotic processes have been implicated in a wide variety of diseases. Excessive apoptosis causes atrophy, whereas an insufficient amount results in uncontrolled cell proliferation, such as cancer. Some factors like Fas receptors and caspases promote apoptosis, while some members of the Bcl-2 family of proteins inhibit apoptosis.

So overall great I thought, aside from the word 'programmed' being littered all throughout the above-quoted Wikipedia verbiage, even going as far as to be included in the abbreviation PCD and the Internet not even attempting to take a stab at why or how and from whom or what this 'programming' came to be, this whole process of cell 'death' seemed like a pretty useful thing. It helped the body form and grow and shape itself. And new cells are created by cell division all the time. So I guess for all the cells that are dying vastly more new cells are being created through cell division. Human marrow produces approximately 500 billion blood cells per day, which join the systemic circulation.

Equilibrium...one big happy system. Cells are dying, cells are being created. Or so one would think. But then I noticed a catch and the shifting of my attention to the following aspect: eventually cells stop dividing, therefore, no new cells are created any longer. The Hayflick limit or Hayflick phenomenon is the number of times a normal human cell population will divide before cell division stops. The concept of the Hayflick limit was advanced by American anatomist Leonard Hayflick in 1961, at the Wistar Institute in Philadelphia, Pennsylvania, US. Hayflick demonstrated that a normal human fetal cell population will divide between 40 and 60 times in cell culture before entering a senescence phase. This finding refuted the contention by Nobel laureate Alexis Carrel that normal cells are immortal. Each time a cell undergoes mitosis, the telomeres on the ends of each chromosome shorten slightly. Cell division will cease once telomeres shorten to a critical length. Hayflick interpreted his discovery to be aging at the cellular level. The aging of cell populations appears to correlate with the overall physical aging of an organism. Hayflick described three phases in the life of normal cultured cells. At the start of his experiment he named the primary culture "phase one". Phase two is defined as the period when cells are proliferating; Hayflick called this the time of "luxuriant growth". After months of doubling the cells eventually reach phase three, a phenomenon he named "senescence", where cell replication rate slows before halting altogether. The Hayflick limit has been found to correlate with the length of the telomeric region at the end of chromosomes. During the process of DNA replication of a chromosome, small segments of DNA within each telomere are unable to be copied and are lost. This occurs due to the uneven nature of DNA replication, where leading and lagging strands are not replicated symmetrically. The telomeric region of DNA does not code for any protein; it is simply a repeated code on the end region of linear eukaryotic chromosomes. After many divisions, the telomeres reach a critical length and the cell becomes senescent. It is at this point that a cell has reached its Hayflick limit. Hayflick was the first to report that only cancer cells are immortal. This could not have been demonstrated until he had shown that only normal cells are mortal. Cellular senescence does not occur in most cancer cells due to the expression of an enzyme called telomerase. This enzyme extends telomeres, preventing the telomeres of cancer cells from shortening and giving them infinite replicative potential. A proposed treatment for cancer is the usage of telomerase inhibitors that would prevent the restoration of the telomere, allowing the cell to die like other body cells. On the other hand, telomerase activators might conceivably repair or extend the telomeres of healthy cells, thus extending their Hayflick limit but giving the cells cancerous properties. Telomerase activation might also lengthen the telomeres of immune system cells enough to prevent cancerous cells from developing from cells with very short telomeres. Comparisons of different species indicate that cellular replicative capacity may correlate primarily with species body mass, but more likely to species lifespan. Thus the limited capacity of cells to replicate in culture may be directly relevant to organismal aging.

Telomerase, also called terminal transferase, is a ribonucleoprotein that adds a species-dependent telomere repeat sequence to the 3' end of telomeres. A telomere is a region of repetitive sequences at each end of eukaryotic chromosomes in most eukaryotes. Telomeres protect the end of the chromosome from DNA damage or from fusion with neighboring chromosomes. Telomerase is a reverse transcriptase enzyme that carries its own RNA molecule (e.g., with the sequence 3'-CCCAAUCCC-5' in Trypanosoma brucei) which is used as a template when it elongates telomeres. (Beyond unicellular organisms) Telomerase is active in normal stem cells and most cancer cells but is normally absent from, or at very low levels in, most somatic cells.

With respect to aging, telomerase replaces short bits of DNA known as telomeres, which are otherwise shortened when a cell divides via mitosis. Embryonic stem cells express telomerase, which allows them to divide repeatedly and form the individual. In adults, telomerase is highly expressed only in cells that need to divide regularly, especially in male sperm cells but also in epidermal cells, in activated T cell and B cell lymphocytes, as well as in certain adult stem cells, but in the great majority of cases somatic cells do not express telomerase. A comparative biology study of mammalian telomeres indicated that telomere length of some mammalian species correlates inversely, rather than directly, with lifespan, and concluded that the contribution of telomere length to lifespan is unresolved. Telomere shortening does not occur with age in some postmitotic tissues, such as in the rat brain. In humans, skeletal muscle telomere lengths remain stable from ages 23 –74. In baboon skeletal muscle, which consists of fully differentiated post-mitotic cells, less than 3% of myonuclei contain damaged telomeres and this percentage does not increase with age. Thus, telomere shortening does not appear to be a major factor in the aging of the differentiated cells of brain or skeletal muscle. In human liver, cholangiocytes and hepatocytes show no age-related telomere shortening. Another study found little evidence that, in humans, telomere length is a significant biomarker of normal aging with respect to important cognitive and physical abilities. Some experiments have raised questions on whether telomerase can be used as an anti-aging therapy, namely, the fact that mice with elevated levels of telomerase have higher cancer incidence and hence do not live longer. Telomerase also favors tumorogenesis, which leads to questions about its potential as an anti-aging therapy.

So then was apoptosis in combination with the Hayflick limit the reason we die? I kept reading further with my mouth dry and lips breaking up as I barely paused to go to the bathroom but not to eat or hydrate myself, which is my common method of functioning when I'm obsessing about shit. Hayflick limit was only the limit as to how many times a cell can divide. The concept of cell division only explained the creation of most somatic cells, other than cells such as blood cells which were created by the bone marrow, but not the reason for their apoptosis or the reason why talomeres shorten after each cell division. Cells use energy, break down nutrients and matter in order to maintain, grow and repair themselves. So, ultimately, why do they start deteriorating and dying? That is, once an organism is fully developed and 'grown' and apoptosis is no longer needed as a mechanism of organism formation and shaping, why don't the cells simply....continue living indefinitely? Why are they not 'programmed' to maintain themselves forever? Logically if enough nutrients are provided the cells should be able to maintain and repair themselves endlessly, no? But clearly that was not the case. As I predicted there were numerous theories as to why cells and by default living organisms age and eventually die.

In 1889, August Weismann theorized that aging was part of life's program because the old need to remove themselves from the theatre to make room for the next generation sustaining the turnover that is necessary for evolution, giving this theory a teleological or goal-driven explanation. In other words, a *purpose* for aging has been identified, but not a *mechanism* by which that purpose could be achieved. Theories suggesting that deterioration and death due to aging are a purposeful result of an organism's evolved design (such as Weismann's "*programmed death*" theory) are referred to as theories of programmed aging or adaptive aging.

The first modern theory of mammal aging was formulated by Peter Medawar in 1952. It formed from discussions in the previous decade with J. B. S. Haldane and the selection shadow concept. Their idea was that aging was a matter of neglect. Nature is a highly competitive place, and almost all animals in nature die before they attain old age. Therefore, there is not much reason why the body should remain fit for the long haul – not much selection pressure for traits that would maintain viability past the time when most animals would be dead anyway, killed by predators, disease, or accident. Medawar's theory is referred to as Mutation Accumulation. The mechanism of action involves random, detrimental germline mutations of a kind that happen to show their effect only late in life. Unlike most detrimental mutations, these would not be efficiently weeded out by natural selection. On the grand scale, senescence would just be the summation of deleterious genes that only present in older individuals. Hence they would 'accumulate' and, perhaps, cause all the decline and damage that we associate with aging.

Extrinsic mortality is the sum of the effects of external factors, such as sunlight and pollutants that contribute to senescence and eventually death. This is opposed to intrinsic mortality, which is the sum of the effects of internal factors, such as mutation due to DNA replication errors such as the Mutation Accumulation theory described above.

A problem with Medawar's theory became apparent in the late 1990s, when genomic analysis became widely available. It turns out that the genes that cause aging are not random mutations; rather, these genes form tight-knit families that have been around as long as eukaryotic life. George C. Williams proposed his own theory, called antagonistic pleiotropy. Pleiotropy means one gene that has two or more effects on the phenotype. In antagonistic pleiotropy, one of these effects is beneficial and another is detrimental. In essence, this refers to genes that offer benefits early in life, but exact a cost later on. If evolution is a race to have the most offspring the fastest, then enhanced early fertility could be selected even if it came with a price tag that included decline and death later on. Because aging was a side effect of necessary functions, Williams considered any alteration of the aging process to be "impossible." Antagonistic pleiotropy is a prevailing theory today, but this is largely by default, and not because the theory has been well verified. In fact, experimental biologists have looked for the genes that cause aging, and since about 1990 the technology has been available to find them efficiently. Of the many aging genes that have been reported, some seem to enhance fertility early in life, or to carry other benefits. But there are other aging genes for which no such corresponding benefit has been identified. This is not what Williams predicted. This may be thought of as partial validation of the theory, but logically it cuts to the core premise: that genetic trade-offs are the root cause of aging.

Another difficulty with antagonistic pleiotropy and other theories that suppose that aging is an adverse side effect of some beneficial function is that the linkage between adverse and beneficial effects would need to be rigid in the sense that the evolution process would not be able to evolve in a way to accomplish the benefit without incurring the adverse effect even over a very long time span. Such a rigid relationship has not been experimentally demonstrated and, in general, evolution is able to independently and individually adjust a myriad of organism characteristics.

Then I came upon a third mainstream theory of aging, the "Disposable soma theory", proposed in 1977 by Thomas Kirkwood, presumes that the body must budget the amount of energy available to it. The body uses food energy for metabolism, for reproduction, and for repair and maintenance. With a finite supply of food, the body must compromise, and do none of these things quite as well as it would like. It is the compromise in allocating energy to the repair function that causes the body gradually to deteriorate with age.

The DNA damage theory of aging is a prominent explanation for aging at the molecular level. This theory postulates that DNA damage is ubiquitous in the biological world and is the primary cause of aging. Consistent with this theory, genetic elements that regulate repair of DNA damage in somatic cells were proposed to have pleiotropic effects that are beneficial during early development but allow deleterious consequences later in life. As an example, studies of mammalian brain and muscle have shown that DNA repair capability is relatively high during early development when cells are dividing mitotically, but declines substantially as cells enter the post-mitotic state. The reduction in DNA repair capability presumably reflects an evolutionary adaptation for diverting resources from cell duplication and repair to more essential neuronal and muscular functions. The effect of reducing the expression of DNA repair capability is to allow increased accumulation of DNA damage. This then impairs gene transcription and causes the progressive loss of cellular and tissue functions that define aging.

The free radical theory of aging (FRTA) states that organisms age because cells accumulate free radical damage over time. A free radical is any atom or molecule that has a single unpaired electron in an outer shell. While a few free radicals such as melanin are not chemically reactive, most biologically relevant free radicals are highly reactive. For most biological structures, free radical damage is closely associated with oxidative damage. Antioxidants are reducing agents, and limit oxidative damage to biological structures by passivating them from free radicals. Strictly speaking, the free radical theory is only concerned with free radicals such as superoxide (O_2^-), but it has since been expanded to encompass oxidative damage from other reactive oxygen species such as hydrogen peroxide (H_2O_2), or peroxynitrite ($OONO^-$). In some model organisms, such as yeast and Drosophila, there is evidence that reducing oxidative damage can extend lifespan. However, in mice, only 1 of the 18 genetic alterations (SOD-1 deletion) that block antioxidant defenses, shortened lifespan. Similarly, in roundworms (Caenorhabditis elegans), blocking the production of the naturally occurring antioxidant superoxide dismutase has recently been shown to increase lifespan. Whether reducing oxidative damage below normal levels is sufficient to extend lifespan remains an open and controversial question.

Ultimately all the theories listed fell into three categories: i) Those who believe in the idea that aging is an unavoidable side effect of some necessary function (antagonistic pleiotropy or disposable soma theories) logically tend to believe that attempts to delay aging would result in unacceptable side effects to the necessary functions. Altering aging is therefore "impossible", and study of aging mechanisms is of only academic interest. ii) Those believing in default theories of multiple maintenance mechanisms tend to believe that ways might be found to enhance the operation of some of those mechanisms. Perhaps they can be assisted by anti-oxidants or other agents. Hence biogerontology the sub-field of gerontology concerned with the biological aging process, its evolutionary origins, and potential means to intervene in the process. iii) Those who believe in programmed aging suppose that ways might be found to interfere with the operation of the part of the aging mechanism that appears to be common to multiple symptoms, essentially "slowing down the clock" and delaying multiple manifestations. Such an effect might be obtained by fooling a sense function. One such effort is an attempt to find a "mimetic" that would "mime" the anti-aging effect of calorie restriction without having to actually radically restrict diet.

Phenoptosis (pheno – showing or demonstrating, ptosis – programmed death), designated by V.P. Skulachev in 1999, signifies the phenomenon of programmed death of an organism, i.e. that an organism's genes include features that under certain circumstances will cause the organism to rapidly degenerate and die off. Recently this has been referred to as "fast phenoptosis" as aging is being explored as "slow phenoptosis". Phenoptosis is a common feature of living species, whose ramifications for humans are still being explored.

Inside of our bodies, worn-out, ineffective cells are dismantled and recycled for the greater good of the whole organism. This is a process called apoptosis. It is believed that phenoptosis is an evolutionary mechanism that culls out the damaged, aged, infectious or those in direct competition with their own offspring for the good of the species. The elimination of parts detrimental to the organism or individuals detrimental to the species has been deemed "The samurai law of biology" – it is better to die than to be wrong. Stress-induced, acute, or fast phenoptosis is the rapid deterioration of an organism induced by a life event such as breeding. Elimination of the parent provides space for fitter offspring. As a species, this has been advantageous particularly to species that die immediately after spawning. Age-induced, soft, or slow phenoptosis is the slow deterioration and death of an organism due to accumulated stresses over long periods of time. In short, it has been proposed that aging, heart disease, cancer, and other age related ailments are means of phenoptosis for humans as spawning is a halmark of phenoptosis for salmon. "Death caused by aging clears the population of ancestors and frees space for progeny carrying new useful traits." It has also been proposed that age provides a selective advantage to brains over brawn. An example made by V. P. Skulachev provides that of two hares, one faster and one smarter, the faster hare may have a selective advantage in youth but as aging occurs and muscles deteriorate it is the smarter hare that now has the selective advantage. According to some by understanding the mechanisms of slow phenoptosis we may be able to halt or even reverse the processes that cause our aging and eventual deaths.

The most likely proposed mechanisms of phenoptosis are: Mitochondrial ROS (reactive oxygen species) – The production of ROS by the mitochondria. This causes oxidative damage to the inner compartment of the mitochondria and the destruction of the mitochondria. Clk1 gene – the gene thought to be responsible for aging due to mitochondrial ROS appears to play an integral role. EF2 kinase – Blocks phosphorylation of elongation factor 2 thus blocking protein synthesis. Glucocorticoid regulation – A common route for phenoptosis is a breakdown of glucocorticoid regulation and inhibition, leading to a massive excess of these corticosteroids in the body.

I had enough facts at this point. I felt my own brain cells starting to die off from information overload. It is an unmistakable feeling I used to have back in school days when my head becomes oversaturated with information and I feel as though no exponential learning progress forward is being achieved, the head feels like a cooking pot ready to boil over and overflow and if anything I feel my knowledge is regressing. I took a break. Then I went over again what I read earlier. Skimmed over it. All the dust in my brain began to settle so I felt as though I can attempt to form some opinions. I read the main proposed theories again of why we age and die. And then again. Although the theory of 'programmed aging' is the only theory officially implementing the word 'programming' in its description, without attempting to explain where the programming part is coming from, other theories didn't really explain their mechanisms of action either in any substantive way in turn more or less also leaving at least this reader under the strong and unmistakable impression that their mechanisms and methods of action are also…. forms of programs. The common theme if you will, at least in my mind was that programmed, purposefully created catalysts, and carefully orchestrated sequences of action, events and tools were biologically and chemically inducing aging and ultimately death of all living species.

I switched my reading back towards cancer again right before bed and that further strengthened my theories. And here is why. A paper published in 2000 titled "The Hallmarks of Cancer" outlined further six factors that are synonymous with cancer and they were as follows: 1. Cancer cells stimulate their own growth (self-sufficiency in growth signals) as oppose to needing hormones and other molecules to stimulate it. 2. They resist inhibitory signals that might otherwise stop their growth (insensitivity to anti-growth signals), containing altered tumor suppressor genes preventing the stoppage of cell division. 3. They resist their programmed cell death (evading apoptosis, and herein again there is the term 'programmed cell death' although apparently now the article only talks about cells being programmed to self-destruct if damaged and for the purposes of growth and body part formation). 4. They can multiply indefinitely (limitless replicative potential). Tumor (different from cancer in that it doesn't spread or metastasize) cells alter the above talked about Hayflick limit in that they disable their pRB and p53 tumor suppressor proteins, which allows them to continue doubling until they reach a stage called crisis, with apoptosis, karyotypic disarray, and the occasional emergence of an immortalized cell that can double without limit. Most tumor cells are immortalized. The counting device for cell doublings is the telomere, which decreases in size (loses nucleotides at the ends of chromosomes) during each cell cycle as I read about already. About 85% of cancers upregulate telomerase to extend their telomeres and the remaining 15% use a method called the Alternative Lengthening of Telomeres. 5. They stimulate the growth of blood vessels to supply nutrients to tumors (sustained angiogenesis), essentially cancer creates its own cardio-vascular system. 6. They invade local tissue and spread to distant sites (metastasis). Besides these six, other potential hallmarks have been identified such as that cancer cells contain deregulated metabolism, have the ability to evade the human immune system via the loss of Interleukin-33, have genome instability and tend to form in the locations of chronic inflammation sites.

More facts. Usually with me when I say I'm done with facts and try to convince myself that I can't bare any more new information I usually end up reading three times more than originally. The sad part is I promise other people that I'm done obsessing and once the promising starts you know I'm lying extra hard. I was officially obsessed. My wife was starting to get exceptionally annoyed. The light of my cell phone late at night was driving her nuts but I, as usual, couldn't help myself. The day was gone, Alicia couldn't distract me or pique my interest with anything else, I was lost. The last thing I read about was the Warburg cancer hypothesis. Warburg hypothesized that cancer growth is caused by tumor cells generating energy (as, e.g., adenosine triphosphate/ATP) mainly by anaerobic breakdown of glucose (known as fermentation, or anaerobic respiration). This is in contrast to healthy cells, which mainly generate energy from oxidative breakdown of pyruvate. Pyruvate is an end product of glycolysis and is oxidized within the mitochondria. Hence, according to Warburg, cancer should be interpreted as mitochondrial dysfunction. Great, now my eyes are burning red, itchy and irritated from staring at the little screen on my iPhone. Good night!

Over the next few days I gave my new found hobby, reading about death and cancer, a rest. Was I a Goth now?! I went to work, gym, ate, slept, essentially I tried to be a normal human being. But I eventually always failed miserably at that. Thoughts of wonder and need for explanations filled my head. I kept reverting back to my new found research. So essentially cancer cells are 'programmed' to resist aging and death as opposed to normal cells which are 'programmed' (regardless of what theory I'm convinced they are all talking about PROGRAMMING) to age and die. And the only way we circumvent being extinct as species is by sex and procreation, new birth, newborns, etc...But if cells eventually stop being able to divide by a circuit breaker called the Hayflick limit or a renegade protein telling them to stop repairing themselves or whatever....are human beings eventually also going to become completely infertile and stop being able to procreate?? There certainly is no indication of that happening yet but following the path of our cells it wouldn't be surprising if this were to happen...

A couple of more days passed. I tried simply focusing on the boring minutiae of everyday routine. However, as I did that the subject I read about extensively for days was not leaving my mind. I was in no way, shape or form able to put any other thought at the forefront. I was even hoping for a 'worry' of some kind to come preoccupy me, just so I would stop thinking about the subject matter turning my already robust primarily cognitive obsessive-compulsive disorder into overdrive. My wife was two months pregnant, couldn't I worry and plan for the baby or something?? It was like when I find something materialistic I like. Eventually the research and 'want' becomes too overwhelming and I end up buying the bloody thing in question. I've become obsessed that all species on Earth are programmed to age and to die. And now what? How do I satisfy this particular obsession?! And....this is the most fucked up thing about it....I've become convinced that the 'programming' part was by no means random, coincidental, gradual, evolutionary, call it what you will. And I was convinced more than ever that it was no God that was the programmer.

Usually in movies at moments of eureka like these a phone rings, or an email arrives, or an SMS message dings on the phone or someone breaks down the front door. The main character having the epiphany moment such as this one is shocked to realize that they have just accidentally broken down the secret screen of conventionally accepted truths and realities, that they have crossed the forbidden wall of knowledge and consciousness allowed to humans and have officially stepped into the territory of taboo and forbidden discoveries. They have crossed the Rubicon. Immediately they become aware of the faction of individuals wanting to help the person in question and the other sinister faction of individuals trying to destroy and silence the main protagonist as they now know too much and have to be stopped from leaking this knowledge to the outside world of otherwise sleepy, amorphous Earth inhabiting biological masses.

Truth be told, and as incredibly obnoxious as this may sound, I spent several intense minutes waiting for just such a phone call, email, text message, with occasional glimpses towards my front door in anticipation of secret agents blasting right through it. To my utter surprise and a horse's hoof kick in the nuts to my ego, no such event occurred. Dammit...how outrageously disappointing.

More days went by and at this point instead of my curiosity regarding the topic at hand waning it became stronger and completely consumed me. This is usually what happens to me. I don't just express mild curiosity towards subjects and matters I get completely eaten up by them. My interests suffocate me. So, I started formulating an idea. What if I, in all my infinite wisdom and responsible glory, went to local Universities and requested a sit-down...'chat' with the head of the Biology and Chemistry Department. And checked out what they would have to say about this, how they would interpret the information I read about aging, death, procreation, etc. How they would explain words such as 'programming', etc...Like with everything a written word deemed intriguing should be discussed with real people, real subject matter experts. I was very arrogant and brash in my assumption that a University professor would sit down with a local engineer bored out of his mind and with apparently nothing else better to do than to chit chat about matters related to life and death. I mean they must have better things to do with their time, research, lectures, tweaking course material slides to appear slightly different than last year. They are fulfilled with their family life and don't crave outside science fiction stimuli. My idea about the sit-down meeting came about from previous experience. My dad had a friend back in Slovenia, this man apparently had an ability to sense things with his hands. Magnetic fields, water, energy. He came up with a glove of some sort made up of proprietary material that would help him sense these things mentioned even more acutely. He wanted a sponsor, someone to fund his invention, to help him mass produce it. And my dad and I went to talk to a University of Central Ontario (where I got my Engineering Degree) professor of Material Science to see if the University would have any interest in funding further research on this topic. The chat was nice, the compliments were flattering, the humoring was exceptional and the answer was a resounding no. This time around I don't even have a goal or a product at hand. I mean seriously what am I even trying to get out of this potential meeting? Will I ask whomever I sit down with for a favour? Am I looking to start funding further research into topics of aging and death? As if they don't have enough of these research experiments ongoing in laboratories all over the world at any given time. That cost millions of dollars by the way. So literally my sole purpose and end result is to...have a pleasant chat for the sake of my...learning. But really to satisfy my obsessions.

CHAPTER 4

RESTLESS BUT SURFACING

I managed to let a few weeks go by, if you can believe it, letting my idea of a scientific conversation with a local University professor simmer. I figure let's be an adult about it and sleep on it for a while. And not telling anyone about the idea. Especially Alicia. Despite my rampant obsessive thoughts and savage impatience, I have managed to acquire a certain ability to be patient in these 34 years on Earth. Maybe it was due to all those times waiting on my father for everything under the Sun. The man, on purpose according to my mother and me although he would never admit it, refused to be on time. He lived for the rush and exhilaration of making people wait for him. No matter what. And I exercised patience this time. And for weeks too. But most of the time, always actually, the patience that I exercise only postpones the inevitable. Which is I end up doing whatever fucked up thing I thought of anyways just......later.

With the only difference being that I don't tell anybody about it. So any repercussions I bare are my own. That's the responsible attribute I've acquired. Keeping my mouth shut. So as time went by I decided to have my insane meet and greet with whatever University professor will spare time and have my aging and death discussion. But I wasn't going to tell my pregnant wife or anyone else about it. So that was settled. Now I had to come up with a plan of how exactly I'll show up to a University administration office, give a valid enough reason so they don't call security and manage to score a sit down with a professor living in Kingston, Ontario. My logical first step was to head on over to King's University. And all of this to satisfy some half baked idea in my head and try to figure out why all species on Earth age, deteriorate and eventually.....die. And then once I get their opinions I can get back to civil engineering, grocery shopping, shitting, pissing, aging and eventually....dying.

Ok, so what do I say to score a sit-down?!?! This is one of those moments I wish I could insert a stupid thinking emoticon. Ok, first things first. WHO do I talk to. I went to King's University website. It seemed pretty easy to navigate. Then I searched under 'Academics', then 'Faculties, Programs and Departments' and honed in on the Department of Biology and the Department of Chemistry. Department Head for Biology was Dr. Sean Williams and for Chemistry it was Dr. Alicia LaChapelle. Same first name as my wife. I also looked under their 'Research Chairs' list and found one Dr. Samuel Charlston who was Chair of Organic Chemistry research. There were other people listed as Chairs of cancer research, biology, etc..I knew I had to try to narrow this down. I couldn't just go around talking to everyone at the university and expect lengthy sitdowns. After all, let's not forget I am a nobody. I had no clue how to score a meeting. I had absolutely nothing any University would want or need. The only thing I could think of that could be worth something would be...money. Like a donation.

Everyone likes donations. Especially Universities. I could make it towards King's University Biology and Chemistry research. I did more digging on their website. Huzzah! University accepts a minimum of $1,000 donations from anyone towards any Faculty and/or research. So my plan was as follows. I call the administrative office and say that I wish to donate $1,000 towards the faculty of either Biology or Chemistry however I do wish to sit down with the Department Head to become more familiar with what exactly the given department is involved with and what precisely my money would be going towards. This is the only thing I could think of that would get me a sit down so I could have my insane chat.

Now the hard part. I had no idea how to keep this from Alicia. I didn't want to worry her hence I was going to omit telling her this. Not for the sake of lying, simply for the purpose of not adding to the resume of why her husband was an imbecile. And I was planning on donating money. $1,000 to be exact so I can scheme some conversation from unsuspecting people. $1,000 at a time when my pregnant wife will soon go down to no hours of work and then mat leave. There was no way I could hide spending $1,000 from her, the hassle from taking the money out of my Tax-Free Savings Account was too involved. So I had to tell her. The way how childishly I'm behaving I think sometimes I forget myself. So I had to explain to my pregnant wife that I'm going borderline insane in my theory that there is something odd and inadequately explained in all the current and modern scientific texts on why all living things on Earth have to age and die. Therefore I need a sit-down with a University prof to hear their opinion and see if they will say something to put my doubts and confusion to rest. Oh, and I also need to waste $1,000 of our money. Apparently, I had absolutely nothing else better to do or to tend to in our daily lives. This could only go well.

I won't elaborate on my discussion with Alicia nor the lunacy that ensued. All I will say is that after two days, several slammed doors on different house levels and numerous sessions of unnecessarily elevated blood pressures later, all entirely caused by me, I got told to take my $1,000 and go screw myself. I took that that my half-ass plan was given a somewhat of a green light by an angry wife who wanted me out of her sights and presence. So I marched forward, even though I despised more than the average man getting the silent treatment and not being on talking terms with her.

The next day I called the Administration Office at King's University. A woman named Suzie answered the phone. If Alicia and I have a daughter, Suzie is not on the list of possible names.

"Hello, you've reached King's University's Biology Department. My name is Suzie. How may I help you?"

"Yes hello, my name is Marcus Stipecic. I am a Civil Engineer working and living here in the city of Kingston. I've been reading a lot about all the involvement that King's University has with various research across all spectra of different disciplines and I am very impressed and would like to help out in a form of a donation. I feel that as a local citizen in good standing I should support our most prestigious University."

"Well hello Mr. Stipecic and thank you for such welcomed and wonderful news! As you know King's University always welcomes monetary donations from local citizens and will be more than happy to do so in your case as well. Where specifically would you like to donate and in what amount?" (what a surprise, something or somebody doesn't refuse receiving free money, I was holding back laughter. Like the time I got a royal tour of the retirement home in downtown Kingston when all I wanted to ask was how much a unit would cost per month for my parents).

"I would like to donate $1,000 to the Department of Biology, towards new research. I hope you can understand that I would very much like to sit down with Dr. Sean Williams to discuss the latest events at the Department and to become even more familiar with the latest research programs so that I could decide on the specific discipline of research to donate towards."

I noticed Suzie's bubbly enthusiasm suddenly drop. She paused for a few moments then replied dryly: "I'm sorry Mr. Stipecic, all donations below $5,000 can be made through me, via cheque in person or a Credit Card payment or direct money transfer, Paypal whichever you prefer. Mr. Williams and the rest of our teaching staff are extremely busy for a face-to-face sitdown, I'm sure you can understand."

I was on my toes and quick to react: "Suzie, I completely understand. However, I hope you can appreciate that I could be persuaded to donate more money if I become even more familiar with the research specifics of your school. And the only way that could happen is if I go straight to the source and sit down with the individuals who are at the head of the research field. Specifically, if I could meet with the Head of Biology Department, Dr. Sean Williams, the Head of Chemistry, Dr. Alicia LaChapelle and Dr. Samuel Charlston, the chair of Organic Chemistry research." I was shooting at all targets with a single dud for a bullet, but I figured what the hell let's go all out.

"Mr. Stipecic...to request a meet with so many of our top staff is highly irregular. How do we know that you are serious about donating any more than $1,000?!"

"Well Suzie as I said I want to help out your institution. There is no doubting that. I am a very reasonable, inquisitive, open minded person, and extremely generous. My wife always says that I'm very easily persuaded into things if only people know how to impress me with their persistence and well though out explanations, haha. I need to be wowed and I light up and tend to get excited about things like a little kid. But anyway if you think that I'm wasting your faculty's time, I understand. Perhaps this was a bad idea...."

"Well hang on Mr. Stipecic. I mean I can see that your interest is genuine. I would hate to dissuade you from becoming a donor. Am I correct in assuming that if I could arrange this meeting you would be open to donating in the future as well? Becoming a regular contributor to the University? Do you know anyone else who might be interested in donating?"

"Oh most definitely. I am certainly looking forward to being continually informed and involved with any future University's activities in the research field. And I have an extensive network of friends and colleagues with various interests in your school." Oh bravo.....

"Alright Mr. Stipecic, you certainly sound very sincere and open minded and I am very impressed with your altruistic nature and interest with the ongoings at our school. Please let me have your contact information and I will get back to you with the details of what I'll be able to arrange."

"Excellent Suzie, and thanks again for your help, I am very much looking forward to you getting back to me and sitting down with your staff. I have no doubt someone as capable as you will be able to arrange something."

After giving Suzie my email and telephone number I hung up the phone.....with a big, sly smile on my face. Aaaa what a manipulative, lying bastard I could be. And how effective. I truly surprised myself and how well I came up with those twists and turns right on the spot. Most people like to write things down that they are planning to say before a conversation, organize their thoughts, to have a skeleton of text. I like to fly by the seat of my pants. I find some of the finest communication experiences I have when I'm the least prepared.

Three days went by since I spoke to Suzie. Three days of my sly smile slowly fading and me coming to the realization that my half baked plan probably went nowhere. Suzie surely realized right after hanging up the phone that she was talking to a prankster, a joker, a dupe. Who was I kidding seriously?! I mean only a child would have bought that story. Random citizen calling out of the blue to donate money to the University?! Right, I'm sure they get a lot of phone calls daily of that nature. People are that wonderful. I wasn't even an Alumni of that school. And how many alumni even donate I wondered. I used to work at a call center at the University of Central Ontario in London, Ontario where I got my Civil Engineering degree. It was a telemarketing gig, I had a few of those in high school too. The sole purpose was to cold call alumni and ask them to donate money to the University. I would explain that their money was vital to our school, for research (haha), new library desks, wireless Internet connection hookups, weird new lighting, snot rags at every laptop station, etc...Since I only worked on the weekends I was usually hungover from the night before too so entire conversations seemed like drunken and hazy hallucinations. I would expect most people to turn me down, hang up the phone, etc..but mostly, surprisingly, they were willing to at least listen to what I had to say. Some were marked as 'repeat donors' and would donate generously every year, at times hundreds of dollars (?!). I couldn't believe it. The school ripped you off with obscene tuition fees and will do even worse for your children and you are willing to give back even more money....Crazy, I could never do it that's for sure. Although I do feel a bit offended that Central never calls me for any donations, I mean I wouldn't give them shit but it would still be nice to be thought of... The people that refused to donate I was supposed to keep on the line as long as possible and convince them to contribute even a one-time small donation. I was horrible at it. Mainly because I felt like a crook trying to convince these people to donate a cent more than what they've already given when they were attending school in the first place. The 'supervisors' at the call center were furious at me, as they would listen in to our conversations to see if we were doing it right. If we weren't they would give us tips on how to improve. It was brutal and after several times of being told how to change my strategy and me not following through....I was fired. I was fired from another telemarketing calling center in high school as well, trying to shove 'free' exterior painting and staining estimates on vinyl siding down people's throats. Simply put, I didn't believe in any of this bullshit and essentially trying to scheme people out of money. And I felt like an utter hypocrite working in these call centers. But it was easy money for me and the job was easy to get because the 'revolving door' effect was extraordinary and people were constantly being let go, or they quit and then others got rehired. At one point I was good at it, used to win prizes for getting most money donated, most 'leads', etc...I enjoyed manipulating and lying to people I've never met, but by University days I had lost all taste for it.

So I felt as though I was in a somewhat similar situation now. Except I wasn't calling people I've never met to beg for money I don't deserve, I was lying and manipulating a University making them believe I was a new donor solely to satisfy some nonsense idea and obsession I had in my head. I was at piece with this.

At first, I explained to myself that Suzie was on to me, she would never call back. Made perfect sense. Shut up Marcus, grow up, focus on being an adult, reliable husband, half-ass engineer, part-time alcoholic, God knows what kind of soon to be father, save your money and move on with your life. But then, like so many times in my crazy ass life, the obsessive thoughts came back with a vengeance. No(!) I said to myself, this bitch owes me an explanation. I totally sounded believable, legit, polite, how dare she?? So even though I was not sincere at all I was defending the honor of my scheming ploy. I was a proud shit that's for sure. In lie or truth. My lies were bulletproof and deserved the respect of some poor soul administrative assistant. I was now stressed out and antsy and

I had a half a mind to call her back to inquire and follow up. I even went as far as to say to my wife that these people today, no one gets back to you, they say they are gonna call and follow up but always disappear and leave you hanging, it was almost like a religion, a way of avoiding conflict as they have nothing good to say, no good news, so don't say anything at all, just disappear….We lived in a culture of flaking out. Instead of saying they might get back to you or just simply refusing to even provide their contact information if they didn't want to, people pushed through synthetic pleasantries, adamantly promised to follow up, gave their real phone numbers all the while knowing they would vanish and would never pick up the phone once called upon. Yet they never missed a cue when it came to providing a snide jab. Needless to say, I hated it. It seemed completely psychopathic to me. I for one was not a psychopath, weird and insane yes, but not a psychopath. Right?! I should probably be more convinced of this than I was.

Alicia got pissed off in a hurry. She was mostly understanding of my criticizing everything under the Sun about the society we live in, country, people, the trials and tribulations of my profession and otherwise, but this time she was quick to remind "You are pissed off because some…Suzie from King's University isn't calling back about your idiotic wannabe meeting with local professors where you are going to waste $1,000 of our hard-earned money so you can have a useless conversation about the science of aging and death that will do absolutely nothing for you, your day to day life and your family?! You should be thanking your lucky stars that she disappeared and hope that she never emerges again for as long as you are alive so that you can focus on being a responsible grown-up and saving money for your soon to be expanded family! God, I married a child!"

She said all that with one breath. I made a terrible mistake of voicing my antsy displeasure to my pregnant and cranky wife. Why was it so hard for me to keep my mouth shut? Weak.....Well at least Alicia and I were on speaking terms again.

I promised myself I was going to forget about the whole thing. And, although not completely forgetting about it, I suppressed it as far down as I possibly could into the deepest recesses of my psyche. As usual in life, or, all the time as truth would have it, the moment you let go of something mentally, let it rest, that something magically reapers. Wherever pressure is released water starts to flow. The next morning, I got a call from Suzie.

"Good morning Mr. Stipecic. I hope you are doing well. I do apologize for being this late in getting back to you, please understand that it's Holiday season and a lot of our teaching and research staff are on vacation. I've had to wait to get a response from all the parties you wish to meet with and several of them took a while to get back to me as they were away with their families. The good news however is that all of them are back and available to meet with you this coming Friday at 10 AM. As you have requested you will be meeting with Head of Biology Department, Dr. Sean Williams, the Head of Chemistry, Dr. Alicia LaChapelle and Dr. Samuel Charlston, the chair of Organic Chemistry research. Will you be available at this time?"

I of course obliged and she set the meeting. It was November, they are starting their vacations already eh... Whatever. Damn, all three of them, I wasn't seriously expecting the entire choir to show up. I guess the wolves never pass up an opportunity to convince a potential sheep of forking over the coin. Regardless nothing short of my wife's water breaking could have made me skip this meeting. And seeing as how Alicia won't be due until June, I was good to go. Especially on a Friday, a day I usually only work half the day anyway and skip out at noon at the latest. So I figured I'd take the morning off and work the afternoon.

I printed out all my Wikipedia and other Internet

documentation. I highlighted the most important, pertinent sticking points and I decided to go in and get the most out of the discussion. Oh and I brought a cheque with my generous $1,000 soon to be donation. On the day of the meeting my wife messaged me from work once again telling me one more time what an outrageous moron I was for blowing a $1,000 on something of this nature and that I should reconsider. Full family team support was rampant so I was going in at maximum bore, confident as all hell.

CHAPTER 5

THEATRE

Friday, 10 AM. I was in a room with three people I've never met who looked like they expected me to thoroughly explain to them why I shouldn't be executed. Or why I deserved parole. Strange, I figured they would be more jovial wanting that cash. After the initial fake pleasantries and greetings the smiles faded and I made an opening statement which I felt at least didn't make me look completely like a blithering jackass and imbecile.

"I would like to say how honored and grateful I am for all of you meeting me today. It speaks a great deal about you as individuals to spare time from your busy schedules to meet with an average Joe like myself. As I have indicated I am very much looking forward to donating to your departments or your respective research fields. I am familiar with quite a lot of your subject matters already and I am very excited about finding out more so that I can determine my final donation amount and area of interest."

"Mr Stipecic it is our pleasure to meet with you. It is always a privilege to meet with potential and new donors regardless of what walk of life they come from. And it is our understanding that you are a Civil Engineer, is this correct?"

"Yes Dr. Williams, I am a Civil Engineer. I specialize in bridge inspections and new bridge design. I am also involved in heritage and historical masonry rehabilitation work."

"Oh how interesting! I love how historical Kingston is and we certainly have many sites that deserve preservation. Good on you to be involved with that."

"Yes it is very interesting work. I enjoy it. My office tries to cover a few different fields and our areas of work are quite versatile so I would say I spend an equal amount of time in the office as I do on site managing different ongoing construction and inspection jobs."

At this point they asked about my background, how long I've been in Canada, why my parents came here. I told them the usual fairly standard fresh off the boat story about how my father came in 1992 due to the political tensions in Slovenia after the civil war in Jugoslavia, how my mother and I came in 1994 once he became more stable and established with his work and how my brother came in 1998 after he finished his University degree back home. I did my high school and University in London, Ontario, worked in Toronto, Calgary, then came to Kingston. I exchanged 7 different companies since I graduated. There were some aaaas and uuuss and good for yous. After all that we all sort of settled in a bit and stared at each other. After nervously changing my eye position several times I started to speak again.

"So please tell me more, each of you, about the most important aspects of research and curriculum that you find are paramount to be developed and explored further and which would benefit the most from a financial contribution. Please spare no details no matter how small as I am extremely curious to be in 'the know' and I want to be sure that I contribute most productively and efficiently. Also, I hope you understand that I have no 'favorite' area I'm interested to contribute towards, no biased research topic that I favor over another, I simply want to contribute to whatever you all feel is pertinent and would benefit the most from more funding."

Each of them spent about 10 minutes talking about the field of research they are involved with and about their respective teaching subjects. As I suspected they would towards the end they sort of started talking to each other and thinking out loud. After several minutes all three of them concluded that the most important and relevant field of research that was in perpetual need of funding was cancer.

"Yes of course. Cancer research can always use more funding. I couldn't agree more. My brother Stan had melanoma. Luckily, if you can call anyone who gets cancer 'lucky', his type of cancer was highly curable and non-life-threatening but many others are nowhere near as fortunate."

After their sympathies I realized I gave myself more credibility now for being a potential donor for cancer research. I made more sense to them. Cancer these days was way too common. Almost all of the people in the room had someone in their immediate or extended family that had cancer or died of cancer. I felt that this was now my moment to try to press the subject matter I was so anxious to discuss and the whole reason for this meeting in the first place.

"You know it is fascinating. And I hope I could trouble you a little bit more if you don't mind before I make my final decision on the amount, as of course it will go towards cancer research. I've become so interested in this subject of cancer and how it manifests itself, how it spreads, grows, etc... and it led me to read about other aspects of our mortality. Of any living Earth species' mortality if you will. And specifically I read about the process of aging and eventual inevitable death. Many different theories abound as to why we age and die, from DNA damage throughout the years and due to the elements on our planet, to accumulated mutations which eventually lead to cancer to.....programmed catalysts which initiate cells to stop repairing themselves, reproducing themselves, to eventually die, apoptose even though their apoptosis no longer serves any growth or body part formation purpose. And then, on the other hand, we have this phenomenon called cancer, this 'ultimate' disease if you will which has the complete opposite characteristics than normal cells. Its cells do not have a limit on how many times they can divide, they seem to ignore anything telling them to die, and essentially they seem to live forever which they would continue to do if their host organisms didn't die. Reading about all this, back to normal cells now, the word 'programmed' seems to be littered all over almost all contemporary explanations. And even the theories which do not speak of 'programmed' cell death per se, to me, are still alluding to some kind of programming. So, I guess I am just curious to hear your take on all this. Since there is no consensus on the exact mechanism of the first spark of life, there doesn't seem to be any particular consensus on any pinpointed spark of death if you will. What are your thoughts on all of this?"

I took out the printed pages I had with me and showed them highlighted sections I deemed most interesting. All three of their sets of eyes seemed to widen gradually as I spoke. They were taken aback by my morphing the subject and heading into something so vastly more complicated, abstract and essentially off-topic. At least I managed to spit it all out without forgetting anything important.

"Mr. Stipecic...you weren't kidding when you said you dug deep into all things related to human biology...to the biology of all species quite frankly. I'm impressed. You have opened up a vast scientific area for discussion and a very interesting topic. We will do our best to try and give you our perspective on what we think is going on."

Alicia talked first. Then Sean and finally Samuel. In short, in an inflated and seemingly purposefully complicated way, they over elaborated the living shit out of facts which I have already printed from the Internet. They regurgitated theoretical nonsense while keeping meaningful and studious faces. And none of what they said in any way shape or form managed to remove the notion of 'deliberate programming' out of aging and dying methodology. At least not from my mind.

In the end, I didn't even know what each of their opinions truly was. Like politicians they philosophized without concluding.

I gave them the $1,000 and almost cried as I was doing it. Their moods dropped when I quickly explained how I have a child on the way and was not in a good enough financial shape to donate more at this time, but will most certainly donate more in the future and will tell my friends to do the same. They looked as if they were slapped across their faces with cold wet cloths and I knew that I would never see any of them again for as long as I live. They would make sure of it. And my child should probably not go to this University one day. They would also make sure Suzie screens future perspective donors much more diligently. My talk of potentially donating thousands was nothing but smoke and mirrors, now officially becoming farts and broken glass.

Walking out of there I didn't at all feel dirty or ashamed or embarrassed. The only thing I felt was my wife's pain of giving away $1,000 to utter and complete bullshit. To get the insight that didn't exist. They are lucky I gave them anything, the audacity of their sunken faces. I almost wanted to go back and get my money back. Fuck, I should have made that cheque out to like $100 tops......

I felt emotionally rained on. I was excited to hear something new, different, revolutionary. I looked forward to that meeting.

And I got nothing out of it. $1,000 short. Unbelievable. And yet I was either losing my mind or feverish with my obsession because I still felt like I was onto something and that actual insight I craved existed…somewhere out there. I wasn't satisfied. My sense of defeat was slowly turning into further ruminations. I already knew I was going to give the whole thing another try. But how?! I just schemed my way into sitting down with three (!) University professors and I got nothing revolutionary from any of them and I squeezed absolutely everything I could out of the Internet so what else was there? I can't possibly run the same scheme at University of Toronto or McGill in Montreal because no way was I going to skip out of work to waste time driving out of town. So, what else was there?

Military College of Canada. That's what was there…They were the other major University right here in Kingston, Ontario which was pretty unique for a city this small. Army base was the reason. They didn't have as many programs as King's, but they had enough. I saw there was a Chemistry department on their website. Research wise they predominantly focused on military related subjects such as Air-Independent Life Support Systems, Air-Independent Propulsion, Canadian Automatic Small Telescopes for Orbital Research, etc..

This was the only other place where I could potentially go and talk to someone else with a scientific background. Without having to take time off work and leave town. And it just so happens to be military based, perhaps they had inside insight into matters a civilian school wouldn't. And they were just dying to share it with a twit like me. The audacity I walked around with.

Of course, there was also the possibility of letting the whole thing go. You know choosing a life of sanity, focusing on my life, work, marriage, upcoming fatherhood. Leaving obsessive thought inspired actions and thought processes far behind me. But I already knew there was no chance of this whatsoever. At the best of times

I can only really postpone my obsessive thoughts for some time, kick the can further down the road, but sooner or later and at times despite my own dreaded fears while going through with it I usually succumb to my impulses and satisfy the deep recesses of my obsessive mind. Whether one day my brain will prove to be a powerful reactor on its way to greater success or whether I will completely self destruct and the people around me and end up in an insane asylum remains to be seen. Either way, I knew that this time like so many others I will again succumb to my obsessions and go against my better judgment and gut instinct.

So what that meant was that I had to concoct another scheme. I kept comforting myself 'common Marcus only ONE more scheme, you can do that holding your breath'. Improvements will be made since last time, no doubt about it. Well, one major improvement for sure. I wasn't going to say a thing to Alicia about this plan. I didn't want a divorce and for her to change her name, take the baby and ensure that I am never able to contact them again. I also wasn't going to spend a dime this time around. So I was proud of myself. For the new found ability to keep my mouth shut nothing else. I was learning to hold more and more of my lunacy inside. At the end of the day, I figured no matter how crazy I am or was about to become, as long as I don't expose others to my contaminated energy and mind that would already be a major behavioral improvement. Everyone was nuts, it was the ability to hide it that differentiated how 'normal' any of us were. It was the best I could do really for I knew that ultimately I was never going to be able to change or control my impulses fully.

The plan this time came remarkably quickly to me and not with too much elaboration and late-night mental conjuring. However, it involved significantly more outright and complicated lying and bullshit. I was going to go to the Military College of Canada, straight to the Department of Chemistry building. I was going to tell them the truth about my profession, that I am a Civil and Structural engineer. But I was going to give them a fake name and say that I work for one of the competitor engineering companies. Real company, real name, just me not actually working there. Then I was going to say that while working on reparative construction work on another building at the Military campus (there was actual restorative work going on, by other companies) I have observed serious deterioration on the outside masonry and water ingress through the exterior with severe mortar joint damage at the Chemistry building. I will then ask to speak with the Dean of the Chemistry department to inquire whether there would be interest in extending our construction services onto the Chemistry building, which of course I would highly recommend, while our company was still mobilized on campus. If only I had put this much effort into my day job or humanitarian work or anything else of tangible and sane significance I could have already made history. Instead crazy is is what crazy does, thank you Forrest Gump.

The plan went quite smoothly. Coming in with my construction equipment on, iron ring visible on my pinky finger, white helmet and all I marched into the Administrative office, cold as ice (literally and figuratively as the weather outside sucked beyond belief with freezing rain converting everything into popsicle sticks) and I presented my story, unrehearsed as usual, to a gentleman named Sal at the front desk. Sal could see the scaffolding of construction work being done on the adjacent buildings quite easily through the windows of the front lobby and he didn't have the slightest inclination of double checking my story with the construction crews outside. Had he wanted to, I would have excused myself to the bathroom and gotten the hell out of there, that was my 'get outta Dodge' plan. Not only did Sal buy my story hook, line and sinker but miraculously he said he will go see if Dr. Jeffrey Madison, Head of the Chemistry Department here at the Military

College would be able to sit down with me this afternoon and go over my proposal. I must admit I was not ready for that.

While Sal was somewhere in the back hallways presumably talking to Dr. Madison I was pacing the front lobby trying to figure out how to go from proposing restorative masonry work at the Chemistry building to talking about chemical and biological processes of aging and dying of all living species on Earth. I was almost hoping that Sal comes back and tells me that I'm shit out of luck and to come back on another day. For a second George Costanza from *Seinfeld* came to my mind when he told Jerry he was scared to death about some scheme they were pulling and to just cancel the whole bloody thing. The 'tippy toe' episode! It looked like I was going to have to use the bathroom for real regardless of how this scenario was about to unfold. Finally, Sal came back. He informed me that Dr. Madison will have about 10 minutes at noon to speak with me and for me to come back then.

I had an hour to kill which was very generous.....from God and life, towards a filthy, lying scumbag such as myself. I took a massive shit, sat on the toilet bowl for a good 20 minutes gyrating my stomach to ensure it was all out, then when I finally re-emerged I went out of the building to the actual construction site adjacent to us. I walked around pretending I was the supervising engineer hoping to give credence to my lies and for Sal to notice me. However, he seemed beyond disinterested. He was already face deep into his computer screen and probably forgot that he ever met me. Fine by me really, quite frankly I would have hated the annoyance of him staring at me the whole time giving me the third degree. At least I got the name of the construction company doing the work on-site if Sal and Jeffrey Madison asked or mention it.

11:55 AM - I came back inside the Chemistry building with a very serious and self-absorbed look on my face. Construction supervision was very hard work, bullshiting and lying my way through life even harder. I checked in with Sal again and all he said was "Ah Mr. Stipecic, right down the hall and the last door on your left, that is Dr. Madison's office, just knock and let yourself in." I thanked him and made my way down the corridor, making noise and leaving mud tracks from my construction boots. I didn't want to look back to see the trail of the mess I was leaving in my wake. Story of my life. I reached the end of the hallway and knocked on the door. There was a cuspidor randomly sitting in the hallway halfway to Madison's office with apparently nothing in it and for some reason, thought of peeing into it came to my disturbed mind. I was a menace.

CHAPTER 6

IN A ROLE

Dr. Madison looked exactly like Santa Claus. At least what most people's idea of what Santa Claus looked like was. The way people dress up like at Christmas time. There are plenty of Internet images so I feel as though I don't need to elaborate further. The hair, the beard, the rosy cheeks, the belly, the works. Absent the suit. And he was grinning from ear to ear. His presence immediately put me at ease while at the same time making me feel rotten to the core for being seconds away from lying to this man.

"Hello Dr. Madison, my name is Shane Stanley, and I just want to thank you for seeing me on such short notice. I know I just sort of barged in here and went to the front desk asking to meet with the head of the Chemistry Department. I didn't think you or anyone would be able to see me so soon. Again, it is much appreciated."

"Please, Shane is it? Let's immediately switch over to the first name basis. Dr and Mr and all the formalities, my God it makes me feel like I'm a patient or subject about to be evaluated for a medical condition, haha."

"Haha, ok fair enough....Jeffrey."

"Jeff will do. Or J, or...you! Haha."

I felt tremendous relief wash over me.

"So Shane what can I do for you young man?"

Man, I almost wanted to sit on his lap and ask him for a train set. Was that weird?? Almost certainly. But then again who dared judge anything in this day and age of universal acceptance of everything that comes to anyone's mind. Whatever that's how I felt at 34 years old and about to become a father.

"So as I mentioned to Sal at the front desk over there I am a Civil Engineer working for Sentinel Engineering here in Kingston, Ontario. The Contractor doing renovations just over at the next building is Stone Temple Masonry. No relation to Stone Temple Pilots, haha (good one jackass). Anyways I am the supervising engineer doing Contract Administration for the client which of course is the Military College. Walking around the whole campus I noticed that this building, in particular, has a lot of cracked and deteriorated stone, deteriorated mortar joints and I can only imagine that the water is leaking through the walls. My thoughts are that if the College is interested I would love to extend our services to this building as well, or any others that might need reparative work on their masonry while the Contractor is still mobilized on site. I could prepare a proposal of our services for your review."

"Well I must say that you are right. We are constantly flooded here in the front lobby hallways. It's driving us nuts! If you walk along the inside walls you can see the water seeping down the stone....It's a mess it is. People and staff are constantly slipping and sliding all over the place I'm just afraid someone will break their neck or back one of these days. Sue the place. So Shane, your proposition makes sense. I think it would be a great idea to get as much work done on the exterior stone restoration as possible, as soon as possible. Is the Contractor able to work through the winter?"

"Ahm, yes. I believe they are scheduled to do just that on the other building. They will cover the work with heated tents between January and March, I imagine work on this building wouldn't start until some time in April. Therefore there would be no need for a heated enclosure so that will undoubtedly bring the price of the work down."

"Splendid. Well then I look forward to seeing your quote. When do you think you might be able to deliver it?"

"So I will propose to compile a maintenance plan, immediate work, 1 year, 5 year and 10 year interval work, with cost breakdown in order of precedence. I think I should be able to put something together by the end of the year. Seeing as how we are almost in December, I hope that's not too late? Would you prefer something sooner?"

"Well if you could hand something in by mid-December that would be ideal so I can slip it into the College Management Board right before the year-end. I know we have some budget allocated still for miscellaneous ventures, if we don't use it they will undoubtedly appropriate it to something else come January."

"I understand completely. I will have something for you by then."

"Excellent young man. Why thank you very much for being so proactive. And making me get off my ass to do something about this school. That's the way to get places in life, no doubt. Now, is there anything else I can do for you this afternoon?"

"Ahm...well..."

For a second I felt like a deer caught in the headlights.....or the sights of a rifle scope more precisely.

"You know....when I was applying to Universities right after high school, every school I sent my applications to I applied to two departments. The department of engineering and the department of science. I liked both equally, my overall science grades were better than my engineering grades."

"Oh is that so? I guess you wanted to make sure you got in somewhere for something. Would you have equally been keen on going down the science route as you were going the engineering route?"

"To be honest engineering was my main goal. At the time I was graduating high school and applying to universities Ontario cancelled Grade 13, Ontario Academic Credit or OAC so I was the last generation to have to go through with it. Therefore at the time of my graduating there were twice as many people graduating high school. The admission averages at all universities went up. That is why I mentioned my science curriculum average was higher than my engineering average. Had I gotten into science, but not into engineering, I probably would have figured out a way to get back into engineering somehow. My passion was bridges. I wanted to design them, build them."

It felt good to tell a bit of truth considering my entire being there was a complete and utter farce and con story. Even though the truth was not exactly flattering to the science field I suppose, I made it seem as my Plan B to engineering. Jeff took it with a good chip on his shoulder.

"You have to follow your passion! There is nothing wrong with that. And you had to play it smart. I don't blame you. I think your interest in engineering is nothing short of extraordinary. And the fact that you were willing to get to it eventually regardless even if you had to go the long way around the barn. Bravo! I'm just curious, let's say you did end up taking the science route, although you have in a way because if engineering is not science I don't know what is, but let's say you took the science curriculum, what path would you have chosen?"

My passion for engineering, once unquestionable, was really being put to the test these days. My father was an engineer as was my brother. They were both electrical. I had no interest in electrical but civil encompassed everything I liked from my childhood. I played with Lego a lot, and Bimo blocks, the cheaper much larger variant back in former Jugoslavija. I was always putting those things together, constructing buildings, bridges, robots, you name it. Going through school I was consistently good at math and physics. So engineering was a good choice. At this point for me, it was a steady grind kind of a job. It consisted of 75% of the time trying to cover your ass like a lawyer and arguing and debating with everyone involved and 25% actual engineering work. And I think I'm being generous. Verbal debates with anyone trying to screw you for money were part of that 75% of the time spent. Specifically contractors, not unlike Stone Temple Masonry already doing work here on campus.

"Well I would have either specialized in Chemistry or Biology. I like to think I had talent for both. And I always had a very good memory, I was able to memorize a lot of facts without having to write the information down. Unlike all my peers."

Really by the end of high school I was highly disappointing in chemistry. So much so I had to take Grade 10 chemistry again in night school to attempt to raise my marks before entering university. It was supposed to have been a breeze. It didn't quite turn out that way. The guy teaching the night class was a hard-ass who specifically made it a point to show everyone that night school was no joke and that if you thought coming here was going to give you higher grades as a given, think twice! My mark ended up being 2 percentage points higher than in my regular high school class! 73%

instead of 71%. Murphy's Law, I get the one night class professor who gave a rat's ass.

"Wonderful. I'd like to think I was a bit of a memory and fact storage sponge myself."

"Well you know, while I was considering Sciences as a career path I specifically became interested in the processes of aging and death. I became a bit obsessed with the mechanics of it all if you will. Why it happens, how, etc.. The whole concept always seemed a bit....programmed to me I suppose. Perhaps it's a bit hard to explain."

Jeff scrunched up his face a bit and said. "Interesting perspective. If I understand what you're trying to say. Can you elaborate a bit further?"

So I did. As best as I knew how. I just happened to have my printed out highlighted notes in my construction vest (no tape measure or pencil, but notes on death were key in the construction world), which I noticed took him by surprise. And so I droned on about how because of my brother I started reading about cancer, and how cancer cells work in the complete opposite way as normal cells and how all the theories about aging and dying always lead me to the same end conclusion of.....programmed death. Deliberate programming. I am careful not to use the words 'intelligent design' as I refuse to be categorized as some sort of religious nut. So I mentioned to Jeff that to me it seemed as though there was very little if any 'randomness' in the process of aging and dying. The whole process in its entirety seemed like a carefully set and timed process. Towards the end 'something' makes us start deteriorating and no one seems to know what. I realized I rushed my thoughts out a bit too quickly as I wanted to vomit it all out as fast as possible so that I'm not taking too much more of his time. When I'm nervous and in a rush then my accent seems considerably more pronounced. Even though I came to Canada at the age of 10 and have been speaking English for 26 years. I hoped everything I wanted to say came out alright, eloquently and not in a too convoluted way. Jeff paused for a moment and then replied.

"Shane do you always walk around with those printouts of scientific facts about aging and biological demise with you to all construction sites?"

He was grinning at me slyly now. All of a sudden he didn't remind me of Santa Claus one bit and I didn't wish to sit on his knee anymore (which was a weird-ass, albeit entirely childishly innocent, impulse in the first place). All of a sudden I don't think I liked him anymore. No, he looked more like the Violator from *Spawn*. It was a remarkable transformation. I've encountered that only a couple of times in my life, this sudden and drastic about-face. It must have been the fact that I was already nervous as all hell about my devious charade, so maybe I was too jittery as is. Maybe I was exaggerating, maybe I was misunderstanding his facial expressions. But then again, I was usually never wrong about these things. His face....looked different.

"Well.....ahm..actually I was talking about this subject just the other day with some of my colleagues from King's University. We... met at the cafeteria at the school and discussed this very subject. It's like a hobby of ours, sometimes we have these debates about how life began, how it will end, and so forth, as we are having some drinks at a bar or playing poker. So I still had these notes in my construction vest since the last time I met with them I came right off of a site. So the notes were still with me."

I always surprised myself at just how well I was able to lie my ass off right on the spot. I had quite the talent for it, especially during job interviews back in the day. This was by no means my finest work, but all things considered, it would have to do.

Jeff now looked like neither Santa Claus nor Violator from Spawn. He retreated into something in between. He was just a fat guy now who seemed not to give a shit. He finally spoke: "Mr. Stanley....." This was already bad as we went away from first name basis. My palms started sweating. "I'm a sufficiently busy individual as I'm sure you are as well. I don't have time for child games. If you have theoretical or scientific questions there is a time and place but this is not the way to go about it."

My sweaty palms quickly spread to sweaty nuts and ass. And cold sweat breaking out on the back of my neck, and at the back of my legs. And feet....then just like that I told myself 'snap out of it you piece of shit, you are 34 years old, you're married, have a child on the way, why are you allowing yourself to be shaken by this tub of lard?! Who gives a shit what he thinks, at the end of the day you walk out, never see this guy again and we all continue with our daily lives.' The problem, of course, was the fact that even though I was 34 years old and married and about to become a father there was something quintessentially juvenile, shameful and utterly irresponsible and idiotic about what I was doing here! I was scheming, lying, putting together theatre style Shakespearean plays to satisfy some prepubescent curiosity for fuck's sake! I mean really in the best possible scenario what am I getting out of this??? If no one suspects anything, if I get away with it all, if I get out of these ploys everything that I was hoping to get out of them......then what?! How will some kind of perceived 'closure' of knowledge make any God damned difference in my life?! In what way? In what way will I become more enlightened, a better husband, father, friend, employee....it will make no difference at all. Any of it. And what closure was I hoping to get? Somebody blurting out something that's not already well documented in all available scientific publications? It was all a useless waste of time and unnecessary stress. In the best-case scenario, I will get confirmation that we, 'we' being the most up to date scientific community don't know our ass from a hole in the ground about a myriad of matters and that the more we think we know we are just becoming aware of just how little we know! That's it! And as many people as many opinions. That's the best-case scenario. So it was hard to be brazen, confident and stoic in front of this man because I was so aware of how I was failing even in front of myself as far as my credibility was concerned. But whatever, I chose to pay it no mind and no matter how idiotic and immature my scheme was I had to see it through! The only way out was with balls, clown or no clown, fuck it, I gotta defend my mischief here!

"You know Jeff (fuck him I'm staying on the first name basis) I came here in good faith. I mean no disrespect, no ill will, no disturbance. I offered engineering services, something that you have found useful, meaningful and practical. We agreed that I was going to provide a quote (I never was) for my company's services (a company I didn't work for) and afterward we moved on to a light-hearted and friendly chat. We opened up some interesting subject matters. I must say I did not foresee that the conversation was going to turn so sour and so suddenly, and upset you in any way. I didn't mean to offend you or to waste your time. I'm not sure why you seem so agitated all of a sudden."

I was swimming well. Again and again I was amazed at my ability to stay cool under pressure, to improvise to overcome to adapt. All the while going through immense psychological and physiological anguish and torture.

Jeff was silent. Motionless, calm, a drone. He enjoyed sitting there in that format for moments, thinking he was making me squirm. However the longer he sat there trying to make me sweat the more I realized he was sitting there desperately trying to make me feel uncomfortable and so I started to...get angry. Except unlike Hulk or some spazzy idiot off the street high on PCP I wasn't going to explode into a fit of rage or flail around trying to morph into some kind of a vicious, bulked up entity (as if that were even possible). I was just going to stand there, confidently and let my anger build up my confidence, my arrogance, my calm. Fuck you motherfucker, no matter what I'm trying to pull here and no matter how idiotic it may be I'll still defend to the death my right to pull this scheme. So, do your worst!

"You got a lot of balls Mr. Stanley. Shane, or whatever the fuck your name is."

Well it sure as shit wasn't Shane Stanley.

Uuuuhhh, we are swearing at each other! Well, actually he is swearing at me. Profusely, unabashedly, arrogantly. A Prof a PhD, reduced to act as an offended weakling little child. It never ceased to amaze me how if you push someone's buttons, even unintentionally, without knowing you are pushing them, people tend to turn into screaming and kicking little children. All it takes is to hit the right buttons, get the passcode right, and you can watch them unravel before you. It was kind of an enjoyable experience for me at this point. Unmasking, unearthing, emotionally undressing people in front of you like that, it was fun, exhilarating, it was an utter and total power trip. All of a sudden the nonsense and the unethical behavior of what I was doing here seemed irrelevant, not as bad, because this man before me, this older experienced PhD who should be my mentor, my superior, my better and someone I should be looking up to has officially lost all of his credibility. At least in my eyes, he was finished. My arrogance could now take over completely because all respect from me towards him was.... gone. Like a fart in the wind.

"Dr. Madison a man with your knowledge, life experience, credentials, how could you allow yourself to sound like a prepubescent child in such a manner? I mean honestly is the swearing necessary? Is the attitude? Is the posturing? At the risk of sounding completely rude, but your attitude turned almost psychotic in a matter of minutes, dare I ask why?"

Not only was I no longer ashamed of my scheme and wasting this idiot's time but I was actually, secretly hoping for this guy to stand up and lunge at me so I could have an excuse to punch him in the face. Now I was officially a teenager with hormones surging and ego flaring wanting this to end up in the most unprofessional manner with cops being called. I could feel the blood pumping through the arteries in my neck and into my temples. I no longer cared for anything.

I could see Jeff get considerably angrier. I could see it in his face, but not anything else. Not in his otherwise demeanor. He didn't move or flinch or twitch or shiver. He just sat there with his arms crossed on his belly. The only thing I noticed was that his stare became a lot more intense, but again this could have just been my perception, and I could have sworn his mouth tightened more and his fingers clenched up in their grip. This lasted for several minutes. But then it faded. It intensified, more and more, climaxed and then dissipated. He did his best to revert to Santa Claus before he finally spoke.

"You know Shane I do have to apologize, I'm not sure what came over me. Been working on some projects here at school and I'm more edgy than usual. You are correct there is nothing wrong in you being inquisitive and starting a side topic. I'm just not being myself.....I'm not in my usual mood for banter. I will try to give you some of my opinions on the matter of the biological clock, aging, death, cancer, as best as I can. And please don't think anything of my agitation, one of these days we should go out for a drink once I get some of these things off my desk."

What proceeded was five minutes or so of Jeffrey Madison pretty much repeating the exact same things that were highlighted on my printed out sheets containing information on matters of life, death and biological processes of living tissue degradation. He said nothing different, new or enlightening, he repeated what I told him that I read.....and rather poorly at that.

"Well I hope I helped quench some of your thirst for curiosity Shane. I'm sorry I can't be of much more help, it is simply because there is so much more we just don't know. Not yet anyway. But stay on the lookout, scientific research is always advancing, always coming up with new theories, conclusions, discoveries. I'm sure in five, ten years we will know a helluva lot more than we do now."

"Well thank you for your time Dr. Madison, it was.......very informative. Again, I am sorry for catching you in a bad time and if I've said anything to offend you."

"Not at all Shane, the apologies once again are and should all be mine. I simply got up on the wrong side of the bed this morning as they say. Anytime you wish to speak with me again don't hesitate to reach out to Sal and he'll set up a meeting. Actually here is my card, with my direct office number, email and cell number on it. Oh, and one more thing, I just remembered. Last staff meeting I had we did discuss the need to renovate all the bathroom facilities in this building. I'm terribly sorry it completely skipped my mind. Again, please notch it up to my distractedness and agitation due to my hectic schedule. Regardless, bearing this in mind I'm fairly certain we cannot accommodate any more renovative work on the exterior of any of our buildings here at the Campus. I'm sorry Shane, it completely slipped my mind. It's an old campus, there are tens of washrooms and they are in a terrible shape, some don't even have properly running water or flushing toilets, some are missing hot and cold water taps, toilet seats, haha, I'm sure you can appreciate the urgency in having something like that fixed and brought back to working order as soon as possible above all else. So I think we should hold off on even reviewing your proposal for masonry restoration until at least later next year. I mean I suppose you could put it together and drop it off at my office anytime, but

I just wanted to give you a heads up that it most likely won't get accepted at this time. I would of course try to review it and put in a good word to the school as soon as possible. So it's up to you, just wanted to be straightforward with you. I hope you understand?"

It was a brilliant exit for both of us. He wanted me to get the fuck out of here as soon as possible and I didn't want to hand in any damn 'fake' proposal either as all of my intentions were insincere and a lie anyway. So it was a good time to pull a parachute cord out of this nightmare.

"Oh I see, well that is unfortunate. But no worries I'll also take a look at my schedule and see when I could put a proposal together. If I can get around to it in between closing off some construction projects I will and leave it with Sal, if not I'll be sure to hand it into your hands before next summer."

"Oh that would be fine Shane, as I said at the very earliest it would be a year from now that we could consider revisiting renovating the exterior again. Take your time with the proposal and we will be in touch."

I found it entertaining how often he enjoyed repeating my… fake name. Almost as if he knew something was amiss.

"Ok sounds good. It was a pleasure to meet you Dr. Madison. I'll have something for you in the near future. Have a good day."

"All the best Shane."

It was always a gymnastics exercise in the talents of psychopathy going back to being nice after a conversation takes a turn for the sinister. First nice, then crazy, then nice again. I've had conversations like these before, mainly on dates with women, with men it was rarer and much more dangerous when they occurred.

I left his office. Leaving the chemistry building took a while longer as I had to take another shit in their dilapidated bathroom facilities (Jeff wasn't lying about that) on the way out, the stress of this showdown had to find release somewhere. The bathrooms really were in a dreadful shape although not in any particularly worse shape than any other bathroom I've ever visited in public, government or restaurant places. Luckily for me I was able to find one stall where the toilet bowl had a seat on it. And this was our military's university. But I sincerely doubted that the school had any plans for renovating them. Jeff Madison was full of it. But he had to get me out of his sight. I was sure that I would never see Jeff Madison again. Sal I could see again but he will be provided with extraordinary instructions on how to screen me much more thoroughly in the future making sure I come nowhere near any of the staff or any person of significance in this building or elsewhere on campus ever again. I guess I'll have to ensure my children never come to this school either. Perhaps not, I never told them my real name.

I got saved by Jeff's raging outburst. I had no intention of providing any renovation proposal. The name I gave was fake, the name of the company I worked for was real but I didn't work there, my involvement with the actual construction works ongoing at the adjacent building was fake. My only hope now was that the actual engineering company that I worked for doesn't get any engineering work involving me at the Military College for years to come. Because if we do, and I have to run it, I'm fucked. I could only imagine my trying to avoid being included and making up a bullshit story to my boss as to why I can't be involved.

Overall I felt fine as I came home. My shenanigans were quite bulletproof. I covered my tracks well. Despite the friction between Jeff and myself, I was fairly certain that nothing else could come of this. Everything I told them including my name was fake. But at the same time very much believable. When lying in life try to stay as close to the real truth as possible. So with nothing there to particularly worry about, I could put all of my focus on Jeff's strange mood swings. My inquiry and chit chat into all things biological as I pulled printed documents out of my construction vest got Jeff eerily suspicious and angry. It was unmistakable. He became shockingly wired, rude...scared. Why was he so rattled and why did that bring him so much rage?! All just because I wasted his time? All because aside from me trying to, albeit dishonestly (which was unbeknownst to him), sell my company's services to also have a philosophical discussion rooted into little known scientific facts. That would piss him off so much? I mean I know I wasted his time but he wasn't aware of any particular lie. Would he get that mad if this was only related to me wasting his time....And then, his shocking about-face, not once but twice, from good to mad to courteous again.

CHAPTER 7

OSCILLATING

In the coming days and weeks my mood fluctuated. And my confidence levels. I went from not caring about my exploits at King's University and Military College and their potential impact to being scared shitless thinking about what if someone finds out what I tried to pull. What if Jeff comes knocking on my home door? At the moment I was in the later frame of mind. I could say nothing to Alicia nor anyone else for I was sure she would pack up and live me and probably go and stay with her parents. Not only did I go behind her back and acted out a highly unseemly and irresponsible ploy for no reason than to satisfy my egoistically obsessive mind, but I also went about it in a reckless way. Every day at work, every time I logged into my email, checked Facebook, LinkedIn or whatever other social media I was expecting to have someone call me out on my behavior at the Military College. Every day I thought I would come home and find a police car in my driveway as Jeffrey decided to report me and they managed to find me. My God, there were probably cameras at that school somewhere...I could barely pay attention at work, at meetings, during conversations with my wife. Attending prenatal education classes was excruciatingly difficult, I could barely memorize anything being told to me. Alicia was furious at me at times, snapping at me, rolling her eyes, saying soon she will have to take care of 'two babies' with attention spans of squirrels. It was rough. As weeks went by and no ramifications happened I slowly started to relax and go back to being myself. Slowly but surely my participation in my day to day life came back. Back to the 'normal' levels of distractedness, paranoia and spacing out. Normal enough that at least people around me recognized me and didn't have the urge to institutionalize me.

With my obsessive interest still unabated and now that I was beginning to feel like no repercussions were going to unfold from my demented lying and orchestrated schemes I went back to thinking about Jeff's weird and overblown anger at me for trying to get his opinion on biological processes of natural deterioration and death and for bringing in all that material with me. I know I must have come off as strange, and even juvenile but to merit such a strong reaction from him was and still is exceptionally shocking. I ran it over in my head numerous times and it still seemed inappropriate, too intense. If anything people in North America are overly polite, can be unnoticeably fake especially in uncomfortable situations and go out of their way to produce a perception that everything is fine, no worries, even if you piss them off beyond imagination. Especially in awkward moments. They strive to water the situation down, minimize the effect. Jeff Madison did not take that route. He wanted to strangle me for daring to start the topic that I started. It was unmistakable. And all these weeks since, I knew I was right. He was out of line, but he was out of line because I seemed to have set off a tripwire. I became convinced of a conspiracy. I really wanted one in my life. I was beginning to live out my own fiction movie. So I started filtering the internet once again. Aging and death scientific articles, Dr. Jeffrey Madison the Military College, age, death, natural degradation, decomposition, why aging causes death, why death happens, why do people like me seemingly randomly go insane... Then I went into aging and death related controversies, etc...my eyes were bloodshot and stinging, I was out of control. Controversial opinions on the subject matter, conspiracy theories, debates, does someone out there insist on one theory over the other, is someone's theory being purposely discredited, ridiculed, bashed. I found....nothing to write home about. It was all vague, all the same, nothing strange, intriguing or peculiar. I went to bed.

A month later at least the fear of people at work finding out about my nonsense shenanigans had almost but completely retreated. I checked with my boss during our bi-weekly project workload overview and any current and upcoming projects were nowhere close to the Military College. Also, nothing involving Stone Temple Masonry either. I slowly retreated into the comfort of my daily work and family routine. I even gave my ever productive research a break. I just....lived. Existed. But as usual and with absolutely everything in my life I got bored again quickly. It still felt nice to give the whole thing a break. Because coming back to something at a later date when a person is fresh and rested from the subject at hand can yield better results, be more productive, crisper, more substantial. You always find something you didn't before even though you were sure you searched everything many times over. So the moment I cleared some real work off my desk just so that my boss didn't think I was a completely useless pustule making the company no money, and setting aside all the other projects that were nowhere near finished but oh well who the fuck cares, I delved again into my research. Rinse and repeat and rinse and repeat, I found nothing new. I did, however, manage to enter into the even more abstract, superstitious and conspiratorial. It led me all the way to religions, to matters such as UFO religions, Scientology, Raelism, ancient aliens. Basically, just as it sounds, theories postulating that life on Earth was indeed 'intelligent design' but not from God, but from a far superior extraterrestrial species much older and more advanced than humans. A guy named Erich von Daniken wrote several books on the subject, famous one being 'Chariots of the Gods?' outlining how aliens must have visited humans thousands of years ago and helped us build the pyramids and other civil engineering wonders, how ancient drawings in caves and ancient paintings depicted flying objects in the sky and humanoids dressed in astronaut suits were extraterrestrial visitors. My dad out of all people actually got me hooked on this stuff. It was super cool for me as a kid finding out about this from him since he was always the most overly and unnecessarily serious, down to Earth and grown-up person I knew. I couldn't get enough reading about it. It totally made sense to me as a potential theory of how we came to be or at least why and how we advanced as a species. It explained many things, sightings, unexplained phenomena, etc. In the end what was more far fetched, that an ancient grandfather with a long white beard and a cane called God sits up in the sky in his armchair created us all, judging who will go to Heaven or Hell, or that an alien extraterrestrial race, far older and more capable than us played 'God', wanted to test their scientific power across the Universe and treated Earth as a Petri dish to see if they can cook up some life on this tennis ball planet of ours. Of course Daniken and others like him have all been heavily debunked by 'experts'. Neither side has any proof of shit but the ones that are debunking are deemed as experts yet the ones claiming the ancient alien theory are deemed as quacks. Nice. Conspiracy theory police were at it again, lurking behind every corner to dissipate any theory other than the ones shoved down our throats like foie gras by organized religion and contemporary science and status quo. And then the 'experts' have to throw in the mix that these alternative theorists such as Daniken are lying, cheating, been threatened with jail time at some point, got involved with fraud, have mental issues, don't think puppies and kitties are all that cute and the discreditation package is then complete. Problem solved, stop reading their shit, go watch your football game and fuck off. Yes sir! And of course I reacted the exact opposite. The more you told me not to do something, not to read something, I'll make sure I won't read anything but. I've learned that especially when someone or something is being bashed and criticized mercilessly then usually there is something much more to the individual being criticized than meets the eye and that there is something highly suspicious about the crew doing all the criticizing. Why I must be a conspiracy theorist. No doubt. How many conspiracy facts out there get completely diluted and flushed down the toilet every damn day by simply being branded conspiracy theories, I wondered. These days in general, you get labeled with something and you can spend the rest of your life defending that the label doesn't belong or fit, but it sticks with you like flees on an ox regardless. Accusations alone encompass trials and verdicts today, looking for real facts is an outdated practice…

I read some more then I finally put the iPhone on airplane mode and went to sleep. Alicia was sleeping in our room in our big king-sized bed, I was in one of the two guest rooms. She was getting bigger by the day and I was a restless sleeper and I needed to toss about 100 times in rapid succession for about half an hour before I could finally settle down and fall asleep. Left side to the back to the right side, repeat, with only staying in one position for maybe a minute. It drove her nuts, especially now that she was pregnant. Maybe I should try sleeping in the washing machine.

One of those giant ones they have at dry cleaners. So just before my trying to fall asleep routine every night, I would read a bit more, that would knock me out. So much so that the act of turning the cell phone off woke me up again. Finally with the phone on charge, airplane mode on I went to sleep at around 11 PM.

The alarm went off at 6:30 AM as usual every day from Monday to Friday. I barely get up around that time during the summer months, now with winter firmly in our bloodstream and a ritual more idiotic than the belief that the Earth is still flat in practice such as the daylight savings time in full effect, I merely used the 6:30AM alarm as a gentle reminder that at some point over the next hour or so I should squeeze my ass out of bed, like an old remnant at the bottom of a toothpaste tube, and attempt my usual morning routine before going to work. Luckily my work was flexible, everyone came and went without being scrutinized and having to lift their hand up to ask for permission like in school. As long as we got our shit done within scheduled time and budget.

7:00 AM - Waking up for the second time I still felt like a piece of constipated crap slowly working my way out. It was still dark, it was fucking cold and leaving my bed felt the same way when I left Europe for Canada when I was 10 years old, traumatic, dreadful and depressing as all hell. Seeing the bed distance itself from me as I went to the bathroom like an astronaut slowly leaving Earth's orbit felt exactly the same as seeing the European land distance itself from my eyes from the airplane that fateful day back in 1994. Tragic. Nothing short of it I tells ya.

Time in the bathroom was uneventful, the shower more eventful but nothing extraordinary. The shaving and nail clipping were more annoying than anything. Now the dressing part. I managed to put on my shirt and underpants and....one sock on. Then I sat on the chair tired from all the ordeals encountered already in the morning and I looked like I was about to pass out all over again with Alicia staring at me laughing her ass off. My God the idea of thirty more years of this until retirement.....

I gathered the pile that was myself off the chair somehow after the socks have been properly placed on the feet. Then with a T-shirt, underwear and socks on I ventured into the closet to pick out pants and a sweater. I was in there for a good five minutes pondering what to wear. It became almost hypnotic after a while. Maybe I could hide in here for the rest of my days I thought. I finally emerged, dressed wouldn't you know it, grabbed my phone and made my way downstairs. As I unplugged my phone off the charger and took it off Airplane Mode I received an instant message that engulfed the entire screen which read "You've been infected with Pseudonym Software and your battery has been drained". I stared at it a little while. It had exclamation marks all over it, a red background that was shooting out away from the text as if to signify explosion and the whole thing was pulsating and blinking. I was in disbelief but I figured yeah right, give me a break, it's gotta be some spyware bullshit. I mean I've encountered a shitload of annoying software in my day but to drain my battery completely, that's a bit far fetched. I exited the screen and was fully expecting that the battery would read '100%' or full charge, however I was unpleasantly surprised. The battery was indicating red and giving a charge percentage of only '5%'. I couldn't believe it?! I turned my phone on and off, waited a couple of minutes, when it came back up again now it was saying battery life at '3%'. I went downstairs.

"Hey Alicia check this shit out."

"Marcus can you please go easy on your intensity and swearing this early in the morning, I mean we just woke up for God's sake. And lower your voice."

"Alright. Just listen though. My phone was on charge all night on the nightstand next to me, the same as every night. Just now I took it off charge and this software pops up on my screen claiming my battery is drained. I thought it was bullshit but look it's freaking drained, 5%?! 3% now that I turned it off and on just to check if it was all a glitch."

Alicia was completely uninterested as she kept preparing oatmeal and washing fruit to cut up and put in it, so that oatmeal wouldn't taste like watery paint chips but like....actual food. It drove me nuts when she ignored me and wasn't giving me the proper undivided attention that a wailing child like me deserved, but instead went about her business. I was extremely agitated..... and turned on at the same time.

"Mhmm. I'm sure you just forgot to plug it in. Happens to me sometimes."

"I 100% plugged it in. I distinctly recall unplugging it from the charger just now before coming downstairs."

"Well then the charger must have fallen out of the wall socket."

Quickly I ran upstairs to check the wall in order to see whether the iPhone charger had perhaps fallen out of the electrical socket. Nope. It was firmly in there. That would have been very surprising now that I gave it a second thought, those chargers fit very firmly and snug into both the wall socket and the phone socket. I ran back downstairs.

"It's plugged in into the wall, not even loose."

"Well then I'm sure you just forgot to plug it into your phone."

I was getting extremely agitated now. "I already told you I unplugged the phone from the charger minutes ago, so it was plugged in just fine."

Silence, more ignoring. To hell with this. I ate my oatmeal, made sandwiches and put together my lunch and headed out to work. The roads were icy as hell, the winters in Ontario weren't as rough as they used to be temperature and precipitation wise but the oscillating temperature changes caused for way more freezing rain and icy conditions. The car was all-wheel drive with winter tires, it handled its own but still, when all four wheels were on ice at the same time AWD or not prayer was the only technique that worked.

I got to work and I couldn't stop thinking about what happened. The first thing I did was I got on the Internet and started Googling 'smartphone battery draining spyware', 'spyware that drains smartphone batteries', 'iPhone battery draining due to malware' but I found pretty much nothing. The only thing that was on some forums was that certain malware might engage applications or search for things online without the owner's knowledge, in turn draining the battery. But this sounded like it was the case of phones that were not plugged in, but were just left idling without the charger plugged into them. And the battery drain wasn't this severe. It certainly wouldn't explain my case which was a smartphone plugged into the charger and on airplane mode all bloody night! My heart started racing, I was panicking. My fear of repercussions from my shenanigans of weeks ago was pretty much completely faded and sure enough, now that I was almost carefree this happens. What could have caused this?! Why?! Was this an accident, does it happen to other people, was it deliberate. Why me...Why couldn't I find an immediate and instantaneous relief on the Internet that something similar happens to other people??

The rest of my day at work was spent in a completely unproductive manner. I pretty much spent most of my day incessantly googling and scouring the Internet looking for some forum, some article that explained how smartphone battery draining malware and spyware was common. That and pretty much going from person to person at work asking if something similar had ever happened to them. Nothing! Everyone looked at me in a weird way and coined the phrase so commonly heard throughout my life "Wow Marcus I've never heard of that before!". The more people said that to me the more my eyes widened and my face turned pale as I went to the next person, and the next. I'm sure the last person I asked about this at work, Amanda in accounting, must have thought I was coming down with tuberculosis by the way my look deteriorated even going as far as to ask "Marcus, are you ok?".

My drive home was hazy and felt like I was driving through a steam sauna. Steam sauna on the road due to the clouds and shit weather, steam sauna in my head. My sweaty palms were making it hard for me to grip and maneuver the steering wheel. I was a mess, no doubt. But I kept driving. Luckily it was Friday. End of the week, it always helped. Just before heading home I had the weekly Friday lunch with people from my company. Good lunch specials, good soup, especially key for winter months. I hated to miss it. However my mind was absent. Ten people or so showed up, and it was lively. Talking about projects, our day to day activities in the office. It was good, light, but unfortunately I was distracted. I kept looking at my cell phone. Searching, digging for the reason my phone went dead for the most bizarre reason, searching for my obsession and items related to my months-long quest on matters of life and death, on matters related to why someone would want to crash my phone on purpose.....that's where I was at this time, this is the corner I hid in. On purpose! People even kept asking me "Marcus common man why are you on your phone all the time?! Talk to us, haha" I was trying my best to field the questions with "Oh common Michael, you are all on your phones too, seriously why am I being singled out?". I was trying my best to be nonchalant about the whole thing, and truthfully everyone else couldn't help but to check their phones every once in a while as well. It was as natural as breathing, check the messages, check the Internet, check the email. But at the same time I knew I was doing it more than anyone else that day. Reaching for that phone, excessively searching, as soon as a thought popped into my mind I had to satisfy it with a quick search. Freaking out. The beer was good and strong, but even that couldn't distract me. It took some serious concentration to get through this Friday's lunch without anyone else suspecting that I was going completely insane.

I made it home, somehow. Distracted, buzzing from that alcohol rich, 8% ale and full of that rich meal with rice, veggies and a Korean flank steak I just ate. Alicia was in a good mood.

"Hey good looking, how was lunch?"

"Ahm, good. It was fun. Lots of people showed up. It was hilarious, we all joked around, planned our ski trip in February. About seven people or so should be going."

"Oh great, I'm glad you had fun. Sounds like the ski trip should be a nice getaway for you guys, I'm sorry I can't make it, you don't want me skiing 5 months pregnant, haha. I'm clumsy enough as it is."

"Of course not. No worries."

I won't lie. I just wanted to come across as sane and regular, of sound thinking and capable of communicating. I didn't want to cause her any undue stress. At the same time, I wanted this conversation to end and quickly. I wanted to hide, and I hope I did, the anxiety that was ripping me apart from the inside. I couldn't wait for us to just eat, sit and watch something on Netflix while I indulged in smashing beers and later smoking some cigars. The never-ending infatuation with all things ultimately bad for us. Too bad the buzz couldn't last forever while we retained the ability to function responsibly. I resolved nothing from my morning worry and usually it didn't take this long. When I worried about something, life, random issues, my obsessive efforts would usually conspire to make me find my peace of mind by the end of the day, or shortly thereafter. Thus far this was still not the case. And I couldn't keep making love with my cell phone all the freaking night as I knew it would drive Alicia nuts. So I sat and put on a face of a man who is not having a near mental breakdown inside and we watched TV. The more beers went down the more they calmed me down.

After about a third or fourth bottle I could feel my stress slowly receding. All of a sudden nothing seemed as worrisome anymore. Figures right, this is why people drink. Ironically tomorrow I was going to pay for this, most likely in a spectacular way. These days at age of 34 my body could barely process three strong beers without being hungover as all Hell the next day. And any worry I had before my drinking binge the day before, which the booze helped suppress, will be threefold the next day. I was going to feel utter depression in the pits of my stomach. But I was paying no mind to such trivial matters now, as I was juiced and feeling great. Short nor long term planning was not at play here and now.

Around 10 PM Alicia was exhausted and went to bed. Me, nicely tuned and glossy-eyed, I went out for a cigar. It was not a pleasant experience. The temperature was dropping, we were supposed to get a half a meter of snow Saturday through Sunday, the wind was howling viciously I felt the entire block of the shanty townhouse complex was going to get airborne like Dorothy's house in Oz and get splattered somewhere into smithereens. I got an inch into the cigar before I chucked it, it was simply too cold and the dropping temperatures and wind were diminishing my buzz. Now I had to go quickly back inside to take a couple of swigs of whiskey to return the drunkenness stolen by rude old man winter and to warm up. Smooth.

I sat my butt at the computer. I said fuck it to any subsequent feverish research. I read all my politics and world affairs earlier so really the only thing left was to play video games. Alicia was fast asleep, I still wanted to stay up a while and enjoy my drunken glow.....as I was biologically disadvantaged in being unable to enjoy a pregnant 'glow' like her. But then again she couldn't enjoy the drunken glow in the state she was in, and which glow is more serene of an experience only time and history will tell.....man I was drunk.

Before logging into Steam I decided to log into Facebook to see what's new in the social spheres. I logged in and the first thing that popped up was a bunch of programming script. It just sat there on the screen and didn't move. I've never seen this before. I was also able to scroll up and down in it. Nothing but a bunch of jumbled programming language. It wasn't going away so I exited the screen. I tried logging in the second time. This time the surprise was shock and fear and not just plain bewilderment. My entire Facebook account was written in what appeared to be some sort of Arabic script. I scrolled up and down frantically.....I was not able to do much else, I couldn't click on any of my photos or change anything on the profile. I was just able to scroll. I logged out the second time and I tried logging in again. This time a message popped up saying that my account has been compromised AND that my password is expired. My heart started racing and my sweet buzz fading. I was starting to get that same old bad feeling I had this morning when my cell phone battery drained randomly. What the fuck now?! Back and forth I went a couple of times. Tried logging in again and again and over again. Nothing! The same message, account compromised, expired password! So I went to contact Facebook Help. I explained my situation and I put in a different, new password. All this time I've been using my University email as my login, which hasn't been valid for years. That means if Facebook wanted to contact me to report to me that my account was compromised they would have sent the message to the old expired email. I never would have gotten shit. This was bad. Or was it? People's accounts are constantly hacked into, get altered, I hear about it all the time. I was trying my best not to freak out and maybe I wouldn't have been overreacting as much as I had was it not for the cell phone battery experience this morning. So I did my best to calm myself but my night was ruined. My buzz now almost completely gone, just the headache remaining, and I didn't feel like wanting to play video games or anything for that matter as all I wanted to do now was to google 'hacked Facebook accounts'. Substitute one obsession with another. I got nowhere other than online forums saying to contact Facebook Help. And then waiting, my favorite hobby. Fuck.

Of course, weeks went by and my Facebook account was still hacked and compromised. I sent out several subsequent messages to Facebook's Help Desk and got no reply whatsoever. I also tried finding a contact number in any of their centers from Toronto to Montreal but conveniently there was nothing of the sort. Then I remembered my second cousin in Slovenia worked for an engineering company who did numerous installation setups for Facebook all over Europe, setting up their data centers. I told him about my predicament and sure enough he said he is friends with one of the Directors of a Facebook Marketing department and that he will get a technician to work on my account as soon as possible. He even gave me the Director's contact information for me to follow up with. The guy replied back instantly! Wow, is it possible that this will get resolved instantaneously as apparently the Director claimed?

Of course not, I mean after all it was me we were talking about here, not someone with average luck. A few more weeks went by, I followed up with the Facebook guy at least three times. Guarantees were made and words 'any day now' were used. I even spoke to the technician who worked on my account directly. Nothing got resolved and finally I said screw it and I created a new Facebook account. It is remarkable in this day and age how the more incapable people are about making something happen the more they staunchly and adamantly swear up and down that they will, in fact, make that something happen for sure and momentarily! Since graduating and receiving my Bachelor's in Civil Engineering I've changed seven different engineering companies. I was driven to keep hopping around by valid reasons (in my opinion) which were mainly a lack of quality engineering work and severe disorganization within all departments I worked in. Oh and I hated living in Toronto, I wanted to get out of there like it was Alcatraz. So I was far beyond driven but the process was a grueling and frustrating grind where all the finest of human nature came to the surface to float....and for me to gulp down as I was swimming around with mouth wide open in a sea of job hunters, ridiculous promises and lies, and listening to endless guarantees that of course never came true. No one can look you in the eye and just say "Sorry we can't help you at this time". Closure, one of the things I crave the most in this life is as reclusive as finding a diamond in a toilet bowl. How 'lucky' I was that it mattered that much to me. Disappearing acts and vanishing into thin air without having the balls of giving you a clear answer was everyone's specialty these days, fine, I get it, but promising the opposite of what you know to be the case was a new development. That took things into the surreal.

Being the genius that I am I put the exact same name on my second Facebook account that I had on my first. So for a while afterward Facebook kept verifying whether it was truly me since the first account with my full first and last name was out there still sitting in the Facebook programmable space, nice, infected and all...

I again went about my life. I slowly started forgetting about the drained cell phone battery, especially since no similar recurrence has reappeared, and the hacked Facebook account. Apparently at least ten other people I knew on the stretch of 401 from London to Kingston had their Facebook accounts hacked in a similar fashion. So hackers were out there, this was common. Neither my cousin nor his Facebook friend knew who or why was doing it all they could say is that the code for the hack came somewhere from "overseas". Remarkable they couldn't retrieve my account...they did however give me some security tips which I adopted.

The winter moved along slowly but uneventfully, still no major snowstorm. Alicia and I were huddled inside playing Risk: Game of

Thrones version. Here and there I was googling the rifle and hand-gun I was planning on getting. I put Alicia at ease as best as I knew how about owning firearms. I will keep them on heavy lockdown in metal lockers in the basement and I will never store ammunition in the house. Whatever ammunition I buy I will use up at the target range. She seemed ok with that. I narrowed down the rifle to a CZ 452 Grand Finale and the handgun to CZ P-09. Best prices, best look, I was satisfied. Stan approved. Especially considering that our mother was Czech it instilled a certain sense of pride knowing that my weapons would be Ceska Zbrojovka and made in the Czech Republic. It was also remarkable that an arms company from Eastern Europe was so highly ranked on all US charts of best quality weapons. I was so excited I went down to the local gun shop and put a down deposit on the rifle. All the stores I contacted between Toronto and Ottawa had one (!) supplier and that one supplier had only one (!) of that rifle left. It was incredible, I felt elated. I put $300 down and off I went. Ah yes, it was a good weekend. I also scored a Bushnell scope, Made in Japan, for $400! Was just sitting there on the shelf, one of the old models left. Ha, I treated myself good. I was looking forward to having some fun target shooting.

CHAPTER 8

BACK TO REGULAR

Coming to work on Monday morning I felt great. My obsessions of the last few months have receded, I started reverting to my day to day life, I stopped worrying my pregnant wife with my childish and ridiculous nonsense and I stopped looking wide-eyed and bewildered whether in front of her or my friends or co-workers or whomever. But obviously that wasn't the reason as to why I felt so good on this fine Monday morning. I put a down deposit on my rifle, that's what was doing it for me. Nothing like a good toy for a man-child like me to put a smile on my face. Gotta utilize one of the few things available in this otherwise minimalistic society, such as the ability to bear arms. And have fun with them at the range. Since I had no intention of becoming a hunter. And let's not kid ourselves, I wasn't buying weapons because I wanted to ensure my family's self-defense capabilities. Canada, at the end of the day, was still as safe as a baby's crib, I was buying guns because I like the way they looked and I wanted to do some shooting for fun. When I found out we were expecting a child, and my initial happiness subsided a bit (and I really was happy, it was a great time in our life, a child felt like an amazing addition) I immediately started thinking what else we could blow money on before the baby comes and we become officially cash strapped. So Alicia decided to get herself a new Mac laptop and I opted for....a gun license and some guns. I dragged Alicia to the gun course with me since I like her to have the ability to participate in my hobbies with me if she so chooses. She was a great sport about it too, a hot broad in early pregnancy in a gun class with a bunch of military guys and me. She took her notes and fed us snacks and worked the guns better than me! The girl was always good with her hands. Very articulate, excellent dexterity. She got higher grades on both the practical and the written tests than me?! I was so turned on I could barely see straight.....

So with glee in my eye I sat at my work computer uncharacteristically chipper. I ate some fruit and made myself a hot cup of coffee and I started sifting through my emails. I spent the morning shoveling the driveway prior to leaving home. The snowblower we bought obviously didn't work since it's been sitting there for a year and it was all rusty and it took turning it on in warmer weather each year for it to unhinge itself from its slumber. So like the idiot that I was when I heard that an unusually cold snowstorm was approaching I forgot to turn the snowblower on in the garage just for practice before the temperatures dropped to -20C all weekend and a foot of snow fell. This morning was too late, so my neighbor and I shoveled our asses off all morning and dug us out. I got my weekend exercise which although tiring also provided for a release of positive endorphins and helped further with my overall good mood already elated due to my gun purchases. I was planning to go to my Muay Thai training on Saturday morning but I was nicely hungover from my beer binging on Friday and I was in no shape for sparring. I went to bed late too, so barely got any sleep and since I was hungover, I could forget training. I couldn't handle hangovers anymore. And having one I could only pray that it didn't make me physically sick. Actually ill, with fever and all. That's what a flower I've become in my old age of 34. So the shoveling was my first vigorous exercise in days.

There were a ton of emails. A swing bridge replacement we designed about an hour West of Kingston was nearing its completion and now the sticking point was the hydraulics and mechanical components that made it turn. The Contractor's sub-consultant was being a pain in the ass. He was 80 years young, owned his own hydraulic company, cared not for deadlines, specifications, standards or proper documentation and made our life a living hell. You can't scare a guy of 80 who's owned his own company most of his life and is one foot in the grave. So we all knew we were stuck with him and his company till the end. With being this close to the finish line, although months delayed, the Client didn't want to pull the plug and get someone else to finish the job as they knew setting that up would delay us another six months at least. So our exercise now was to babysit this guy through to the finish line regardless of how cranky and filled with pompous attitude and outright defiance he was. So the emails and teleconferences were daily and as frequent as possible since our own hydraulic and mechanical sub-consultant pretty much had to do the Contractor's sub's work while the rest of us had to witness it and be available for constant feedback and support. My inbox was fast approaching it's 9 Gb size and Leslie the Administrative Assistant was going to have to help me store thousands of emails onto our archive program.

Around 9:30AM, I just happened to receive a phone call from Leslie at the front desk.

"Leslie! How's it going? I was just thinking about you. When you get some time can you please help me archive a bunch of emails? I'm constantly getting reminders that my Inbox is almost at its limit and Oxington Swing Bridge project is still kicking and screaming and flooding me with emails. So just let me know when you start transferring them and I'll give you remote access to my computer so just start the process whenever in the background as we both work on other things. Start from the oldest emails and work your way to the newest ones. But stop about two months ago as I'd like those emails accessible."

I darted into that rant rather rudely since I didn't even ask Leslie how her weekend was or why she was calling. I wasn't trying to be rude or obnoxious I just simply had so much energy this morning and was in the mood to get some actual work done that I wanted to utilize that and waste as little time as possible. Plus if I didn't stick right to the point Leslie might drone on about other things and we would be stuck in a never ending loop of pointless post-weekend blather.

"Morning to you too Marcus. You were thinking about me? Well keep dreaming loser, haha. Did you maybe put too much sugar in your coffee? You seem very hyper, hahaha."

She managed to steer off the clear task at hand and throw in some smartass jokes. Leslie was always a ball breaker.

This morning however I enjoyed her wisecracks.

"Yeah I'm not even sure why I'm in such a good mood to be honest with you Leslie. Maybe I'm just anxious talking to you so I come across jittery. Stop making me nervous dammit! Haha."

"Hahaha, yeah right. You are probably still just hungover from the weekend, which is what I wish I were."

Had she said that to me two days earlier she would have been spot on.

"Hungover? You? You are probably drunk right now. Hahaha."

"Hahaha, again, I wish! Anyways I promise I'll get to your

emails at some point after lunch today. Now the reason I called is twofold. First, you owe me lottery money for the office pool. You were paid up till the end of last week. Second of all your 10 AM appointment is here."

"I'll give you lotto money on lunch break. I have to take out some cash. What 10 AM appointment Leslie? Now I'm really starting to believe you are drunk, haha." As I was saying that just to be safe I checked my calendar on the computer in Outlook and indeed no 10 AM appointment was scheduled.

"Ahm Marcus a Dr. Jeffrey Madison is here, from the Military College of Canada. He says he is here to talk about a project you two discussed recently. Stone renovations at the Chemistry building on campus, or something. I don't particularly know the details."

Well, there went my good mood like diarrhea down the toilet. I could feel my pupils dilating. The palms broke out in sweat instantaneously, as did my back and armpits. Some 'diligent' frugal employee managed to turn the heat down in the office, which was an ongoing annoying occurrence during winter months (like unwashed dishes in the common kitchen on any given day) so my shivering was already commencing prior to this. My armpits now dripped with cold sweat like faucets with broken gaskets. When I spoke again I'm sure I must have sounded like a prepubescent punk whose voice was still changing due to gradually descending testicles.

"Oh...aaahhm, ou..ahh..."

"Wow sounds like those magic mushrooms you ingested are finally kicking in, hahahaha. Everything alright there champ? You taking a crap?" I was about to. "No...I mean I'm fine. Yeah, Dr. Jeffrey of course. Where can I speak with him? Main boardroom?" The other alternative to going along with the scene unfolding before me was to get up off my chair, start crying and screaming with maximum hand gesturing and running out the door.

"Yeah, let me check to see if it's free...yup you should be good to go until about 11 AM. But someone else has the room booked at that time."

"Oh ok. Well tell him I'm just quickly finishing up an email and should be with him in a few minutes."

"Alright no worries, I mean it is only 9:45 AM, even he said that he's aware that he came a bit early."

I thanked her and hung up the phone. Feeling completely inebriated, mainly from my own fear sweat, I somehow stumbled to the bathroom, in the process knocking over shit at my desk, bumping into cubicle walls and almost accidentally running into my boss, Sean.

"Whoa Marcus where's the fire?" He was chuckling as usual his cheeks red from the cold.

"Oh sorry Sean...it's just my wife on the phone, pregnancy related."

"Say no more son, and, be even quicker about it, haha. You don't want to piss off a pregnant woman."

"No, haha, thanks for understanding."

Literally one second later I no longer even remembered the conversation I just had with him. I barged into the bathroom and hopped into the first available stall, took my pants off and sat down, just in case I start shitting myself from fear. Why on Earth couldn't constipation be the natural response to anxiety?! I was a quirk away from having a full blown panic attack. I was feeling intense palpitations and rapid quick blackouts in front of my eyes. Like blinking shutters. Luckily temporary, for now. I quickly put my pants back on and ran to the sink, I ran cold water on my wrists to calm down my pulse and washed my face with it several times over. Then I went back into the stall, took the pants off again and sat down again. The cold water helped. Greatly. It stopped the spinning that I was starting to feel as if I was intoxicated. The heart rate calmed down and my vision stabilized. I had to pull myself together. I couldn't stay in here forever either! I knew I was petrified as fuck and highly disoriented when I couldn't even quickly jerk off to calm myself down. The scene from Wall Street was replaying in my head over and over again when Charlie Sheen's character, Bud, comes into work and everyone is staring at him until he finally gets to his office to get arrested. Another scene also came to mind, which was Jeff Daniels destroying the toilet in Dumb and Dumber and then being incapable of leaving the bathroom as the toilet couldn't flush. Luckily for me Dr. Madison apparently didn't come with cops in tow and the toilet I was sitting on had fully functional flushing capabilities. Well....as functional as these low flow toilets were in North America. You could take a shit, just don't go nuts about it as the water pressure won't be able to handle it. Nor the volume of the pipes. So a good plunger was always a much needed necessity right near any toilet especially in the case of a colossal bullshitter like myself. I had several at home too, and they have come in handy numerous times already. I had to start rationalizing. I had to start dissecting the heap of shit situation I was in. Dr. Jeffrey Madison was in my office!! The worst of my fears from weeks ago came true. What the fuck did he want?! Ok cops were not with him, good. No military personnel either for my potential trip down to Guantanamo Bay...or whatever the Canadian, Ontario alternative was...Windsor maybe. Also....my boss Sean seemed completely out of the loop and clueless about this meeting. Leslie only told me about it, Sean just showed up to work and didn't mention it. Luckily no other work intervened in this particular moment in time. Ok....well alright, fine maybe Dr. Madison dug me up on Facebook, or LinkedIn or whatever other social media I registered my idiotic face on these days. It wasn't that hard to find people. Plus he worked at a military educational facility, he probably had other means to find me with. Not that he would need them. I guess...ok so maybe he's just here because of that bullshit proposal

I was going to put together for him. For the stone rehabilitation of the chemistry building at the Military College. No big deal, maybe that's it. I figured if he wanted to rat me out to my boss he would have done so already. I had no work proposal for him but I suppose I could slap something together quickly. At the end of the day if he actually wants our business I could easily spin the story to my boss as to how I met him, how we got to talking about stone rehab at the College, etc..My boss would be happy if anything that I'm soliciting more work for our company. Ok, yeah. I was slowly starting to get color back in my face. I might survive this thing. Ok....maybe it was time for my pants to slowly come back up again and for me to venture out into the brave world existing outside of the bathroom. But wait. I distinctly told Jeffrey Madison a wrong company name. I didn't tell him the name of the actual company I worked for! I also didn't tell him my real name either! Fuck! He'll surely ask about that. So what the hell do I say to that?! The made up names and the actual names sounded nothing alike either, I couldn't exactly pretend that he heard me wrong. I had no idea what to say to that. I think I'll have to spin some ridiculous tale about how I have my own mini-consulting firm on the side. Or something along those lines. How it's a start-up and I'm trying to win some business for myself and grow clientèle and how my boss is fully aware and ok with this arrangement. Well that will have to do I suppose. I will have no excuse for why I lied about my own name. I'm running my side company with a pseudonym??! That wouldn't fly. I had a weird feeling. Only ten minutes went by since the time Leslie called me. It seemed like I've been in this bathroom for days. Bye bye toilets, wish me luck. Now I just needed to make sure I didn't pass out upon seeing Jeffrey Madison.

CHAPTER 9

TURBULENCE

Jeff was standing next to Leslie's desk which happened to be adjacent right up against the main office entrance and the main boardroom where we were to sit down and talk. He was dressed business casual, had a briefcase with him (perhaps containing a syringe filled with either bleach or cancer cells to inject me with, we would surely find out soon) and looked sharp, but jovial. He looked like a business Santa. His stare was kind and his smile friendly and genuine. Man this guy could act.

"Marcus, hello sir! Good to see you again. I promise I will not take up much of your time. I just want to go over the proposal you left with me. I signed and approved it. So let's just quickly go over the details."

Everything he just said was a total and utter lie. Word for word. I was beside myself. Now I actually believed that as soon as we step foot into that boardroom he will inject me with something. But I had no choice than to go in. I couldn't run away to the bathroom again and I couldn't go home crying to my wife. Or to Sean my boss. Oh God if only Alicia were to see me now.....in the situation I was in caused by my bullshit lies and child's play especially seeing how important my job was at this time in our lives considering the baby on the way and her inability to work full time. I was a royal piece of shit. There was nowhere to hide, nowhere to run. I had to see what this guy wanted from me and what exactly I got myself into. I looked at the boardroom walls, luckily they were covered with big windows, with blinds on them. All the blinds were up for some reason. That means that Jeffrey and I, although in a closed space, would be visible to anyone outside. This worked in my favor, I would try to sit opposite of him across the big table. There is no way he could lunge that syringe at me that way. If he tries anything everyone will see. And if he tries pulling the blinds down I'll tell him not to and run screaming out of that boardroom, fuck it all.

We entered the boardroom, closed the door and sat down opposite each other.

"Now Marcus you little rascal, this is how this will play out. I will pull a bunch of papers from my briefcase and hand them over to you. Well, three pages really. You will pretend to look at them and sign them. We will exchange a few words and shake our heads, smile and gesture, and then I will leave. Then what I want you to do is to meet me at Jim Mortons coffee place on Princess Street and Macdonnell Street close to downtown tomorrow at 2 PM. I will explain everything then. Don't worry about signing the pages in front of you, they are filled with random gibberish text. They are useless pages. I also only announced myself to Leslie at the front, I spoke to no one else. Luckily you were able to see me so quickly and readily. I'm not your enemy Marcus and I wish you no ill will nor harm. I will explain everything tomorrow. Can you meet then?"

"Ok, what is this?" I was now certain this was a practical joke, most likely put together by Leslie. I looked outside, Leslie appeared to be transferring my emails. I was certain this was a ploy and it started to make me feel better. I felt like this huge feeling of relief washed over me. I also remembered immediately that Kim, a mechanical technologist working in a cubicle close to mine had all of her items in her cubicle wrapped in Christmas wrapping paper right before the Christmas break, computer, monitor, etc, as a practical joke. I forgot to ask her if she ever got to the bottom of who exactly did it but regardless it was a joke played by someone from our office. So they were clearly common. "This is a practical joke right? Leslie put you up to it?" As I was saying this I almost immediately realized that it made no sense. How the hell would Leslie know Jeffrey Madison?!? I mean sure if she engaged someone from the office to team up with and pull a prank on me fine, or even one of our sub-consultants with whom we worked with frequently, but not this guy.

We stared at each other. Jeffrey had a concerned look of a father talking to a drugged-out son on his face. I looked around through the windows of the boardroom. Everyone at the office went about their business. Leslie was unfazed staring at the computer screen. I was jittery as all can be.

"It's not a joke is it? You are actually serious? Look I'm sorry for coming to your school and bugging you and wasting your time. Really it was an innocent and stupid thing I have been researching lately and I went on some tangent mission to find out more about it. There is nothing else to it I swear to God. My wife knows about it and she kept telling me to let it go, to stop wasting people's time to quite frankly fuck off and start behaving like an adult. I got a kid on the way too. But I get fixated on things and I just couldn't let up. My visit to your school she is completely clueless about. I sat down with some faculty at King's University and had a similar meeting. About the biology of dying, about aging, etc..I even donated money to them just to get some insight. I lied to you, I'm sorry I wasn't honest and more mature about the whole thing. Again, in the end, it was all a meaningless, childish little pet project of mine. I hope you can let this go Dr. Madison, really. Is there anything I can do? I just don't want my boss to find out. Or my family for that matter."

I went all out into panic mode. Total crumbling of the façade I had going for me when I was in my own confident element meeting this guy for the first time weeks ago. Now I was a little whining bitch. I felt two years old right now. I was an embarrassment to adults, husbands, men and would be fathers everywhere.

Jeffrey Madison was keen to put me at ease.

"Marcus, as it turns out your meaningless and childish pet project as you call it isn't as meaningless and childish as you think. I can't say more about it right now my friend. But again I'll stress that our meeting tomorrow will explain a lot more. It will be nothing more than an informative session. Since you are so curious, I will try to give you just that, a partial satisfaction of your curiosity. I have no intention of getting you into any kind of trouble, speaking with your boss, wife, I mean that. I have no patience or time for that nonsense. So please, can we meet tomorrow?"

I didn't know what I felt anymore. Fear, confusion, nausea, hallucinations...possibly a bit of relief? Nah. I needed to extricate myself from this conversation as I felt like I was about to puke. I needed to stop talking for a while. And I needed to get out of this boardroom and away from this guy for the time being.

"Alright let's meet tomorrow at 2 PM at the specified Jim Mortons." It seemed as though someone else said this and not me.

We shook hands, I grabbed useless sheets of paper he gave me and he left. I went back to the bathroom to recuperate myself. I washed my face with cold water so much that at one point I thought

I was going to start getting frostbite on my skin. The faucet started condensing that's how cold this water got.

I needed to pull myself together. I needed to manage communicating with people at work, with my boss, I still had a full day of work ahead of me. And then coming home to Alicia and not looking like a ghost. Oh God how the hell was I going to pull this off?! How was I going to sleep for a minute tonight??

I made it to lunch doing my best hiding in between cubicle walls and avoiding talking to anyone. I grabbed my lunch and ate it in my car as I didn't want to sit at my desk or to have it in the lunch room. I was in no shape to socialize with anyone. Anxiety beat hunger like paper beat rock. Every bite I took I felt I was going to vomit out immediately. The outside temperature was -20C and I had the heat on full blast. I parked in some random neighborhood away from my office so that I could be as far away from everyone as possible and there would be zero chance of anyone seeing me or running into me and starting a conversation. If the cell phone rang I would ignore it easily. Finishing my lunch I could certainly sympathize with those poor ducks going through the foie gras process. I don't know how I held any of that food down. Afterward, I ventured out for a walk, -20C or not I desperately needed to move. I couldn't sit still for a second.

What the hell was going on? What the fuck exactly just happened?? I looked around and the same old aluminum sided box buildings surrounded me common to any average Canadian city, same gloomy January weather, same boring work awaited, about to become exciting family life at home. And now this. So, I wondered, did I just completely imagine this *Matrix* style scene which just transpired? Seriously did I hallucinate all of this? Jeffrey Madison in my office? At 10 AM today? Did any of that just occur?! I mean he left no card, no number, maybe he doesn't exist, maybe I'm just turning schizophrenic. One could only hope right? I'd rather be a psycho than have this twilight zone play out.....wow I'm gonna be such a great and responsible father one day, I can't fucking wait! The baby will comfort…me! I was brimming with responsibility and sound, rational thinking.

I was so distracted with my predicament that I failed to realize that I almost walked all the way back to my work from where I was parked! Luckily I came back down from whatever hallucinogenic my brain was releasing in the last minute to see the building where I worked well in front of me. I stopped. Coming back to reality also made me aware of how insanely cold it was outside. And now I had to walk all the way back to the car. I turned around and backtracked. It was brutal. The snow felt like soft flour, it was like walking on a treadmill moving in one spot without advancing anywhere, and neither the road nor the sidewalk were properly cleaned. It was simply too cold and the accumulation was immense. The salt was doing nothing to melt the snow, it was way too frigid. As I walked back I was amazed at the colossal and imposing heap piles of snow that the snowplows had created, some of them must have been four or five meters tall at least. I felt as if I was walking between fjords or through an ice exhibit somewhere up in Scandinavia. Thankfully the torture of the walk back was all somewhat distracting for me which felt great as I needed the distraction.

I finally made it back to the car and drove myself back to work. The walk helped. It felt like a defibrillator.

It was exactly 1 PM when I made it back to the office. I got lucky with work. I was supposed to start modeling a swing bridge we were replacing up in Peterborough, Ontario in software called CSiBridge 2017. I've already modelled the same bridge in software called S-Frame but now I wanted to try a different program, supposedly more powerful and significantly more versatile and easier to use. Although the IT department installed the software onto my computer as well as several upgrades to S-Frame, CSiBridge was crapping out on me. It couldn't acquire a license or something....it was weird but like anything computer related and Marcus Stipecic, it took forever to figure out and fix with the IT or whoever else saying "well we've never seen this before Marcus". Sometimes I wonder how I even look like a 'regular' human being and not like some mutant as everything else about me, my life experiences, shit that happened to me, when telling it to another person the reaction is always "wow, I've never heard of that before". I was 'special'. In all the right, useful ways. So IT was spending all day remotely controlling my computer trying to figure out why CSiBridge 2017 wasn't working. The second day they spent all day doing this. Therefore my hands were tied, I had no choice but to sit there, trying not to freak out about the events that have transpired earlier in the day caused by my idiocy, and not do any actual work. I was going to charge these two days to overhead as it was simply not billable time. And I told my boss Sean about it, he was fine with it. I said look I can go back using the old software but then we'll never master the new one and I won't be able to train others in the new software either. So as much of a pain in the ass this all was and a waste of time and company's money, it was for the long term greater good. Sean agreed. I was surprised how convincing I sounded, I was surprised at the eloquence of my words considering what internal hell and upheaval I was going through. So I basically counted the minutes and hours until 5 PM blankly staring at my computer screen watching the IT guys turn every file and folder upside down trying to figure out how to make this software work. I couldn't really do anything else. I couldn't possibly distract myself with any other Internet research or anything on my phone. I couldn't talk to anyone to kill time, people were busy. All I could do is stare. And pray to be left alone. And God answered my prayers.

The home situation was significantly more difficult. Alicia was very chatty and upbeat, she wanted to plan for the baby, start buying things, rearrange rooms, furniture, buy new stuff, etc...I was distracted as ever. I asked her at least three times to repeat whatever she said. Questions she asked me I asked her to repeat three times as well and when she did and I understood every word as best as I thought I did I still didn't understand the meaning of the composed question. She was getting agitated.

"Marcus what is wrong with you? Are you drunk?? You are ridiculously zoned out even for you. I feel I would get a better partner in conversation from this wall cabinet than with you! Why are you ignoring me?? Why are you so disinterested in anything I have to say??"

"Alicia would you relax please?! I've had a rough day at work. Tons of emails to sift through plus this software IT issue. I've been incredibly unproductive for two days now. It's worrying me. It's on my mind. Just give me a break."

She did not give me any break. Instead, she just stopped talking to me. I guess it would take anyone a certain number of times of being ignored before they completely lost any will in conversing with the ignorant fool.

I was too stressed out, self-absorbed and in a jam to even pretend like I cared. So I decided to take advantage of the situation at hand. I didn't have to worry about conversing with Alicia for the rest of the night so I could focus on trying to survive till the morning with my brain. With Alicia safely ignoring me in her room I could go nuts turning and tossing in mine, pacing even, trying to come up with contingency plans, ways out, lies, stories, defenses before, during and after my infamous meeting with Jeffrey Madison coming up tomorrow. At best I could tell myself that we would be in an open space, with people around and that I most likely wasn't getting arrested as I committed no criminal act, that I wasn't going to get raped, beaten or sold off for organ transplants. Ok, so I had quite a bit to work with here. I was slowly starting to feel good about my prospects of..... managing to fall asleep tonight. Surviving tomorrow was another story but sleeping tonight was starting to look more and more like a definite possibility. I paced so much my legs were starting to hurt, I also ran cold water down my wrists several times in the bathroom. The whole package induced serious yawning. No matter how candid or friendly this meeting was going to be, was there any kind of a chance that this was about to be a one-time thing and me being let off the hook.....I doubted it. That thought just now made me stop yawning and brought me out of my slowly setting tranquil mood. This was not going to be a one-time thing was it? It just felt like it wasn't... My God, what the hell did I get myself into?! I ran back to the bathroom and ran cold water on my wrists until I lost all feeling in my fingers. I wish I could jump into an icy bath. I contemplated drawing myself a bath and throwing some ice into it for a second before I realized that could not have been pulled off without waking Alicia up and expediting my probably already inevitably pending divorce. Also going down to swim in Ontario lake at 3 AM wasn't gonna happen either like a Christian Orthodox epiphany. So I went back to my room and kept rotating my wrists until I got the feeling of blood flow back. One day, somehow, this all would pass, and I would get drunk as hell to celebrate its passing. Whether I would drink in celebration at a positive resolution or in misery to drown out the sorrows of my ruined life would be determined, either way, I would be poisoning my body with sweet lady liquor.

CHAPTER 10

FURTHER DOWN THE TUNNEL

The night was spent more or less in my familiar way. Eventually I fell asleep. The complete opposite of Alicia who went into one position on her side and then passed out in it for hours almost instantaneously. I spun like a rotisserie pig for hours. Eventually there was not a single cool spot left in the bed, it was all hot and melted sheets from my sweat and somersaulting turns. It was a rough night. It seemed like my entire life hung on the precipice of some impending dread and doom I was helplessly hurtling towards.

I must have tossed and turned at least five times more frequently than usual for what seemed like hours. Eventually I completely uncovered myself in order to cool down and pass out. If as though I blinked, when I opened up my eyes again I noticed that it was all of sudden 3:13AM and I was freezing. But success, I passed out. I slept. Thank God. Now even if I couldn't fall back asleep for the rest of the night it wouldn't be such a big deal. With that in mind and the pressure of 'having' to sleep off my shoulders, I passed out again and sure enough woke up at 6:30 AM as per my usual morning routine. I made it to the morning, that's all that mattered. Everything else I could manage as long as I didn't have a panic attack at some point during the day.

Alicia was still in a pissy mood. I decided to take the easy, capitulatory route.

"Look Alicia I'm sorry for being so distracted lately and distant during our conversations. More so than usual that is. I'm done making excuses as to why I'm like this so I promise I will try and be more attentive going forward. And I'm sorry for raising my voice so often in our arguments, it's completely uncalled for and it causes you undue stress especially now that you're pregnant."

After about a minute she replied. I was pretty much ready to not even give it a second attempt but to just leave her be and leave for work.

"Well thank you for saying that. I was stressed out all night and had pains in my tummy because of our nonsense. I barely slept. You know this is not good for the baby. We have to change our dynamic before the kid comes."

"I know you are right. Again I'm sorry for making you stressed out all night and I'll really try to be more attentive and less tense."

"Alright. Well, it is what it is now. Let's just eat and I'll make you sandwiches for lunch."

We had oatmeal with fruit as usual. She made me sandwiches and packed a bunch of fruit and a yoghurt. Her bottom lip retreated which was a good sign, we were making progress. Now that she was pregnant it was quite a funny sight to see her belly sticking out and then when she was mad her bottom lip too. Super cute though. I'll be sure to tell her that if I come back from all of this alive.

I took the lunch, kissed her and left. Perhaps forever.......

Of course in the haze of insanity that I was going through I forgot to turn the car on before eating breakfast. So the -20C seats provided my ass and prostate with a memorable shock therapy. Luckily the seat and steering wheel warmers engaged quickly.

I arrived at work on time, 8 AM sharp. It dawned on me that my meeting with Jeffrey was not until 2 PM so there was still a whole lot of cold sweat torture and clammy hands time ahead of me. Combined with frequent bathroom breaks. When I sat down Leslie promptly called me from the front desk. As I saw her name pop up on my Skype (no more phones, only headphones and Skype calling, money-saving 101) I broke out in even more sweat and immediately started to smell my armpits as I was convinced that Jeffrey Madison had rolled up to the office again, this time with RCMP in tow.

"Marcus did I just see you come into the office?"

"It wasn't me, it was my evil twin...Jonesy", I managed to brake balls.

"Good one smartass. Anyways, I thought you had your site visit today. I booked you a rental car last week?!"

I got reminded of the scene from Indiana Jones when he exchanges the gold statue with a sack of sand. I swapped my cold sweaty pits and clammy hands with an immediate urge to take an explosive, wet crap. It was an extremely identifiable problem for me. The switch was instantaneous. My fucking site visit! Fuck!! It was to be an important meeting too before the official winter shutdown (even though it was pretty much February and work had continued throughout half the winter), there wasn't supposed to be another one until Spring. I quickly printed the minutes from the last meeting, shoved them in my briefcase, grabbed my construction winter jacket and ran.....to the can. I tried to make the bathroom visit as quick as possible but it was a messy one and the wiping of my hairy behind took longer than usual. I should really carry a portable bidet with me at all times. Now I finally ran out the door. I wasn't going to take the rental car as the rental place was in the opposite direction so I took mine. I called the rental place and canceled, they seemed cool about it and said there would be no last-minute cancellation charge. I rushed and weaved through snow flurries with my car windows fogging up due to the extreme cold, I couldn't get the right temperature settings in the Infiniti. I was stressed out beyond belief and could not properly fathom the situation that I was finding myself in. At the moment what was more important to me, my job or some creepy meeting with Jeffrey Madison?! The weather I was driving in was more of a problem as was the fact that I needed to focus on the meeting I was about to chair. I did my best to minimize the significance of my meeting with Jeff to be nothing more than a quick, in and out, coffee break sitdown that I would try and wrap up in a haste. You are going to be a father soon I kept telling myself, you cannot keep on being such a chicken shit.

My new-found bravery oscillated and competed intermittently with my ongoing pop up bouts of extreme fear in an infinite never-ending loop. And rehashing things in my head over and over again. As I sat through the meeting I found myself going from paying extreme attention to what the Client and the Contractor were saying to completely zoning out for minutes at a time. A couple of times I got asked a direct question and all I could say was "Well... we'll see" as I didn't hear the fucking question let alone know what the hell we were talking about! Then I had to figure out what to put in the meeting notes since I had no idea what conversation had just transpired. I somehow made it through it all, walked the site with the Client at -15C, marginally registered his questions and barely engaging him in conversation, said bye to everyone and got the hell out of there. At least the clouds cleared up so although still bitterly cold I had a smooth drive back to Kingston.

It was exactly 12:30 PM when I left the site. I made it a point to tell everyone present when I arrived that I had another work-related 'meeting' at 2 PM and that I had to leave the site at 12:30 PM at the latest. Everyone seemed to understand. The Contractor was ridiculously late with completing the job and the Client, at least from the emails, seemed ultra pissed off about the whole thing. But now with all of us here, not a whole lot was said and what was said was brief and easy going. No conflicts. Good, I needed peace and quiet. When, where, what can you commit to, etc...The Client only mentioned that the public was getting somewhat agitated as they kept telling them the bridge will open at a certain date only for the construction finish date to keep being postponed. I guess all the anger got vented through the emails. Everyone was brave behind electronic walls. Face to face the fake pleasantries, aided with clenched teeth smiles, were carefully maintained.

The road back was clean and almost completely dry. Traffic eastbound was always good as people were driving away from the black hole called Toronto. My thoughts were completely focused on Jeffrey Madison now. Nothing else. The site visit actually worked out well for me as I wouldn't have to skip out of work randomly at 1:30 PM to meet with Jeff and then come back God knows when if at all.....This way I would come back whenever to the office, maybe even tomorrow morning and simply say that the meeting dragged on way longer than expected as there were numerous items to cover seeing as the next meeting won't be until Spring.

So now, with all the other distractions out of the way...What the hell did Jeffrey Madison want? Really...What could this have possibly been about?! I played a prank on him, I was aware, over some nonsense research I was doing. He got pissed off and agitated and ushered me out of his office. Then he digs me up, sees right through my bullshit and shows up at my work telling me my nonsense research was not such nonsense after all and come talk to me in Jim Mortons in one of the most run-down parts of town. Unfortunately for me I was not coming up with anything even as a remote possibility. I simply had to meet this guy and find out in person. Either that or not meet him at all, ignore him, disappear and hope he somehow forgets about me and doesn't show up at my work again or worse yet doesn't tell my boss Sean what transpired at the Military College. But I could not opt out for the second option. The risk was too great. My livelihood was at stake, my marriage, everything pretty much. So I had no choice but to meet him.

It was 1:40 PM as I was pulling up at the coffee shop. My timing was excellent, no issues on the road whatsoever. As I was looking for a parking spot I was overwhelmed with a different kind of fear and that was whether my Infiniti would get broken into, stolen or scratched up by the mutated zombies that hung out in front of this particular coffee shop. They lingered and milled around drinking their 40 ouncers of Olde English, smoking their cigarettes and now even smoking weed all over the place since it became legal. They were at it 24/7. And here I was with my fancy little car. Being a vane, snobbish piece of crap. Good for me. Even when feeling like I was in utter danger I managed to worry about the finer things in my shitty little life. So what I did is I parked in the farthest spot in the lot, as far away from the Jim Mortons building and as close to the sidewalk of the main road. The zombies seemed to have tapered off that far out, the gravity of Jim Mortons didn't let them venture out quite that far. They needed the warmth and the proximity of the shitting facilities that it offered. And warm coffee. I even went as far as to put the steering wheel lock on, just in case! God, I was such a piece of shit.

I rolled up onto the dirty ass floor of the coffee shop, making it even dirtier with my construction boots dragging mud and snow all over it. I felt no remorse whatsoever. I didn't want to be here no matter how you swung it. I didn't like the location, the place or the company I was about to entertain. I had my worn-out work jeans on and my construction winter jacket with reflective stripes, my hair was all over the place because of the toque and construction helmet and I looked pale as whiteout. From both winter and dread. So, aesthetically, I felt like I fit right in this joint. I looked around. Remnants of human society, nothing else. Like a diner from Fallout. I didn't see Jeffrey Madison anywhere. So I went to the can to take a piss and wash my hands. While in there I debated wetting my hair to try and make it look representable, but I decided against it. I thought fuck it, I'll look as pathetic and run down as possible, maybe he would take it easy on me. When I came out of the washroom I saw Jeffrey sitting in the corner directly opposite of where I stood. He saw me and waved with a big smile on his face. He had jeans and an Adidas zip-up sweater on. Like a Balkan mobster. His winter jacket was draped over the chair he was sitting on and the bottom of it was mopping up the dirty freaking floor underneath. He definitely looked like he didn't belong here. Although I have to admit his greeting and grin did somewhat put me at ease. I needed that, like a kid watching the reaction on their parent's face after they've done something wrong and assessing the amount of punishment that's about to come their way. Although sometimes a parent would be smiling in a psychotic way in anticipation of how nicely they were about to lay down the beat down. I slowly approached him, I gradually sped up as I got closer, like a cat. I hoped when I spoke that I wasn't going to sound like a little bitch. I also hoped a bullet wasn't going to whizz through the window and finalize its journey in my skull. My hope not to sound like a little bitch was in vain. I had to clear my throat three times before any audible non-screeching sound started to come out.

"Jeff....Dr. Madison...h..hi, hello."

"Marcus, good to see you! Thanks for coming my friend. Please sit down. Can I get you anything? Hot tea? Are you catching a cold? Is your throat ok?"

He was laying on the charm and 'caring dad' offensive a bit too thick. I was certain secret intelligence agents did it like this before they chopped off your head and shat down your throat. Any more of this and I was going to jump behind the service counter and tell one of the brain dead teenagers serving coffee to call the cops. I'm screwed though, no way any of them knew how to dial a phone. No way any of them knew the devices in their hands they stared at all day long were.....phones.

"Ahm, yeah no worries. I'm good, I don't need anything.... thanks."

"Are you sure? It's damn cold out there and you seem like you could use a hot drink."

"Well, alright I guess, I suppose I could use a hot tea."

"Tea, yes! Good idea, we'll both have a cup of tea. Anything to eat?"

"No thank you, just tea will do."

In the situation I was finding myself in I couldn't possibly contemplate any solid food, my stomach was completely in knots. However my throat was tickling a bit, what from the cold and site visit and what from the stress of this nonsense unfolding before me. Which I caused. So I was looking forward to some hot tea. I didn't want coffee, I was afraid it was going to make me way too jittery and I was already having enough of an issue coordinating my movements and desperately trying not to knock things off the table, that's how jumpy I was. So the idea was that tea would calm me down as well as help out with my throat. Jeff went up to grab the tea, as he did I even had the guts to tell him to ask for some lemon slices. He complied. I knew that the stress of the situation I was finding myself in, plus the seasonal weather had a good chance of actually getting me sick. Fever sick. So to try to mitigate it in any formidable way I had to overload myself with teas, honey, lemons, garlic, the works. Worst case scenario whatever I was bound to catch wouldn't last as long.....I hoped. I didn't want to get Alicia sick especially now that she was pregnant.

Teas were now on the table, Jeff even grabbed us two chocolate dipped doughnuts even though I specifically asked for no food. Although I did eat mine and it tasted pretty darn good. I was hungry I just wasn't aware of it. I've had enough of the introductory song and dance, my uneasiness and antsiness were getting the better of me. With some food and a few sips of tea in me, my voice at least sounded normal now.

"Jeff, can you please tell me what this is all about?"

He answered my questions quickly, there were no long, unnecessary and theatrical pauses, I guess he didn't want to torture me with anticipation. He knew I didn't handle it well.

"Marcus this meeting is about the leisure research you have been doing."

"What about it? I already told you I'm sorry for wasting your time. I'm sorry for misrepresenting myself, giving you fake information. And I'm assuming you are upset with me. But in all honesty and fairness at the end of the day I didn't commit a crime. I didn't steal anything from you, cheated you out of anything, money or whatever. If anything let's say you wanted my actual company to do a masonry renovation assessment of the Chemistry building over at the Military College, we could, we are in a position to do that. My boss would be happy that I successfully offered our services to others and that we have more work coming our way. So that part could very much become legitimate if you were interested. Seriously. I'm not sure what else I can say."

"No, no it's nothing like that Marcus. I don't need your company's services, well not at this time anyways as I said the University's budget is limited with respect to any further exterior rehabilitation work for the time being. I meant that. So perhaps in the future we could talk about it but not at this time. And I know the company you actually work for can provide these services, I've looked you guys up and I'm aware of the work you offer, it's impressive. Also, as I said before I am not mad or upset nor do I have any intention to tell your boss about what happened in my office. Or your wife, or whomever. This is not some childish revenge ploy. I certainly would not have bothered to find you and come out of my way to sit down and talk to you if I had only been annoyed with what you were trying to pull at the College. This is not what this is about."

I was officially clueless.

"Well I know I mentioned to you that I ran a similar scheme at the other University in the city, and that I donated some money just to make myself look more legitimate just so I could find out more information. If you are expecting me to donate money again, I can't. My wife would kill me, we are not well off or anything like that. Plus we are expecting a child sometime in the summer and she can't work as much so we need to save our money."

"Oh well congratulations! I don't think I properly wished you all the best when I saw you at the office. That's wonderful news. When is your wife's due date? And do you know the sex of the baby yet?"

"I don't recall whether I mentioned that my wife is pregnant when we talked in your office. I'm almost certain that I didn't. Anyways the due date is early June. We find out the sex next week."

"It must be so exciting for you guys. I have two boys myself. Ah that brings me back to those days of anticipation, early beginnings, finding out..."

I would have to take many washroom breaks if this conversation was to continue in such a manner. My irritable bowel syndrome was having a field day. I simply couldn't take the pointless and platonic drivel any longer.

"Jeff please forgive me for interrupting and sounding rude but can you tell me what you want from me?"

"Nothing specific Marcus. And nothing really. Or, more specifically, nothing unless you ultimately so choose. I intended to let you know that your leisure research has stumbled upon something. Something that a certain group of scientists and researchers have stumbled upon a while ago and there is a, for a lack of a better word, a 'secretly' funded and organized program put in place dedicated precisely to that research. So this meeting was more meant to be a preliminary informative session for you, or partially informative I should say, and see if you would be interested in hearing certain things, highly unorthodox things outside of the box of anything official you have ever heard."

"Seriously Jeff, is this some kind of a joke? I mean people in my office are being played pranks on pretty regularly these days, I know for certain Leslie is in on it. Common just let me know, what's the play here? Did she put you up to this?"

This had to have been some fake scenario like from the movie *The Game*, I must have fallen trap to an organization of pranksters who do this for a living. There had to have been a hidden camera somewhere very nearby. Perhaps I was on *Just for Laughs*. The only thing I was fairly certain of was that I was not on the show *Punk'd* since I was a complete nobody. I had no time nor patience for pranks.

"Marcus please work with me here. This is not a prank and you are not in trouble. This is....something else. Can we please accept that fact and move on? We will save a lot of time that way. And I can eventually prove all of this. If you are incapable of believing that, I can also just walk away and leave you alone. And I won't bother you again. Please let me know if that is what you prefer. Maybe you are just not ready yet."

Yup, this pretty much felt like about most movies Hollywood pumps out regularly.

What the hell do I do with this guy? Now he is even telling me I could just walk away and he'll leave me alone. Should I? A smarter, wiser and more responsible person would. Also, a less childish one who doesn't instinctually fall for the trap of wanting to do the exact opposite of what he is offered. This guy was applying basic infant reverse psychology with me. So now, at the presented opportunity that I could just extradite myself from this unseemly mess, I was all of a sudden afraid of leaving it all behind and going back to my mundane life. I was completely nuts.

He spoke again before I could say anything.

"Marcus I simply want to know if you would be comfortable and strong enough mentally, to learn certain things. Things that fall right out of the realm of regular and usually accepted. I want nothing from you. Well not exactly, nothing materialistic certainly... my job is to sort of recruit and scout for individuals, intellectuals, whoever, that can learn, accept and live with certain....alternate possibilities and truths. Quite frankly isn't the entire reason you embarked on this 'research' project of yours precisely because that is what you are after?"

"Jeff what on God's Earth are you talking about?"

"God's Earth. Interesting concept. Certainly has been around for a while. I wonder how much longer it will remain around for."

"What?"

"Marcus, please. A simple yes or no. Do you wish to hear what I have to say?"

Crossroads. Like in the movie called.....real life! But what do I do? I was intrigued. But scared. Story of my life. I mean after all my entire 'research project' as he put it on the matter of aging and death was spurned by my insatiable thirst for alternative knowledge and things poorly conventionally explained. I wanted to hear alternative explanations and reasons than the norm served in school and universities. And this guy apparently was offering just that. I just wasn't sure in regards to what subject exactly. Was it to do with something else not related to what I was inquiring about? Well that was clearly impossible since he already specifically indicated that our meeting had to do with my 'research project'. He swears that he is not upset with me, doesn't wish to ruin my career, rat me out, he doesn't want money, he is not a prankster (well the jury was still out on this one). I know where he works too, so worst case I could cause problems for him at his place of business need be. So maybe I should just hear out what this guy had to say. I decided to probe a bit more.

"I have to tell you Jeff...I'm sort of on the fence here. I mean, try to put yourself in my shoes, you show up at my work lying about why you came to see me, then setting this second meeting on neutral ground telling me about some secret information, knowledge, whatever... This is all very weird and suspicious. It's surreal."

"Well now you know how I felt when you showed up in my office, talking about biological process, chemistry etc... You are looking for the surreal. Are you not? How is my showing up at your place of work under false pretenses any different? You went out fishing Marcus, for something different, now that something different is pulling on your hook you are weirded out by the whole thing. Peculiar don't you think?"

Touché Jeff, touché. You've just earned your worth. And I was fully aware of my own hypocrisy in this situation. Further to this I loved to lecture others on the necessity of acting like an adult while at the same time secretly playing an immature adventure seeker behind the scenes, as in this case. Although in my defence (and I always loved saying 'in my defence') I was nowhere near the worst hypocrite in my family. I'm not sure why this knowledge would matter to Jeff but it was a nice pat on the back for me. In the end,

I had to love myself, always and forever. In this situation though, it was more of a case of being a scared shitless chicken who couldn't handle the results of his own actions than being a hypocrite but I still preferred Jeff think of me as a hypocrite than a coward.

"You have a point Jeff. I'm sorry for sounding like a hypocrite. This information you have to tell me.....is this like one of those things you'll tell me but then you'll have to kill me down the line or something? Or I'm going to be on the hook or something to have to do a favor or participate in something, I don't know...maybe I've seen too many movies but at the same time I know there are numerous societies out there in real life that once you join....you can't exactly leave. And once you hear something you have certain responsibilities, certain duties you acquire, things you can never again step away from. And I have to tell you I don't need nor want that in my life. So if whatever you are about to tell me is along those lines, I don't want to hear it." When I was younger I used to fantasize one day about having a meeting like this with someone. To be on the brink of discovering 'something' outside of the norm, to be included in some secret, I lived for a moment like this. And now that it was here, that I managed to summon it, I was behaving and acting like a complete pussy. I was chickening out hard, full bore. My ass, my wife's ass, my future kids' ass were on the line. And I was playing it safe all of a sudden. Or was I being responsible? What did I want to be? Responsible and 'safe' or living on the edge? Couldn't I just be somewhere in the middle? Was that at all possible? Somehow I doubted it.

"Well the way I figure it I could tell you a small introductory spiel, nothing requiring commitment in return, with the possibility of you finding out more at a later time and at a different place if you choose to do so. There is not much you could really do with what I would tell you. You can't harm me in any way. You can't go to the media with it either. You could try, but you would be ridiculed, laughed at and embarrassed and you don't strike me like the kind of guy who would want that in his life. Quite frankly your status and other's respect for you seem very important to you. What the world and your family will think of you. So the way I figure it, what I'm about to tell you you can't do anything with. Nothing negative for me or the people that I represent. And if you choose to do something about it, I hope that something would only be positive, meaning I could involve you further into certain things, at no harm to you or your family of course."

"Ok........well then why don't you just try me out. Say something already, let's stop this courtship."

I regrew....one nut back. He was a smooth and intriguing talker and I bit into the bait, hook, line and sinker. Fuck it. Let's live a little.

"Hahaha, courtship. I like that. So much song and dance in this life before anything tangible happens eh? Alright Marcus let's see how wide your eyes get at what I'm about to say."

My eyes remained the same but my intestines started percolating and my throat hurting more. It would be one of the fiercest testaments to my mental and physical strengths if I manage to make it through this sit down without descending into a nervous breakdown.

"Ok, go for it."

"Marcus, have you noticed anything unusual lately? Think of the seemingly insignificant but at the same time noticeable things that may have happened over the past month, since you've come to my office, in any aspect of your life. Things you found strange or intriguing."

This guy was nuts and this whole thing now felt like an introduction into a horror theatre play. I should just get up and walk out the door. My life was fine, aside from my own theatrics of playing pranks at universities and this guy's office, everything else was regular. I worked a boring job, I took a shit every morning, I annoyed the hell out of my wife who often thought I was a moron and I paid my taxes. That's it that's all. I was about to have a baby. Babies, one of the most efficient excuses for adults to make moronic sounds without being committed to an insane asylum. I surfed the Internet, googled stupid shit and trivia every chance I got..... wait......googling my phone. My phone. My phone which had an unexplained battery crash. Furthermore to this, my Facebook account that crashed even more unexpectedly. That's what this guy was going on about wasn't it. It had to have been. He already knew.

"Let me guess you are talking about my cell phone's battery and Facebook account crashing aren't you?"

I was trying to sound serious and composed but I was struggling majestically not to vent a massive fart building up in my gut. It was excruciatingly exhausting maintaining a solid outer shell when the insides were a pressure cooker of fear and anxiety. This guy had to have been working for the CIA. My intrigue gave way to a sense of incredible danger again.

"Is that what it was for you? A phone and a Facebook thing? Interesting."

"What do you mean? 'Was for me?' What are you trying to say?"

"Marcus, you got.....recognized so to speak. You got 'picked up' by the filter screen. I am a part of a certain organization. The organization I'm involved with scans the Internet for individuals they feel might be like-minded. The 'search' not only depends on the material that individual searches, but it also depends on the pattern of search, how you probe, the questions you ask whichever search engine. For me I noticed my email crashing. For others it's something entirely different. But there is always a 'tell'. The organization gives you a hint that it recognized you. Shortly afterwards you get a personal visit from someone like…myself." What an outrageous intrusion of privacy I thought. Like the seizure inducing, but otherwise highly inefficient, Emergency Response System implemented in Ontario infecting our cell phones whenever it so chooses.

"I see. Would you please excuse me I just have to go to the bathroom. It's the tea, it runs right through me."

"Not at all Marcus."

I failed miserably to make it through the meeting without visiting the stalls or coming up with a better excuse as to why I had to leave the table for a few minutes. As I sat there on the toilet bowl I had an extremely hard time comprehending how the sound of me farting didn't make it all the way across the street let alone to Jeff and everyone at the coffee shop. It was impossible. I suppose for the time being I was just happy that the paper mache walls this fine building was composed of, like most infrastructure in North America, didn't come crashing down upon me due to the acoustical and wind pressures exerted by my flatulence.

People assumed I was a sarcastic pessimist. I resented that. I was perfectly optimistic about things that didn't suck. A hardcore realist yes, pessimist no. I just always wanted the whole picture. I simply ask not to discuss sunshine without the darkness that's behind it, don't talk to me about spreading joy and happiness without awareness that evil and fire spread just as well and even more efficiently. Focus solely on the pleasant and ignoring the unpleasant only makes the unpleasant grow unabated and pounce more unpredictably. Learning to truly embrace and love the whole picture is how one becomes leader of men.

My bathroom visit was mainly vocal, all nervous airhorns.

I returned after about five minutes or so and tried to look dignified.

"Sorry about that Jeff. No more tea for me, haha. Ok now where were we? I got picked up by the scanners of a secret organization you are involved with correct?"

I almost burst out laughing as I was saying that. I was now again convinced that there had to have been a candid camera somewhere on me. This thing I was going through could not have possibly been real. No way, never.

"Yes Marcus. I'm happy I'm able to give you a good laugh."

Shit, I guess I must have been at least grinning like a jackass as I said that.

"I'm sorry, I can't help it, this is all too surreal. Ok, why? What is the reason? What is the reason why I got picked up by this.... secret organization?"

"It's related to the subject that you have been so feverishly researching over the past couple of months or so."

"Ok, I've been researching about aging and death. Why we age and why we die."

"Precisely. But millions of people wonder about that. It's the specifics and nature of your research that got you tagged."

"Ok. What specifically?"

"Your insistence on the word 'programmed'. In your searches, and during your conversation with me."

"I don't understand anything."

"Oh stop playing dumb Marcus. The organization that I am involved with...has discovered something. And we are generously funded by various parties to get to the bottom of it."

"Oh?"

"I will give you the short of it. And the preliminary introduction. Anything further than that, more elaborative, will depend on your reaction and willingness to get involved. And commitment. Again, you are not obliged to do so. You are not obliged to do anything."

"Ok...whatever go ahead, speak."

This time I will make it, I will succeed in not running to the can with anxiety! I can do this!

"Marcus, the organization that I am involved with has discovered that the main gene that acts as a catalyst for cells to stop repairing themselves and in turn start destroying themselves is the same gene that causes the cells to stop dividing. The gene produces an enzyme to which we both assigned the same name, Clk1, dual-specificity protein kinase. Enzymes, as you may have read are macromolecular biological catalysts. The gene is also known as 'Clock-1'. This gene is thought to be responsible for aging due to mitochondrial ROS, also known as Reactive Oxygen Species, which are chemically reactive oxygen species containing oxygen. Examples include peroxides, superoxide, hydroxyl radical, singlet oxygen, and alpha-oxygen. Now in a biological context, ROS are formed as a natural by-product of the normal metabolism of oxygen and have important roles in cell signaling and homeostasis. However, during times of environmental stress, such as UV or any kind of heat exposure, ROS levels can increase dramatically. This results in significant damage to cell structures, ruins their ability to repair themselves and eventually makes them stop dividing."

"Jeff, I don't mean to sound like an ass but did you somehow manage to get a hold of my research history off of my laptop and are now regurgitating it back to me? I feel like I'm having a serious case of deja vu here, all this stuff I read off of Wikipedia. I already knew this. What are you trying to tell me? That the organization you are involved with is responsible for the information given on Wikipedia? You guys feed Wikipedia articles?"

"Bear with me Marcus. Indeed, everything I just mentioned you've already read. And I know you've read about concepts such as panspermia, a hypothesis that life exists throughout the Universe and is distributed by space dust, meteoroids, asteroids, comets, planetoids and also by spacecraft carrying unintended contamination by microorganisms, correct?"

"Yup, in great depth. It's one of the hypotheses. Just like Clk1 is one of the hypotheses of what exactly kick-starts the process of death."

"Well Marcus, the exact same protein, enzyme and gene found in the family of Clk1 in its current composition and form observed here on Earth has been found on another body in the Solar System, close to Earth."

Something instantly popped into my mind and it seemed plausible so I decided to throw it out there as a reply without being rude as hell.

"What do you mean, like on an old abandoned satellite left behind in Earth's orbit or something? That doesn't seem all that surprising, I'm sure it's just human contamination. We put those things up there so obviously they have our crap, fingerprints, dead skin cells and even DNA littered all over them."

Jeff sat on what I just said a good few moments, at least thirty seconds before he spoke again.

"No Marcus, the traces were not found on an old satellite, or any man-made hunk of metal floating aimlessly through space. The traces were found on a Solar System body that has not been contacted or interacted with by a human until recently. Other than just being registered as existing. And these compounds were already there before the contact."

Ah fuck I knew cutting down on drinking was a bad idea. I mean what is the point anyway?! Being sober is boring 90% of the time. This is what I tried explaining to my father. And to Alicia. My dad always thought that me getting sauced in University was because I was depressed, running away from my problems and drinking my sorrows away. "Don't drink your troubles away son" he used to tell me. If I needed help to let him know, he'll get me professional help, he would go on. And I used to tell him "I drink because I'm bored of being sober old man. Sobriety...BORES ME!" He wasn't buying it. He kept reverting to the whole 'drinking my troubles away' notion. I wonder how one gets help at a rehab center if you tell them that your primary reason for drinking is in fact because you are painfully and brutally bored with being sober. What do they prescribe for that? What advice do they give?? Hey look over here, do this and you'll have so much fucking fun and excitement while doing it, go to Canada's Wonderland at least three times a week that should cure your boredom. Yeah....sure I'll do it.... but I would have even more fun doing it ragingly drunk! It never fails. Boredom was a big issue for me. And a defense mechanism in a way. This is the reason why I could never become an addict, or an alcoholic. Quite frankly with time, I would get bored with it. Most definitely though at the given moment listening to Jeff telling me science fiction stories would have been a lot more fun if the tea I was slurping in through a straw was instead whiskey."

"Ok Jeff. I'll bite. Where did they find traces of this....gene? I'm guessing it wasn't the Moon?"

Now I was just being a smartass.

"They found it on a near-Earth asteroid designated as 162173 Ryugu, approximately fifteen years ago. The asteroid itself was discovered in 1999."

I didn't skip a beat and kept following up with questions so that I don't lose my train of thought.

"How was this discovered on this asteroid? By what means?"

"About three years after the asteroid's discovery, in 2002, a mining company called Tredarious Corporation lobbied United Nations to be the first to get mining rights on the asteroid. Initial international probes sent to the rock soon after its discovery showed that the surface was rich with nickel, iron, cobalt and ice of unknown composition. This was only the surface however. Most other industries lost interest as they felt the surface was not containing enough lucrative precious metals worth exploring further. Tredarious, on the other hand, wanted to send more sophisticated equipment and dig deep into the asteroid as something like that has never been done before. They were speculating that the interior of the 800m diameter chunk of dirt might contain more precious metals, such as gold and platinum. So in 2004 they attached customized mining and research equipment to refurbished obsolete rockets from various space agencies around the world they were able to purchase relatively cheap, and landed on the asteroid successfully. The launch was performed from a classified launch pad in an undisclosed location but with US and Russian governments having full knowledge of it. All the machinery was remotely operated from Earth, no human has stepped on the asteroid's surface as of yet."

"Hang on, how big did you say this asteroid is?"

"About 800 meters in diameter. Its shape is quite extraordinary....it's shaped almost exactly and symmetrically......like an industrially shaped diamond. Its geometry makes it fairly easy to land on and to explore."

"Ok so I don't get it, a golf ball about a kilometer in diameter, that's about a chunk of a mountain. Why spend all the money and resources on a rock like this, isn't there plenty of ground and rock still left on Earth to explore? Much bigger in size, capacity and yield? Much cheaper losses to recover in case the mission fails and discovers nothing? I mean are we about to completely run out of resources here on Earth so now we have to explore debris floating in the Solar System?"

"Well we are not quite yet out of space and resources here on Earth, but one thing that's a problem for so many mining and resource companies is the fact that the International Environmental Regulations are extraordinarily rigorous. Getting worse by the year in fact. The costs of Environmental Assessments have skyrocketed, some companies had to shut down as their budgets and profit margins simply wouldn't cover the EA, and related insurance policies. Rocks floating in space no one cares about. Deep drilling equipment is already available here on Earth and is capable of being remotely operated, all these companies' need is simply to launch it into space and ensure it has plenty of fuel. State of the art electronics, that's the biggest cost. That and the launch itself. And these days, this is cheaper than all of the Environmental mumbo jumbo, bureaucracy and paperwork necessary for Earth exploration. Not to mention the wait involved in receiving permits. It can take decades at times. Private companies like SpaceX and others, there are a few in Russia and even China and India now, complete these launches for relative bargains that these companies can easily afford. And what one does to a rock floating in Space is nobody's care or business. So if it's determined that a given asteroid in space is worth a significant amount of money, 162173 Ryugu was estimated to be valued at about US\$82.76 billion in mining resources, paying even up to \$57 million for launches is negligent. And currently, Tredarious Metals runs the show up there, no one else is anywhere near. Their connections with the US government and others run deep. Aside from the launch costs, equipment operating costs, etc... everything else is pure profit for them, and whoever else happens to be their powerful and close friends in the world governments. Overall, very lucrative indeed."

I was following what he was saying. It made sense. I've heard of companies all over the world expressing interest in mining the Moon, or Mars one day. I also heard of probes and spacecraft being landed on other asteroids and meteors for exploratory purposes. But I had no clue that an exploratory mission managed to get this far.

"So as I was saying initial exploration was only superficial, a surface exploration that's it. But then Tredarious sent deep drill probes. And that's where the real fun started. The traces of genes, proteins and enzymes, not just the aforementioned Clk1, but other carbon-based molecules were found as well. And they were found not on the surface, but at about 100 meters below. And that wasn't all."

"It wasn't?" I had a feeling I wasn't going to get an answer to this question.

"No. They found out that 162173 Ryugu was not an asteroid at all. That's all I can say at this time."

Drum roll please. Silence. And no I wasn't going to be stupid enough to blurt out 'Ahm is it a really miniature planet maybe?'. However at the risk of sounding like a wide-eyed school child I came out with the obvious: "Well what is it then?"

"Marcus I think you would agree that I have shared quite a substantial amount of information with you wouldn't you say? We had a bit of a rocky start but we finally got a nice chat going, and I hope I was informative enough for you and that I have managed to spark your attention. I would like to formally encourage you.... invite you if you will to come find out more, but this will have to be done at a different place, at a different time."

"Not here? Why not? Why not share everything? And why did we meet here in the first place, in this dump?"

"More information will require more commitment from you. To our....scientific society. We have to know that you can be trusted. You know quite a bit already but everything aside from the few peculiar bits I've mentioned is public knowledge. So you blabbing around that some piece of turd floating somewhere in the vicinity of Earth is not an asteroid and contains biological debris won't exactly spark anyone's attention. There is more to this story. Much more. But as I said this will require a significant commitment from you. As to why I chose this place...well I suppose it is perfectly inconspicuous in an utterly run-down neighborhood somewhere in between where both of us work. Furthermore, our organization has a certain field frequency, electro-magnetic interference blocking cloak on this building. No one other than 'us' can hack into our cell phones in this location."

"We are being listened to right now?"

"Only by the people I represent. But no one else. "

"So what kind of a commitment are we talking about here?"

"Membership in our society is a commitment for life Marcus. Such as with the Truemasons organization. I assure you before joining you would have a full overview of our interests and what we are all about. I would be very much surprised if you didn't feel like you have finally found a place where you belong. As I know you've felt out of place for a long time. Since you've left Europe as a child if I'm not mistaken. Out of place with everything, people, society, work, etc...Please take a few days, hell, take a few weeks to think it over, ok?"

I dared not even ask what ominous protocols transpire and are set in motion in case someone tries to leave this 'organization'. I figured whatever reply, if any, I got there was no way it would have been truth to the fullest extent.

"Alright I will. By the way, I have to let you know I've had a chance to join the Truemasons a couple of years ago when I lived in the Toronto area. I worked with a man who was a member. I got spooked by the whole 'for life' requirement. Even though I've never heard of anyone complaining about it or reporting horror stories from being a member. But I've always thought of myself as a free thinker, free shooter, free arrow well you get the point. Somehow signing up for a 'team' for life sort of goes against that, in my mind. Quite frankly it freaks me out. I hope you can understand. So I will think about it, but similar concerns are already popping up in my head."

"Marcus many things in this life are 'for life'. Eating, sleeping, breathing, working. Try to look at it that way. At the same time and again I stress that you've always felt like you wanted to belong with a group of like-minded people isn't this true? Haven't you felt that whether it was during your life in Slovenia or your life here in Canada that there are so few people you connect with? Men or women? Don't you rave about how everything sucks how people don't understand anything, the way of the world, the politics, the geopolitical games, etc...Don't you say how nice it would be to have a 'crew' to connect with? I mean aren't these your words?"

"Well I guess you have me and my whole life completely bugged. So you are trying to reassure me but you are actually freaking me out more. I have to tell you now that I am aware of just how much you know about me doesn't exactly make me want to join your cult, or club or whatever it is. You are feeding right into my fears and paranoia, you are not reassuring me in the slightest."

"Marcus, we found out enough about your personality and life to know that you would fit in well within our circle. If you choose to go your own way and you and I never speak again, we will never impact your life in the slightest. You will be leery at first as you'll think I'm lying to you just now and that we will use all sorts of dirty tricks and tactics, good or bad, to persuade you to come and join us. Intimidation tactics. But as weeks and months go by you will see that this won't be the case. Now, that being said, if you decide to embrace our realm you will find most of the answers and the comfort you have been looking for your entire life. You know very well every single human being these days is under surveillance. There isn't a government out there that isn't spying on its citizens. Collecting data on them, observing their patterns, thought processes, habits, reading their messages, emails. But for bullshit purposes, control, money, power, brainwashing. Therefore why not join something that although wanting commitment from you will also make it worth your while? And, protect you from surveillance from anyone else for the rest of your life. So, since you can't beat them, join them, if not them then us. I assure you a lot of things will begin to make more sense to you. I can't say anything more than that at this time."

"What is the name of your organization?"

"I'm sorry I can't tell you that. I've told you everything I can or should at this stage of our acquaintance. Just enough to spark your interest, but not enough to disclose more than allowed, to get either of us in trouble. Everything you know thus far can't harm you or 'us' if you choose never to meet with me again. Anything more and I will have crossed the threshold of no return, for both of us."

"How did you get involved with these people? Or how long have you been involved?"

"Similar to how we are trying to involve you. I got 'observed' and the organization in question liked my character, way of thinking, reasoning. They felt I would make a good addition. I have been a member for 17 years."

"And how exactly did this....'organization' get involved with Space, matters of life and death, etc...?"

"Like any powerful organization that's been around for decades and has significant influence, money, pull, they get interested in all sorts of matters, biological, technological. Anything related to the well being or non well being of the humankind, species on Earth, the Universe. Many famous individuals and entities you've heard of are part of this organization."

"And what did you say is the name of this organization?" I tried again. "Again Marcus I'm not at the liberty to divulge that. And unlike other religions or organizations you may have heard of we do not have our own blurb on Wikipedia. Our people have gone through great lengths to ensure just that, anonymity."

"How many people are involved? How old is it?"

"We've officially formed in 1949, a couple of years after the Roswell UFO incident. So exactly 70 years young. Since the official formation we've now grown to just over 300,000 members."

"That is quite sizeable. Like a medium-sized city. Reading....or should I say hearing between the lines of everything you are saying, I'm supposing this organization you are part of also investigates UFO phenomena?"

"Oh sure, but we are not unique in that field per say. More details to come Marcus, if you grace us and yourself with your life-long attendance and presence."

"I just don't see how I can make this work. I mean, I couldn't possibly not tell my wife Alicia about it and hide this from her for the rest of my life. On the other hand, she will never sign up for this with me. I know her. She will divorce me over this. Plus we have a child on the way too, she will think I'm getting involved with some insane cult and that I'm either doped up or losing my mind or something. I just don't know how to even contemplate this."

"Marcus your wife is a like-minded individual in many ways... to yourself, to our organization. But she is nowhere near as radical, outspoken, easily agitated, such as yourself, due to her frustrations. She doesn't obsess about alternative knowledge. However, I know she cares about some obvious concerns in our modern world. Out-rageous prices of pretty much everything these days, mortgages, food, clothes. What if I told you our organization could be of great help to you, her, your entire growing family?"

"Now it sounds like you are just flat out trying to bribe me. You know Jeff you sure spin a ripping good yarn, and you make yourself sound like the greatest thing since sliced bread, but other than your word, fairy tale assurances and some very interesting sci-fi hints, what tangibles do I have to go by? I gotta tell ya, my wife will surely be asking this. How do we know we are not signing our life away on a bunch of cooked up fantasies? Isn't this how so many people get suckered into joining cults, spending their life savings, and so forth? You could easily be one of those pranksters, con artists, thieves. Or you can be a Satanic nut job. And any more

I probe you just come back with 'You gotta join to find out more'. Like this, the chances I join are 2%. Sorry Jeff, at this very moment sitting here in this shithole of an establishment potential risks of what you speak of, in my mind, tremendously outweigh the potential rewards."

Pause. Long. But sort of overdue as I felt like we've been yammering nonstop for over an hour. Considering the specifics and the theme of the conversation from start to end, I am sincerely surprised this pow wow went on as long and just flowed so uninterrupted as it did. Only interrupted by my bathroom break that is. Jeff finally spoke again.

"Marcus the only thing left for you to do is to think this over as I'm fairly certain you have exhausted all the research you'll ever be able to do. There is nothing left to research. The information about the asteroid in question and everything related to it which I told you about is readily available online, but it will give you neither the extra information you just got from me nor any further information that I and our organization would be able to give you. You can try and waste your time but I assure you that you will find nothing. Think it over first, decide for yourself. Then let me know. You know where to find me."

We shook hands and went our ways. It was a strong drug withdrawal syndrome kind of feeling as I had so many more questions to ask I found it hard to breathe. I bet involved, warm and fuzzy hugs will come standard only if I join their organization.

As I left the place I realized that it was 4:30 PM. I was there for two and a half hours somehow and it was getting dark out. I was no longer tracking wet mud all over the floor I was now dispersing dried up and crumbling dirt all over it which was stuck like paint on and beneath my construction boots. I wasn't sure which scenario was worse for them to clean. Honestly, I didn't care. I had my head so far up my ass with my issues and living in my own world on any given day usually, today I was surprised I still even registered where I was walking. There was a good chance someone was going to find me wandering next to Lake Ontario about 20km away from Kingston at some point in the middle of the night.

I had no intention of going back to work for any reason whatsoever, it was the end of the day anyways. So it would have been useless and I was way too distracted and jarred to risk falling into a socializing trap with anyone from work. For a guy who spent most of his life distracted, this was by far the most I have ever been distracted in my entire life.

As I drove home I couldn't turn on the music or think about anything. I wasn't even thinking about the meeting that just transpired. I was simply too exhausted mentally to think anymore. I was shivering from the outside cold, the freezing car and stress all at the same time. I felt as though my immunity had dropped so low over the past couple of hours that I was going to be burning a fever by the time I came home. It was going to be another rough night of me trying to pretend like everything was fine and not being distracted while I talk to my wife and feel the kicks of our unborn child. I wondered how many more of these moments I outmaneuver before she snaps and runs away from me for good. This double life was lunacy. I was on the edge and I knew it. Tiptoeing a fine line. Like with so many things and countless times in my life. Most of my life had been spent in this state.

I replaced the anxiety of dreading a meeting with Jeffrey Madison, especially after the mysterious way he showed up at my work, with a new dread and anxiety of regurgitating what he said to me in my head over and over again. The implications....of his implications, hints, drops of information. That combined with the fact that in order to know anything more, which I wanted my whole life, I needed to become a member of some secret organization?! How on Earth will I ever sell this to myself, let alone to my wife or my parents? I simply was not cut out for this, had no fortitude for it.

I hallucinated and stumbled through the evening in a haze, although a surprisingly articulate one. I focused on all the questions coming from Alicia and I answered them correctly and in a sound way. One of the first things I mentioned was how the site visit was long and cold, with many issues being brought up to the table by the Client. I said it was the longest site visit I've had thus far on this project and that I was overall dead tired. So all subsequent questions coming from Alicia were nice and easy. She was caring and loving and took pity on me. And I felt like shit for exaggerating my work situation as the reason why I wasn't myself. But how could I possibly tell her the truth? At least at this moment in time. Even later if I ever manage to sort all this out in my head I will never be able to explain the intricacies and details of the predicament I was finding myself in to anyone in my family. Worst-case scenario if I end up being sick I will blame it on the site visit. Not on the stress of my side life. The stress of my capability to always add a pile of issues to my life just at a time when my life was already stressful and busy to the max.

I was tired early as was Alicia since she worked half a day. She was getting bigger and bigger and she could only tolerate half days at work. I didn't want her to work at all anymore but it wasn't that simple. She was a nurse and the hospital she worked in was severely understaffed and the staff that were available were dangerously overworked. We were lucky that they agreed to reduce the number of days she worked and the ones she did we cut down to half days. Patients were coming by the tens every day, a lot of them demanding and difficult cases. Alicia had to help position them, move them, almost act as their crutch, at least to the ones that were really sick and/or elderly. It was a lot for her to handle, especially considering she was now five months pregnant. So she was beat.

Overall it did us both good to go to bed early. Unlike her though, I would be lucky if I fell asleep at all tonight.

I made it to bed. I started thinking. First I had to calm myself down. Jeff Madison at least seemed legitimate in one aspect. He didn't mean me any harm. Had he wished me any harm this already would have manifested itself. Bottom line, if I choose to never reach out to him again, I was free as a bird. To go back to my day to day life, work, family. Alicia would never have to know anything. Neither would my work. Or the rest of my family. It would be like nothing ever happened. So, no matter what, if I don't decide to go with anything Jeff suggested, I was free, free out of the mess I've made. Ha! That was good enough for me for tonight, the anxiety faded completely and I passed out. I learned to live in the moment and not to freak out as much for the long term. Some of the times at least. So tonight I pretended like I was going to turn Jeff down and never see him again. My ass and my family's asses were for sure protected, my sanity intact.

CHAPTER 11

SAFETY IN STATUS QUO

I slept like a baby. I woke up feeling refreshed. It was one of those dreamless nights of sleep. I found a comfortable thought pattern last night and it was sufficient to put me out. The morning was pretty relaxed as well. As rested as I was I found it easy to converse with Alicia, to hug her and kiss her (which it seemed as if I hadn't done in ages). Our conversation was light and breezy, we laughed and joked around, I rubbed her belly, kissed it. Felt the baby kick inside. I decided that morning to focus on other things. I decided to be normal. We had the twenty-week Ultrasound coming up for our baby and this was going to occupy all of my attention. I was going to work, work out, come home and spend time with my family. The upcoming Ultrasound was major, they would look at the anatomy, inside and out and tell us the sex. Jeff Madison and our nonsense conversations as well as my childish adventures over the past few months I decided to put into a vault inside my mind. I decided to deflect the whole thing like it never happened and like I didn't have to do anything about it anytime soon. Which I didn't even have to. Jeff clearly said for me to think about all of this over the next 'few weeks'. So, like writing exams in University, I decided to pretend like they didn't even exist up until the last couple of days prior. I gave myself a three week time period. I will live my life normally, average Joe, and only remind myself of Jeff, the organization, etc…a couple of days before the three-week deadline. Starting today. I put the remainder into my phone, and I unplugged myself from that issue.

The following week Alicia and I found out we were having a girl! And by the looks of it thus far at five months along, a very healthy one at that. The anatomy scan showed everything looking healthy and strong. It took me by surprise how much I loved the fact the we were having a girl and not a boy. I don't know why that is, maybe I needed a girl to soften me up a bit, to make me more sensitive and caring. All the territorial male pissings between my dad, brother and me played their toll and were getting on my last fucking nerve. All my life growing up I wanted a little sister. I had a feeling it was going to be a girl anyway, as did everyone else in my family and Alicia's family. The only one that thought it would be a boy was Alicia . Oh well, after laughs and cute bets we could all now rest knowing the sex of our child. And a little girl would make an amazing addition to our family. It was a great feeling for us. And not a moment too soon either. Alicia and I were both in our mid-thirties and waiting any longer would not have been wise biologically speaking. Plus our families were getting ever more curious as to when we were planning on expanding our family. We've been together for over ten years, married for almost nine, we've done the schooling and the traveling and the 'me' time. Now it was time to worry and care for something or someone other than ourselves.

We both felt ready. There are only so many material goods you can buy, so many times you can stay at hotels and travel here and there before you have a clear sense that something is missing in your life. That an addition is very much needed, progress. And only then can you go back to enjoying these other things that you've enjoyed a million times before in a renewed way, with new found enthusiasm.

Both families were upbeat and energized by the news. A lot of people needed this in their lives. My parents, her parents. First grandkid in the family. Let the record show that I've done something responsible too. Something memorable, something to be proud of, a legacy left behind. Alicia became almost a different person instantaneously. And I mean that in the most positive and complementary way imaginable. All of her good qualities were accentuated tenfold. The way she conversed, the way she sent SMS messages, replied to questions, got up in the morning, went to bed at night, hummed and sang randomly, etc...she was beaming with optimism, positivity, love, care. She was going to become a wonderful mother and I couldn't wait to witness it. I had great hopes for our daughter. Mainly I wished she would make me a better man, help me grow up even more. God knows I needed it. I've come a long way since ten years ago but I still felt there could be major improvements made. Maybe I was wrong though, the shenanigans that I was pulling the last few months, Marcus from ten years ago would never dare.

With the daughter on the way and Alicia beaming I was fully on the feel-good bandwagon as well. I truly felt good. Genuinely. I felt happy, I felt all the things Alicia felt. Everything in my life all of a sudden seemed more interesting, day to day things, work, people around me, my hobbies. I found myself considerably more interested in other people's stories, specifically about family and kids, water cooler or coffee machine talks didn't seem as bland, uninspiring and utterly mind numbing anymore. I was a model train enthusiast, I had two massive full O scale locomotives in the basement just waiting to be set up on some fancy and interesting track layout around the perimeter wall of the basement. I had it all planned out, I found a company in the US that manufacturers custom steel bridges for this hobby, I found a company in the UK that makes custom buildings for this scale. Now with the kid on the way a hobby like this made even more sense as I was sure a child would be mesmerized by it. Especially during Christmas time. Perhaps a son would have been more fascinated but I was sure a little girl would love it at least in those early years. If I couldn't get our daughter into model trains or shooting they would be my little side adventures. But I would try to see if she would be interested. It doesn't hurt to teach her how to shoot and fish. By the way, I am again undecided about which handgun to buy. But that's another story not deserving any time to itself...

I was in this haze of delight, wonder and dreaming about the future and my daughter for a few weeks. I have decided to completely drop my extracurricular research and everything Jeffrey Madison ever told me, himself included, out of my memory. After my initial three week deadline which I gave myself to tell Jeff my decision had expired, I easily told myself that I wasn't going to make any decision regarding Jeff's proposal at that time either. I simply decided to leave it open-ended. I didn't owe him anything and he wasn't in a need of an answer from me anyways. The whole thing was a bunch of far fetched nonsense I told myself. I replayed my own actions before even meeting him in my head, then I replayed meeting him at the College, him showing up at my work, our conversation at the coffee shop. At moments I explained the whole thing from start to finish as a complete and utter scheme, played upon me due to my irresponsible and juvenile behavior. Asteroids, extraterrestrial proteins, my God that man was full of it. This is how they prey upon fullish and careless individuals like myself, who despite their childish adventures are still ultimately just innocent saps poking around their noses where they shouldn't. I was proud of myself for reaching such a conclusion. I felt like I've matured, grown, learned to decipher right from wrong, real from fake. This would help me with fatherhood, Alicia and my daughter could depend on me better this way. In this confident frame of mind weeks went by quickly.

However right around the time that Alicia entered the third trimester in her pregnancy, with less than three months left to go till the delivery date, I started to get restless. I began wondering again. Eventually, with everything, I get restless. I knew I would. And I started questioning whether abandoning my quest and my compadre Jeff Madison was the right thing to do. Was he really a bullshitter? Was everything he said a complete lie? Was he a con artist? He must have been. All the things he said, these were things of movies and fairytales, he had to have been lying. Who falls for schemes like that? Had I agreed to join the 'organization' or whatever cult he was advertising I surely would have regretted it. They would have taken my money, freedom, God knows what else. Stories like these were common, documentaries were made regarding these subjects all the time. Various Church affiliations, cults, abusing people, taking their possessions, lawsuits for years to come. People try to leave, they are not allowed, etc...I was better off leaving this beehive alone! Or was I??? My incapability to be at peace with my decisions was debilitating. My father never would have struggled back and forth like this. I was nuts. I lived by the adage of 'It's only romantic because it didn't happen'. Or at times, almost because I instinctually knew that something wouldn't work out. I had to get to the bottom of everything otherwise it would stay with me for the rest of my life asking me silently at night from the depths of my psyche...what could have been? And would it have been great?

So what if he wasn't lying? What if he was telling the truth? What if I'm missing out on something that is a once in a lifetime opportunity? To break free from the daily minutia of mediocrity and regularity and boredom. Maybe it would be an incredible chance to have access to a different lifestyle, information, people, way of thinking. Since I recalled myself I craved a different way of thinking, my thirst for it was overwhelming, it was almost as if I was lacking an essential nutrient of life. Will I spend the rest of my life wondering what could have been? Bottom line I had no guts to call Jeff, not even to chat with him a bit more and see if I could maybe get some more information, to confirm the legitimacy of his story without officially joining some Satanic club. I couldn't do it. And he sure as hell wasn't calling, he was giving me my time. With the kid on the way I was simply too scared to reach out to him. The potential repercussions were too dire and heavy. I had no choice, I was doomed to spend the rest of my life wondering what might have been...maybe this was all a dream that I would wake up from momentarily.

CHAPTER 12

EXPANDING THE WEB

On Tuesday afternoon Alicia came home incredibly excited. At first, I thought that it was her usual pregnancy glow and overall cheerful glee but then I realized that she had some interesting news. She barely took off her coat and shoes before she went right into it.

"Marcus you will not believe what a great day at work I just had!"

"Let me guess, no patients came in and you just sat there rubbing your belly the whole time?"

"That's hilaaaaarrrriousss! Plenty of patients came in thank you very much, but it was one patient that mattered. And to think you didn't want me to work at all anymore because of the pregnancy. If I had stopped working a month ago I never would have met this lady that walked into our hospital today!" she quipped.

"Yup, fair enough. I am a terrible husband for caring about

you and the baby and wanting you to stop work ahead of time so you can be home and rest while I go grocery shopping, tend to all of your needs, etc…My God how will you survive the outrage you have suffered from your unthoughtful husband?" I was laying on the sarcasm thick and heavy, like I usually like to do. Luckily for me she was in such a good mood all she did was run up, correction waddled up, and hugged and kissed me and didn't bother with the usual calling me out on my nonsense protocol. I was relieved, I was taking a bit of an advantage of Alicia's good mood lately I have to admit, I felt as though I could get away with a lot more bullshit than I used to be. She just trooped through everything with a smile on her face and a great chip on her shoulder and didn't dwell on any of it. I could have sworn other husbands would say their wives become severely more agitated and noticeably less patient with them while pregnant, but everything was opposite in life for me, as in this scenario, this time entirely in my favor.

"Marcus you will never believe what happened today. So these patients and difficult cases keep coming in and out all day right, I was starting to lose my mind slowly but steadily" well this certainly had a good start to it I thought as she continued; "but then this woman walks in, her name is Shauna…I forgot her last name but she gave me her business card. So anyways it turned out her company contacts random places of business and asks the owners or managers and bosses, whoever is in charge, whether they employ any expecting mothers. She enters these places of business into a draw and out of I believe she said twenty random places of business she picks three. Again all of the places she even enters into a draw have to have expecting mothers or mothers working in them. So my hospital got picked!!!"

At this stage she was staring at me wide-eyed, gently squatting with arms wide open. She appeared ready to try her luck at long distance jumping, or early labor I couldn't quite determine which, and her being pregnant and all made the whole thing look extra comical. A few moments passed before I said: "Ok......ahm....yeah, great!!!" Luckily she quickly realized that she forgot the punchline. "So" she continued, "I just won a 75% discount to any daycare in the city for the duration of our child's attendance AND, oh my God Marcus I can't believe this, $10,000 to our child's future tuition!!!" She screamed out a little towards the end there. And holy shit she should have! This was really unbelievable.

"What?? Holly crap, really??? Alicia are you for real? This is incredible!" I hugged her, kissed her, hugged her again, we were both overjoyed with brimming and positive disbelief. I busted out some homemade brandy that I bring from Slovenia every year and I had a shot, she was content just looking at me drink it. Soon though I had to ask: "Ok, so are you and your work certain that this isn't some kind of a scheme? Like a prank, Kingston's funniest videos, stuff like that? You don't hear things like these every day. Especially not happening to us Alicia."

"No it isn't. My boss confirmed her legitimacy and her company's. Here let me dig up her card, ok here it is. Shauna Tressler. New Horizon Incorporated. Head office in Toronto, phone number, fax, website, email. My boss mentioned that she reached out to our place of business months ago and they agreed to be part of the draw. He checked her credentials several times and wanted to keep it a surprise. He said he didn't want to say anything in case we didn't get picked, I mean the chances were pretty slim, and if we did get picked he was going to....well...surprise me with it! Which he did. I mean screw a raise he hasn't given me for three years straight, this is better than that! Do you have any idea how much money we are going to save on daycare?? Our daughter will be there for at least three years prior to JK, we are talking tens of thousands of dollars Marcus!! And then the $10,000 on top of that towards her University education?! This is insane, this is like winning the lottery! We could invest that money, let it build up, by the time she will enter University hopefully it triples, quadruples. I can't believe that something like this fell into our laps. Us! Shit like this never happens to us Marcus! Can you believe it?"

Indeed I couldn't. I actually really couldn't. I simply would not let go of the notion that this must be a prank of some kind. I had deep paranoid phobias and now, considering everything else unfolding with me, was certainly not the time I would let go of any of them.

"This is amazing news baby, I am at a loss for words" I exclaimed again and hugged her. We were feeling as if on Cloud 9 for the next hour or so, went for a walk, came back called our parents immediately to tell them this incredible news. Winning the lottery that's how it felt. I called my parents even though it was midnight for them in Slovenia, and during the week so not our usual weekend talk time. My father couldn't resist asking "Marcus, this is great, but are you absolutely sure that it couldn't have waited until the weekend?" My mother immediately criticized him "Stop it you big oaf! Your child is calling with exciting news! Are you registering what he is saying? Can't you be happy? Thank God he called about this. Why must you always be on such a precise schedule?! What is he disturbing your upcoming news coverage?" She was a trooper my mother, unfortunately for her she didn't have much staying power. Soon enough they both focused on how Alicia and I should triple check this situation at hand and try to ensure over and over again that this is not some fraudulent scheme at play. I described that it didn't seem like it was (even though I was scared to death myself) but they were not listening, they were adamant. My joy and thrill of wanting to share this news with them soon turned to complete anxiety and frustration and I couldn't wait to get off the phone. They had a talent for bursting bubbles and finding a negative in everything and further reinforcing my own fears never dissipating them.

I came downstairs with a slight headache after talking to them. But as it turned out Alicia 's parents were just as wary of our little 'gift from God' after initially expressing excitement over it. They reiterated twice, whereas my parents reiterated five times, that we need to make sure this whole thing wasn't a scam. So now my dull headache spread into a migraine wildfire as instead of making fun of my parents and their paranoia with Alicia and comparing it to her parents' usual upbeat, encouraging and optimistic demeanor about pretty much anything, Alicia and I were instead sinking in the quick sand of primal fear. Brilliant! Gotta love immigrant parents. Don't trust anyone or anything, spend your time in paranoia and anxiety, if something sounds too good to be true it probably is, everyone is out to screw you, if a great opportunity knocks on the door run away from it, etc...I've spent countless hours and days trying to decipher how much this sort of approach in life actually aids in one's safety, decision making, good physical and mental health. Or whether it is completely debilitating. I've determined that it is mainly the later. It hinders a person big time. It envelops you in this perpetual dark cloud of negative energy, dread and weariness and it causes you to never reach your full potential and to step out of the mould of being a pathetic and overworked ant. It completely locks you in mental chains. You spend all your time and energy analyzing and looking over your shoulder. Dreading bad things happening to you only invites more bad things to happen to you. Tell a person something bad will happen to them and then it does and then you can spend your days telling them "I told you so". My parent's parenting technique in a nutshell.

Despite my rationalizing and minimizing both our parent's efforts to try and instill fear and to encourage us to indulge in our usual paranoia, both Alicia and I succumbed to their fear-mongering and delved deep into research. Alicia pulled out Shauna Tressler's business card, and we both started to frantically search her and New Horizon Incorporated on the Internet. I was digging into Shauna, LinkedIn profiles, Facebook, Google, Alicia was all over New Horizon Incorporated. Everything was coming up quick and easy. I dug up Shauna instantly on both Facebook and LinkedIn. Married, mother of two, a double degree in economics and psychology from the University of Michigan, moved to Toronto 15 years ago, husband from Canada. Even creeped him out, University of Toronto grad, cardiologist! A++. Works at Sunnybrook Hospital. So far so good. New Horizon Incorporated, been around for thirty-three years. Enterprise comprising of baby products, formulas, nonprofit organization, charity, R&D into early child development, etc....CEO Russell Newitt of Indianapolis, Indiana. Offices primarily in the States, Germany, Mexico and Canada. Canadian headquarters in Toronto.

Both Alicia and I started to breathe a sigh of relief. The ease with which we were able to confirm the legitimacy of Shauna and her company was instantly reassuring and comforting. As we were searching we were quickly screen saving everything that popped up on our computers and phones and like school children instantly sent it to our mommies and daddies to reassure them. Don't worry mom and dad everything will be just fine! And we didn't really properly start to rest and unwind until we got replies from our parents giving us the thumbs up and telling us 'Good job kids!' on research well done. We were finally relieved. Funny enough my parents seemed to have been up late this particular night as if seriously freaked out about a scam being run against us. I sent them messages of 'reassurance' around 8 PM my time so that would have made it 2 AM Slovenian time, and they replied instantly. I guess we were all children tonight, needing some guarantees about the world we live in. Now we could all sleep tight, ages 34 - 69.

Waking up in the morning I felt hungover. Stress headache was there, unmistakable, and Alicia felt about the same. We didn't know anymore whether we were happy or sad, or scared, or somewhere in between. Emotions were mixed, even though we just got served with an incredible gift the day before. We found it hard to be truly happy, with guard down, at least I did because I was certain that I was going to be bitten in the ass the moment I felt that way. My life's experience. Couldn't let the walls down ever really, the hyenas lurking outside immediately pounced. If they didn't our own fears and paranoias would finish us off. So now I trod through life permanently vaccinated from ever feeling pure, unabated happiness and calm. Everything, no matter how joyous, was five minutes of happiness, ten minutes of anxiety and dread over what wrong can go down.

So as we ate our breakfast Alicia and I didn't know whether to feel reassured or whether still to worry or what. Our bubbles were burst. We didn't even know whether we should tell anyone at my work about the handout from Shauna and New Horizon. We decided, until we proved beyond a reasonable doubt that Shauna and Alicia's work and New Horizon were coming through for us as they promised, that we would say nothing at all to anyone at my work or any of our friends, acquaintances or extended family members.

As days went by we decided not to say anything even if Shauna and New Horizon came through as promised. Which by the way would only be truly proven once our daughter was born and actually started going to daycare. We decided that news like these to average folk would not be welcomed, even if legitimate. People are prickly and flaky, envious and turn snooty easily. They would feel like we were rubbing their noses with the fact that life is giving us such generous handouts as they struggle, with child costs, mortgages, house renovations, etc....It was best to keep our mouths shut. Permanently.

Shauna and Alicia's work were in touch over the next few days and weeks. They provided paperwork, they brought in lawyers guaranteeing everything Shauna was talking about. We couldn't believe it. Somebody going out of their way reassuring us that they are legitimate. Going out of their way holding themselves accountable to their promises! Alicia and I checked the law companies they came in with, we even got our own independent lawyer to look over the paperwork provided by New Horizon just to make sure they are for real. Everything checked out fine. Our lawyer knew of that company as well and was involved in litigation on their behalf years ago. The whole thing was too perfect. Alicia was completely reassured. She was more trusting than me. After the whole run-around she started referring to Shauna as if she were a saint. She spoke of her as a deity of some sort. "Can you believe it Marcus?" she would say, "someone like her comes into our life and turns it upside down for the positive?". I would just add "Ok Alicia let's just wait and see if this thing really works out the way she says it will before we start canonizing her." But Alicia wouldn't have it; "Why do you have to be so distrustful Marcus?", she would go on "This is coming from your family, they distrust everyone, all the time, you even distrust me, you have to drill me with questions a million times in a thousand different ways before you finally take at face value what I'm telling you." It always drove me nuts how she had a tendency at times to make everything personal, back to us, while at the same time always telling me not to personalize things.

"Alicia, take it easy", I began with my most diplomatic and composed tone of voice which I have adopted recently, especially since I found out she was pregnant. "You don't need to be Shauna's advocate. I'm not attacking her in any way, I'm just saying let's be careful before we frame her picture above our bed. And don't throw me and my family to the dogs right off the bat. Your family didn't trust her or her story either when they first heard about it. They wanted us to double and triple check everything as well and they were only able to rest easy once we did. Both of our parents are immigrants, they ate and shoveled shit for many years and got screwed over by countless hordes of jackasses in the process. So let's keep things in perspective. It's good to err on the side of caution."

"Marcus, we debunked all of that" she continued almost unabated. "And once we did and once we proved that everything she was saying was true, there is no need to keep doubting her and not think of her as anything but a wonderful person who came so unexpectedly into our life. So please enough with the paranoia."

"Alicia " I also continued unabated as I'll be damned if I don't go out in a blaze trying to prove my point "all I'm saying is let's just act in a measured way. There is no need to keep doubting her as we did in the beginning, true. But there is also no need to start praying to her every day either. She seems on the level, legit, we will be forever grateful to her once the time for that has come. We'll give her a gift basket, take her out to dinner, whatever. Until then let's just be calm and composed, that's all I'm saying."

"I cannot believe how ungrateful you are being Marcus" oh fuck my life I thought to myself; "After all she's done that's all you have to say!"

"Alicia I'm going to work out. This is ridiculous. How you managed to turn this into an argument between you and me I'll never know but just know it was all you who caused it. I didn't do anything wrong, you are arguing with yourself."

I picked up my gym bag and left. She muttered "Whatever"

and that was easy enough to take I suppose. I just needed to get out of that conversation trap.

The gym helped. I was punching and kicking the bags with additional ferocity and both the bag I was torturing and my sweat were bouncing and flying into other people's space around me. I didn't care, I had to let off some steam. It had been an exciting past nine months that's for sure. We got back from our vacation in Greece, Alicia became pregnant, I teetered on the edge of sanity with research into human biological processes of living and dying and courting shadowy societies, Jeffrey Madison hallucinated about asteroids and proteins from outer space and a woman named Shauna was dishing out heavy coin and goodies for random children and their future, because hey why not. As the Chinese would say, may you live in interesting times. It dawned on me that I hadn't seen a movie in months, or anything fictional on TV, I didn't need to, I was living in fiction. I was on the verge of completely losing it.

Days and weeks flowed by again. We settled into our life. Alicia's belly kept growing like a subtly inflating yet perfectly shaped balloon and since we were close to the finish line apparently the baby's auditory senses were now coming online. So I spent time talking into Alicia's belly more and I must say as much as I used to think that shit was corny, I was having tons of fun with it. I also told Alicia that if her and I were arguing she can pout and turn her head away from me all she wants but I still must be allowed to talk to the tummy and the baby. She laughed out loud at that as I was tickling her. We haven't had any useless arguments in weeks. It felt nice. We were too busy trekking through the winter and crappy spring and measuring out our bedroom to see how we will fit in the crib, changing station and a chest of drawers. We moved our bed, rearranged other furniture, etc....something to do every day. In the upcoming weekend we were making a trip to IKEA to pick up more items and maybe a baby stroller with a car seat as well.

Alicia and I both called into work today and said we weren't coming in as we were informed of a severe snow system heading our way that was bound to deliver 30cm of snow between Tue-Wed. We thought we were being extremely proactive and responsible since the weather forecast was calling for '100%' precipitation by the hour well into tomorrow morning. Sure enough as we milled around the house the snow quantities were pathetically unimpressive all day with only about 2cm accumulation by 3 PM. We were surely both going to get flak for this at work tomorrow and I was even more 'enthused' since I took a non-pay leave day because I didn't want to use up any of my vacation days. Murphy's Law was the Bible of my life. Had I gone to work than the snow would have piled up to the rooftops, which happened to me numerous times before when I braved the weather forecast since I figured they were full of it. And my drive to work turned into a prayer marathon for me not to die. As usual however everything was always the opposite of what I expected or prepared for. It was a safety mechanism in a way, one that ended up killing spontaneity and joy numerous times. I had to constantly walk around with awareness of the possibility of the worst happening in order for things to work out fine. Daunting way to live. But in my mythological mind it prevented impending doom at every corner. Anyways, whatever, skipping a workday for a snow day like back in school was damn fun.

All of the snow fell during the early morning hours of Wednesday. It made for a fun dig out session Wednesday morning. We were well armed for such an occasion, we bought two new shovels just this year. Alicia picked up the one for $40, ergonomic handle and shaft, huge scoop, very easy on the back. She made sure to put it in the house at the end of every day since she didn't want it stolen?! I kept telling her that pretty much everyone in the neighborhood had the exact same shovel and was leaving it outside on their porch. But she was adamant about putting it in the house during the night. "You never know" she would insist "that one wandering vagabond might scoop it up during the night". I wasn't quite sure which 'wandering vagabond' would be wandering at -20C during the night stealing shovels, they would be mainly looking for a warm shelter of some sort before anything else, but once Alicia got something stuck in her head you couldn't dislodge it if your life depended on it. Whatever I thought, it was easy enough to put it into the front hallway during the night. I didn't want to argue over this issue, it seemed utterly irrelevant at the end of the day.

So I shoveled the porch, cleaned the cars, put them on the road, and snowblowed the driveway since I got the snowblower to work.. Alicia helped God bless her pregnant soul. She also made my lunch. I showered after the snow session, ate and headed for work.

As I drove down barely cleaned roads in the warmth of my car I felt like I could dose off. I felt dead tired since a shoveling session was a heck of an exercise in the cold and barren tundra that was Kingston in the Winter. Showering off, having some warm milk with honey then sitting in my warm vehicle made me tuckered out like a baby. I never knew how on Earth so many people exercised in the morning?! I mean what the hell was that anyways...Get up at five in the morning, especially in the Winter, in pitch darkness, go to the gym, then shower and go to work ready to.....work?! Seriously. I would be under my desk with a pillow and a sleeping bag catching zzz's before I could even turn on my computer. I was most certainly not a morning person. Less so every day as I got older. Some of my best sleep was between 4-6AM and I didn't see that changing anytime soon. Especially not in Winter.

As I strolled into the office the Engineer in Training that I helped hire, Sylvia, was already bragging about her morning workout session. She was chipper as hell holding her half a liter cup of coffee and standing in the middle of her cubicle with a giant Aladdin's carpet wrapped around her neck that she insisted was in actuality a scarf, latest fashion design, and with her hair completely wet from a recent post-workout shower.

"Good morning Marcus", she started with an energetic intensity "I'm so happy I made it to the spin class this morning. I missed it the last couple of times and I was super pissed at myself."

"Yeah God forbid you stayed at home...and...slept another couple of hours" I added slyly literally unable to hide cynical sarcasm. It was too damn early in the morning and my filters of political correctness, already severely malfunctioning on any given day, were simply not working at all.

"Thanks for the sarcasm grumpy pants" she went on seemingly cheerfully amused with my tone of voice. She was used to me by now. Bottom line I really liked the girl, she had an incredibly polite, upbeat personality but not in any kind of a fake, bullshit way. She genuinely felt good about the world around her. She was still optimistic about it. Oh God how I wish I could go back to those days. But I was too far up shitburger creek. She was punctual, old school in all the right ways, very smart and we all loved having her around in the office. She was a great addition to our team.

"How do you not catch a cold with your hair wet every morning in the middle of the winter?" oh man I felt bad but for some reason I just felt like picking on her. "I remember girls on my bus to high school every morning with completely wet hair in the middle of the winter, I would always cringe, it would send shivers down my spine whenever I would see that." I droned on in my jackass way.

"Well I don't know what to tell you" she replied dryly "I've never heard of anyone catching a cold or becoming sick due to wet hair and cold." Now I noticed her enthusiasm fade as she sat down and turned towards her computer screen. Good I thought, it's the fucking morning after a snow storm, no one should be anything but miserable! And oh by the way she was full of it about the whole cold and sickness thing as I could distinctly hear her starting to sniffle and cough. She was coming down with something for sure and good luck telling me that it had nothing to do with her wet hair parties after working out and exhausting her body. They seemed to relish in classifying common sense as 'old wives' tales' here. It was a strange phenomenon. Everything was simply...opposite of my logic. I was a bitter old crank this morning and no one could really snap me out of it.

I booted up my computer quickly, chowed through some fruit and yogurt and promptly stood up and went to make myself some coffee. I had to break apart this dream state I was in. Otherwise, I was actually debating going into my car, having the engine on and passing out for an hour or so. Just to 'blink with the eyes' so to speak.

The coffee didn't help at all. It never helped with my feeling of being tired. That, I thought, was a legitimate old wives' tale. I simply drank it because it was a habit I got into since everyone else was doing it. The same way I got into smoking back in the day, it was a social habit, nothing else and nothing more. I never felt that I 'craved' nicotine or whatever other bullshit they made people believe here. I did it because I was bored and it was a habit of movement, holding it with my fingers, exhaling smoke, talking with it in my hands, flicking the ashes and eventually the butt, etc....Once the weekend drinking sessions were over I would never contemplate actually smoking on my own time, sober, at random times of the day. Well maybe once in a Blue Moon, but not as a general rule of thumb. Drinking and cigarettes went like milk and honey for me in those days. Once sober the cigarettes only added to my already raging anxiety. Coffee was similar, I drank it since everyone else did, it was the movement of lifting the cup up and down like an idiot, like one of those 'drinking water' bird toys that seemed to compliment my already never ending leg twitching tick due to my excess of energy. Plus I'll be honest in the winter months the warmth of it did feel nice. But otherwise it did nothing else, it didn't wake me up, it didn't really make me wired if I had too much of it, all it really did was make my stomach feel heavy and crampy and kept me running to the bathroom like a race horse. So I substituted it with hot tea as much as I could.

CHAPTER 13

TOO DEEP

I had to start checking the connections for the new swing bridge we were designing. The budget was already completely blown and the deadline was fast approaching for it to be submitted to the client. Common occurrence these days in all the companies I've ever worked for. I had all the possible design software installed on my computer. I got it approved with no problems or roadblocks at this company unlike at all other companies I've ever worked for. Good place I was at, finally, after changing seven companies since graduating University eleven years ago. So I had no excuse not to hammer this out properly. I opened my design excel sheet for this project and started the 'Connections' section as I had my S-Frame model opened on the other screen. I was too far along using S-Frame on this bridge to transition to start modeling it with

CSiBridge, an otherwise significantly more powerful software I just recently had installed.

I was finally starting to get into the focus of things (if you count me checking my phone every two minutes like I was in highschool being in focus) when Leslie called.

"Hey you loser, I got someone on the other line for you", I wondered at what exact moment in time did Leslie and I get so familiarized as for her to open up a greeting with me in such a way. Like we used to fling crap at each other back in Kindergarten. Except she was almost twice my age and she didn't know shit about me and likewise me about her.

"Well, hello to you too Leslie, next time why don't you just come to my cubicle and kick me in the nuts instead" she was laughing her ass off on the other line. "Alright, transfer them through" I said. I was in no mood to continue this farting contest of wits with her. Not today. As I told her to just transfer the caller I didn't even notice that I hadn't asked who it was on the other line.

"Hello Marcus, how are you this fine early spring morning? If you can call this beginning of Spring, haha." said the voice on the other line. I have to admit I thought that it must have been one of the Contractors from one of the jobs I was involved with. Before I answered anything I was cycling through all the people from site that this voice probably belonged to. Once the brain goes down one alley it's hard to direct it elsewhere, it decided it must be one of the Contractors and that's the way it had to be. Then I figured it must be one of the Clients. Before I could figure it out the voice continued; "I hope you still remember me sir, I mean I've grown more handsome and much younger since our meeting at the coffee house but I'm sure my tone of voice is still the same, haha."

Jeffrey fucking Madison. Well, the coffee might not have had a wake up effect on me but this phone call just now did the trick just fine. Also, my percolation issue went right into overdrive. I must have had full-blown irritable bowel syndrome by now. Literally everything gave me the shits these days. Well most things anyways. Work-related things, socializing with other humans, etc... And of course myself. My own brain. And my own actions. For a guy who had anxiety issues I was very talented at creating and putting myself in situations that caused me considerably more anxiety. I suppose I wanted to give myself exposure therapy and vaccinate myself against all the things that made me anxious by tackling them head on. Facing them. Dealing with them. I can honestly say that I was doubtful if the method worked at all or made the whole thing worse. Some things made me more resilient, others just wore my nerves further down to nubs. This whole theatre show I pulled off with my leisure research over the past few months was also shock therapy for an anxious prick like myself. I have absolutely no idea where I found the balls to embark on such a ridiculous adventure. And most certainly it wasn't helping me get 'nerves of steel', I felt like a bigger little bitch than ever. I wanted to hide beneath the kitchen table and cry. Whatever doesn't kill you makes you stronger. But with severe scars, if you survive. That's the second part of that saying they don't tell you about. And Jeffrey Madison, well he was that anti-constipation pill that I really didn't need in the first place. Now I desperately needed a portable toilet with me all the time. I got what I deserved, this is why you don't leave the house, don't ask questions, don't step out of the box and do not shit disturb. It causes more time spent in the bathroom praying your heart won't jump out of your throat. Leave the already dangerously taut nerves alone. Get into a mortgage and start home decorations (otherwise the exact uninspired antithesis of what I've ever wanted) and feel the hypertension steadily ascend, that's normal and socially accepted. Not sci-fi matters related to the most cooked up conspiracy theories that have ever existed or been thought of. Stress ordinary folk go through, group stress, not unique individual stress that no one else identifies with including your loved ones.

What did this fucking guy want, I wondered. Probably one of the most idiotic questions I've ever asked myself since a second later it dawned on me that I knew exactly what he wanted. I tried my best to calm down and not squeal like a cat with its tail run over. Ok, I told myself, he is calling to see about my decision. I was supposed to contact him and let him know a couple of months ago, and I never did. I decided to never call him and basically I hoped that he would forget about me and go away. Classic shit disturber I was. I figured he would never contact me if I had simply vanished. He seemed busy and important enough, both with teaching and other apparent extracurricular activities he told me about, and he already went out of his way to reach out to me after my initial contact. I thought a person like that would reach out only once. If I chickened out and essentially denied to join his brotherhood, or ganghood, he would surely disappear, right? I mean who the hell was I in the grand scheme of things anyway?! It made no sense for him to persistently chase after me. Apparently, I was wrong. Dead wrong.....and I sincerely doubted that he was calling to engage my company with stone renovation work over at the College.

"Jeff...", I started pathetically "Ahm, I mean, Jeffrey...Dr. Madison", my voice was dry, I had no spit in my mouth, although my shirt was instantaneously drenched in sweat. "Yes, I am good. How....how have you been? What's new?" I was so utterly aware of how moronic I sounded. It felt like trying to make small talk banter with a cop who just arrested you for robbing a convenience store with topics completely non-related to the matter at hand. I had no idea what to say. Leave me alone! I don't want to play anymore...

"Marcus I am fine. Busy here at school, went on vacation, down to Florida for almost a month. It was nice to take the family out of this polar vortex nonsense, haha. So I'm just getting back into the swing of things."

How nice I thought. These freaking college and university professors and their time off. All we got in the private consulting industry was three weeks vacation a year. With a chance of gaining the fourth week after ten years in the industry. Pathetic. I should have been a university professor. There it is again, only romantic because it didn't happen. Alright I should really focus on why he is calling as opposed to experiencing envy towards his livelihood, perks and benefits. How easily I got distracted.

"Oh nice" I tried to keep up even though my stomach was now in knots and I couldn't wait to hang up the phone so I could retool, "yeah a few people from my work went down south during the winter. Mexico, Cuba. Some went back in November, some in December, and some are going now. Reading week is usually a good time so people go with their kids."

"Exactly!" quipped Jeffrey. "My boys are done school, just traveling around a bit before they start looking for jobs so I took them with me." he continued.

"Will they follow in their father's teaching footsteps?" I asked.

"Nah," said Jeffrey, "the younger one finished for Tool & Die and the older one is opening up his own Auto Mechanic shop. They were never very enthused with academia, books and studiousness. I can't blame them. Let them do things with their hands, forget this world, it's dull as a baseball bat."

Even though Jeffrey was trying to sound upbeat about his sons' vastly different career paths than his own I could detect an unmistakable trace of disappointment in his voice. He was insincere in his portrayal of happiness for them and their career paths. I could only imagine the days and nights he spent convincing them to pursue a university-educated career, for little Johnny and Bobby to become a lawyer, doctor, engineer, chemist, dentist, etc....But it was not to be. My father immediately popped to mind. What would he have done had I told him that I don't want to attend University but instead wanted to go to college, be a Technician or Technologist of some kind. He would have lost his mind, I knew it. I never gave him any such trouble luckily, the way I was raised not finishing University was never an option for me, quite frankly I wouldn't have been able to live with myself. That's how strong University education was engraved in my blood. It was a Socialist thing I guess, coming from ex Yugoslavia. Everyone was asking who finished what, who got what degree. Engineers and doctors were revered the most. You would command more respect back home as a homeless doctor than as a millionaire shoemaker who only had a high school diploma. Such was the mentality. Nothing could change it.

"Well I'm sure they'll be able to find great jobs, maybe even have their own businesses" I tried sounding optimistic and upbeat. I found myself boosting this guy up regarding the career paths his kids took even though he was calling me for God knows what reason to shake up my otherwise mind-numbingly ordinary existence. "To be honest" I kept going "many times these days I wish I didn't attend University, that I went to College instead, became a technician or an electrician or got some Trades program diploma. It would have been a more hands-on curriculum, easier to find a job and quite frankly better money to be made." As I was saying this I got sad since I realized that my pointless gibberish was 100% true. It indeed took me forever to find a job out of University, even with my engineering degree. No one wanted to hire a green novice without practical experience. And I was stupid enough not to take co-op during the summer breaks, I was too busy drinking, working at a local auto mechanic shop and Canadian Superstore meat department part-time. I didn't want to sacrifice my precious time off. What can I say I was an idiot. Half the people that took co-op ended up working for the companies they did co-op with right out of school. Then once I finally got hired the first company (out of the seven I've changed since graduating) didn't have the time nor the money to give me proper training, everyone expected me to be Leonardo Da Vinci of civil engineering right out of the gate. Anyway, now thinking back to my early career beginnings added to my already severe anxiety caused by this conversation.

"Marcus you are exactly right!" I felt Jeffrey was actually being sincere as he said this, and genuinely boosted by my pep talk "you are absolutely right! David has already gotten two job offers and Sam has an interview next month in Calgary. I'll be sad to have him leave Ontario if he decides to take that offer but in the end I won't stand in his way. They'll both be fine, I'm sure of it!"

"I'm sure of it too." I said. We were both stalling whatever actual subject matter was meant to be discussed.

"Ahm, how is work? Other things?" I couldn't resist but to stall some more.

"Fine Marcus, everything else is just fine." replied Jeffrey rather dryly. I could tell that he was now itching to get into the real reason for this phone call.

"Marcus" he began, "have you given much thought to our conversation months ago?" as he said that he literally sounded like a Mafia don. Flat, emotionless, deadpan delivery. He might as well have said "Marcus the time has come for you to repay me a favor" in Marlon Brando style from the first *Godfather* movie. He instilled instant fear in me as he said that. I paused, I frantically looked around my office. If only the people around me knew what I was going through right now as they mindlessly went on about their business on their stupid computers. I would have traded my spot with any of them in an instant. How I craved right now to be one of the regular Joes, left alone to go about my boring ass life as I waited for eventual sweet death to come my way. How I longed at times to leave this shitty planet, and I was a shit on it.

I decided to be honest with him. Now is the time. Get it over with Marcus I said to myself. Quick, like a Band-Aid! The sooner you tell him the truth the better. He will go and try to recruit someone else and get out of my life for good. And I would never try something like this as long as I live! I will make it my life's mission to be the most boring motherfucker alive. I will be a daddy, hubby, home renovator and I'll calm the fuck down. I was such a pussy at this very moment but I couldn't help it, I was aware that I simply had to get out of this mess I made.

"Jeffrey", I started trying my best to hold my voice steady, "I apologize for not getting back to you. Honestly, life just got in the way. I don't think I can accept your offer for joining your organization. I have too much on my plate with the baby on the way. I'm busy at work, my wife needs my help, I simply cannot take on any more commitments. Especially life long commitments. I am very grateful for our conversation and you trying to open up my eyes to unorthodox things. I am truly sorry for the inconvenient way that I came into your life, I know it must have all been a tremendous waste of your time. But again I will have to pass on your offer. I hope you can understand."

I wasn't really happy about the way that came out. I was very aware of my nervousness, jitters, shaky voice, everything. But the gist was there. And the gist was I was scared to death so please leave me alone before I cry, hide under my desk and get beaten up and divorced by my wife, all at the same time! My ego would never forgive me for this one day but at the given moment I was chickening out hardcore.

Moments passed that felt like an eternity as I waited for Jeff to utter something like "Ok Marcus, no worries, all the best. Have a nice and boring life." out of his mouth. Or anything close to that would have worked. But those sweet words of salvation never came. Instead, Jeffrey completely ignored what I uttered and went on by saying:

"Marcus I have someone else with me here. I hope you won't mind if I put her on the speakerphone as well and the three of us chat together would you?"

The torture continued. It was like a never-ending bad dream. It reminded me of the time when I was ten years old with a broken femur in the hospital after having been plowed down by a BMW at a pedestrian crossing. I won't go into the details of my surgery and titanium plate placement and removal but I remember when they tried finding a good vein to hook up the IV to me. I was so scared and traumatized that no vein they tried yielded a good enough through-put. And they kept trying for another one and another one and another one. This went on for a good hour. Afterward, I looked like a ten year old heroin addict with both inside elbows pricked at least ten times and they still couldn't find a good vein. Finally they just decided to inject me with IV supplements in the form of daily injections. The torture I was going through at the moment was shaping up to be an almost identical experience.

"Well" I began, "I suppose I don't mind. Please Jeff I don't mean to be rude but I do have to mention that I have a lot on my plate today work wise and I have a teleconference for a very important project in fifteen minutes so I won't be able to stay on the phone much longer."

"Not to worry Marcus" he went on "I really just want you to say hi to someone and for her to say hi to you."

I sure hoped to God that he didn't have Alicia tied up next to him and was about to put her on the phone crying and screaming.

"Hello Marcus", a female voice came on. It wasn't my wife, I knew that much. So I was relieved. My guessing at least didn't last for long as the woman introduced herself.

"It's Shauna Marcus. Shauna Tressler."

I could feel the color of my face starting to fade to white as I instantly realized what was going on. Shauna, Jeff, New Horizon, gifts for Alicia and our child, daycare discount, money for college. It was all the Organization! I was becoming coated with sweat all over, I was so stressed out I didn't even have a sensation to go to the bathroom anymore, this was beyond that. I could feel my clothes slowly get drenched. I was as stiff as a door knob. I don't think any part of my body functioned properly in the given moment, I was shutting down. I could barely breathe save for the shallow breaths that I was mustering, let alone believe what was happening. My double life has officially infiltrated my family. I didn't know what to say. Shauna tried to help me out.

"Marcus please relax, I know what you are thinking", she went on "Please know we mean no harm, this is the honest truth. To your family, your wife, yourself. We are simply using a bit of...the power of persuasion if you will to help convince you that you and your family belong in a community and amongst people such as us. Your life will be so much better than it is now, you will know things that you have been dying to know most of your life, you will make sense of things that you have wanted to make sense of since you were a teenager. And we can provide other conveniences in life to make the daily struggle easier. As we have shown. Think of all the times you've felt betrayed by everything around you, your employers, government, social services, how many times you've felt you don't understand ordinary people around you, and vice versa. I wish you would believe me that you have nothing to lose by becoming one of us, and everything to gain. Just look at how happy your wife is."

Oh how uplifting I thought. Like a line of blow. She talked fast but without mistakes, maybe she was reading off of a piece of paper or talking cards. She tried to get in a formidable sized shot of tranquilizer to placate me. But I was too numb. And scared to death even more of their persuasion tactics. We both just sat there for what seemed like an eternity. She kept talking.

"Marcus no matter what you decide the things we have provided to your family and your soon to be newborn child will stay in place. No matter what your decision. We will not ask for a favor back. And there will be no caveats or catches associated with it. That whole thing was simply an example of what we can do for you. A very small example of that. It was an incentive. A bribe sounds too ridiculous to me as we offer a lifetime of better living, it's not just a one-time thing. So I refuse to regard an offer of a better life as a bribe. I'm asking you to trust us. I'm asking for a leap of faith from you."

I suddenly felt a surge of bravery rush through me that I haven't felt in days. "I can't talk here," I said, "Give me a number to call you back on. I will go talk on my cell phone." Jeffrey provided a number and I rushed outside and sat in my car. I called them back. They were both still there.

"Look" I started "I can't join your 'organization'. I am very sorry, but this whole thing sounds like a cult to me. The way you speak, the way you persistently convince, the way you use the word 'we', the way you guarantee a better life, better things, sense of belonging, whatever, it sounds exactly and I mean exactly like every possible documentary I've heard or seen about cults in history. And I just cannot think of anything that will persuade me or convince me otherwise. My wife would divorce me in a heartbeat if she knew I was even contemplating this. There would be no amount of incentives, money, whatnot of convincing her. What you did for us is incredibly generous, I mean it, thank you ever so much! But I will never use any of that money. I won't touch it. I'm too scared to. Quite frankly I don't believe you. I don't believe that you won't ask for anything in return. I wasted your time and that wasn't right.

I will repay you whatever you feel is worth me wasting your time. I'll do a one time favor if it's reasonable. But after that I ask that you get out of my life. And retract the gifts you've assigned to our child. Make up something, anything, Alicia will believe it. Say your company went bankrupt or something. Please, I'm begging you. Let's come to an agreement and then please stop contacting my work or my family."

I was panicking. I was pathetic, wide-eyed, pale and an absolute pile of human cowardice and everything I've ever despised about human kind. If Jeffrey and Shauna could actually see me right now in person (although for all I knew they probably could as they had cameras all over everywhere) they might have just told themselves to forget about me once and for all. A pathetic acting and looking biological specimen that I was in this very moment could not possibly be a good addition to anything on this Earth, no organization nor cause. In the state I was in I could only 'aid' a team of psychiatrists at some institute studying weird and strange human behaviors, phobias, specifically a flight or fight response to unforeseen or uncomfortable circumstances. I retreated into behaving as a worse chickenshit than I was before I set out on this quest of mine. I had less balls now than when I was a child.

"Marcus please settle down", now Jeff piped in. I felt like the two of them were tag teaming me mercilessly and not in any fun way whatsoever. "Get a hold of yourself young man. We understand you are uncomfortable, and scared, out of your element. Ok, let me throw the word 'we' out of the vocabulary to make you feel less uncomfortable. I know how you feel. I felt the same way when I was approached. Almost everyone that joined felt the same way."

"I did too." said Shauna. I didn't believe them for a second. For all I knew they were eternal beings from Outer Space.

"Guys, Jeff, Shauna, please listen to me, again I just can't. You have to understand I would need way more proof of your legitimacy, of your benevolence if you will. And I will never get that, I'm asking for too much in advance I know that. You have said some interesting things Jeff, and you have done some amazing things Shauna, but at the risk of sounding like an ungrateful piece of shit, it's not enough for me to join permanently! I can't commit for life to this thing. I'm still uncertain about a million things, I'm not sure really why you want me, what's so special about me, what you still want to show me, tell me, again why me?! I need more...."

"Marcus I'm sorry I cannot provide more," said Shauna. "We have provided a very generous incentive. Jeff has told you some pretty fascinating inside information. It is on you now to reciprocate. All we want is your attendance, your commitment to something that from knowing everything about you and your personality and life thus far Marcus, and we know a lot, will fulfill you and make you feel as if you are living for a cause. Living for a purpose, amongst like minded individuals. But you have to take that leap of faith. There is no other way. Ask yourself, will you not spend the rest of your life wondering what could have been? I know I couldn't live with that. That was the main reason that I joined, and I haven't looked back. And neither will you."

My head was spinning. I was getting panicky and felt my feet burning. I needed this to end. It reminded me of my younger days in my twenties when I turned down several job offers because I was too scared to leave the proximity of my parents, the comfort of my friends, the familiarity of it all. And I regretted it afterward, did I ever. This felt similar, it's as if my gut instincts were telling me that I was a fool to chicken out but still the fear was too overwhelming, and differentiating between gut feelings and fear was damn near impossible more often than not. This time again it seemed fear was winning the poker game. The loss of my comfort zone was too unacceptable. I ran with fear, it took me by the hand and kidnapped me like a parent kidnapping a toddler after a custody dispute. Oh

God I thought, Alicia will do that with our child after she finds out about the lunacy I have gotten myself into here.

"I'm sorry I can't," I said flatly "my answer is no. I don't want to join. I can't and I won't. Please leave me alone. You are not saying anything different to put me at ease here you are just repeating the same clichés and slogans endlessly."

"Marcus how many times in your life have you spoken, thought and dreamt of wanting to be disassociated with the norms and habits of everyday life, work, cliché conversations? Too many to count? How many nights in your 34 years do you go to bed at night praying that 'something' different occurs the next day? How many times do you wonder rhetorically if this is all that there is in life? And if so, how boring the rest of this life will be? Think. These thoughts are constantly with you, every day, week, months, years. No matter what you have on your plate, work related, privately, leisurely, these thoughts never leave your psyche. And they never will. And now the opportunity is here, the time is here, the right people are here, and you are about to throw it all away and then what?!?! What will you do Marcus?? Go back to thoughts and prayers of wishing something exciting to happen, to turn your world upside down, to have something good to die for so life can be beautiful to live. But now with the additional knowledge that you could have had all that but turned it all down?? Nothing will change or diminish your cravings Marcus. Not your work, not socializing, not fatherhood. Your thirst, your cravings for something more will only intensify, not taper off. But now there will be that never ending thorn at your side nagging at you that you could have embraced an opportunity presented to you and you passed it up, and that knowledge combined with your never-ending desire for all things unconventional and above the norm will be a terrible cocktail to live with. I wish you luck, but it will bury you under its weight. I guarantee it."

God damn, these hyenas sure knew how to blab. I couldn't

disagree with anything he was saying. He was spot on about everything. He summarized me and my life and my entire mindset in five minutes of elaboration. I don't know how to describe what I felt. Butt naked for sure for one. I felt incredible unease about the fact that he knew me inside and out, or the fact that I have been spied on, studied and psychoanalyzed for years like Jim Carrey's Truman by a team of weirdos in some secret organization. I felt incredibly petrified. I was amazed that my heart didn't just burst like a bird's or rabbit's in extreme fear. There is something to be said about people who wish for something so badly and so feverishly to happen in their life, something so extraordinary and out of the norm but who completely fail to prepare for the possibility of their wish actually coming true. And that was me. I was completely and utterly unprepared for anything of this sort. Because you simply don't think it will ever happen. It's too far-fetched. Dreams and nonsense of this sort never come to fruition. It's like wishing you'll encounter a UFO or actually meet little grey men but then stroking out when you actually do. And now I realized the folly of my ill preparation. I was beyond ill prepared. I was an embarrassment to my own dreams, aspirations and desires, to myself. All those times I looked down my disgusting, pompous nose at everyone else around me, thinking how I was different, braver, bolder, more adventurous, it turns out I'm nowhere near any different than anyone else. I was a chicken shit member of the masses, and I belonged right there somewhere in the middle of the herd of human penguins all huddled up in the middle of Antarctica getting ready to weather the winter storm that is life.

We all just set on the line there quietly, not saying anything. I had no clue what to say. I knew that I couldn't ask them to give me more time to think about everything because first of all, it would have been incredibly rude after I spent two months procrastinating on it and they would laugh in my face, and second of all I knew that nothing would change in my calculus. Bottom line I was scared to death and I would need considerably more incentive to even seriously contemplate joining. None of that was going to happen and we all needed to simply stop wasting each other's time.

"Jeff, Shauna" I started "everything you are saying is true, Jeff you are dead on, spot on with every last sentence, word, comma, behind the lines message. But in the end, I'm chickening out, and I know I am. And I am sorry but I don't know what would ever make me change my way of thinking. Ever. Maybe if I wasn't married, didn't have a child on the way, wasn't so scared to death about jeopardizing my livelihood...but even then I have to be honest it would be a hard sell. So, again, with deep regret and apologies, I have to turn you down. My fight or flight response right now is through the roof and it's set hard on the flight."

As I was pushing back I started to gradually feel better. I felt as if I was regaining confidence and manhood that I have lost throughout the process of talking to them. I started to believe in my cause. Fuck them! I have a family, soon to be a father, responsibilities, who are they?! Pranksters, fakes, cheats, God knows what I would encounter and experience if I listened to them and their 'guarantees'. I've gotten screwed over in similar ways before. A company in Calgary sprung to mind I interviewed with. Very similar. What have you got to be afraid of Marcus? Why not step out of the box Marcus? Don't you want to try something different Marcus? Aren't you going to regret it afterward?? They turned out to be con artists. Thinking of that experience definitely helped me solidify my decision greatly right now. And a serene peace came over me.

But Jeff was not going away that easily.

"Marcus, some very great minds are with us. Why wouldn't you want to meet them? To freely talk to them about matters that are not allowed to be discussed within the life you live right now. Some people that are part of us you already know. They are already in your life. Wouldn't it be wonderful to recognize them, to talk to them about things other than politics, sports, work and other minutia of everyday existence?"

This was starting to worry me. "You are pestering me now Jeff", I said "you are officially being pushy, now I want to say no to you even more. Look if you want to keep doing this I don't care, I'll go to the cops, I'll tell them everything, I'll tell my wife everything, my boss. I don't give a shit, but I will not let you blackmail me. I'll survive. Do your worst."

"Marcus please stop being hysterical. Exercise a little more restraint." said Shauna.

"Great diplomacy Shauna! I've said everything I got to say" I added. "I'm not sure what else there is. Your tactics are agonizing. What, I'm supposed to now bite and ask who is it that I already know that is part of your organization?? Well I won't. You are not convincing me or enticing me any further. I don't care if Clint Eastwood is part of your club." I was sounding very agitated now. "Why are you so insistent on getting me to join??"

"Marcus your whole life you've wanted to be recognized as unique and different from the rest. And now that you do and you whine why you?!" said Jeff.

They were rubbing in my cowardice hard.

"Not just anyone Marcus, people in your family as well. Your father for one." Shauna shot out before I could even catch a breath from my agitated rant.

"What did you say?" I retorted. "What kind of a bullshit tactic is this?? Are you trying to say you are going to go after my father, my family?!?" that's not what she said or meant but as a person in utter panic usually would I was overreacting and not listening properly.

"No Marcus, that's not what I said. If you would just try and calm down you could understand properly. What I'm saying, and I am giving you way too much information here, is that you father is part of our organization, has been for years."

I hated their condescending tones in talking to me. I was being addressed like I was a flailing child. So I told them to "Stop talking to me like I'm some sort of a flailing child who just shat his diaper" and continued with "if any conversation is going to continue between us and you don't want me to hang up this phone right now, then talk to me like a grown man! You are unloading a lot of extravagant shit on me, have been for a while, so excuse me for not reacting to it in a casual, calm and non nonchalant way. OK?"

"Ok Marcus, allright, we apologize, you are right, let's talk like equals." said Shauna.

"Alright" I continued "so you are telling me that my father, an Eastern European immigrant who lives the cheapest, most modest lifestyle in the world, is suspicious of my mom's soup contents let alone anything else and has been a pain in the ass all of his paranoid life is part of your organization of enlightened individuals?? I don't believe you for a second. This is just another cheap ploy to get me to join."

"Marcus, look into it some more. That's all we will say. Please understand we also have other things to do than to spend all day trying to convince you. Goodbye, for now" said Jeff.

"I'm surprised you spent this amount of time on me already!" I shot back before they abruptly ended the call. Dammit! Leave me hanging why don't you...

I wanted to throw my cell phone across the parking lot. I was livid! I ran to the washroom downstairs and washed my face with cold water to calm down. Although I preferred the emotional state I was in right now much more over the previous one. I was angry now, pissed off royally, before I was scared shitless. Anger was good, anger provided strength, armor, shield and a sword, fear did nothing but impede basic functioning.

I had to snap out of this mental paralysis, I had to get through a day of work. How I still had a job and a wife I'll never know, my distraction has been at an all-time high these past few months. I was a walking zoned out corpse. I had to get my head out of my ass before becoming a father, otherwise I will leave that baby somewhere and forget where she is. I had to shape up, I had to resolve this crazy situation I was finding myself in. I didn't know what was worse. The continual anguish I lived with or having to fake regularity and trying to focus at work and at home for those people not to suspect anything. I walked with a harlequin mask on, it was an excruciating effort. Being and acting fake was not my cup of tea. I morphed over the years into something that resembled a synthesis of one quarter good, one quarter evil, one quarter actor and one quarter something I cannot even identify. That was me in a nutshell. Perhaps 'evil' created 'good' as an illusionary concept. Or maybe neither existed and there were only random emotions and acts that served to endlessly advance and conquer.

Jeff and his crew were now officially worrying me. Should I actually contact the cops? Were they lying unabashedly about everything?! To mention my father and imply he was part of them, did I just hear that correctly? That had to have been a ruse. My father was the most paranoid, high strung, distrustful human being on Earth, who played by the rules, despised the unknown and out of the ordinary and had worse OCDs than me. There was simply no way that he would have signed up for something like this. Haha, yeah, no way, nice try Jeff! What an outrageous and desperate lie. Good one! Not to mention that my father lived like a broken down immigrant the entire time he was in Canada. We rented a two-bedroom apartment while he saved money like a beaver stores logs for my outrageous tuition and his and mom's life as pensioners. My parents had to retire and move back to Slovenia because life for them in Canada in retirement would have been overwhelmingly too expensive, and completely unaffordable. So my parents were most certainly not coming across like they had any extra perks in their life as a result of being part of some secret organization. Yup, this whole thing was clearly bullshit, I was convinced of it. But that still leaves the question of how to get them off my back for good...

I pulled myself together and was able to get through the rest of the day at work. Like making it through a day in solitary confinement. Of my mind. Surprisingly by 5PM the mental clouds subsided and I felt completely at ease. I felt like I was myself again. Regular and functional. Not overly brave, I have never been that, but at the same time not a scared little mouse. So I came home with a clear head, spoke to Alicia like a normal human being, didn't zone out once, I rubbed her belly, we even felt our unborn daughter inside kicking and moving. It was surreal, my hand literally bounced off of Alicia 's belly from the baby shifting inside. The miracle of life, it truly was a thing of mesmerizing natural science. I couldn't wait to become a father, I felt like I was ready for it, like I needed it right now in my life. I could only imagine Alicia felt the same way. Come whatever may on any front in my life, but this child should be born.

Yet again I retreated into my day to day life. I decided I cared even less now to ever contact Jeff or Shauna or whoever else about some nonsense organization. They'll find me again I'm sure, and my answer will be the same. A resounding no! So let them waste their time. But what to tell Alicia about the money Shauna had promised for our child? I decided to keep my mouth shut for now. I figured it will be years before that moment of truth comes knocking on our door, I'll simply push it aside. And then I hoped, that by that time, Jeff and Shauna or whoever else will be sufficiently pissed off at me for ignoring their calls and invitations that they will retract their offers, make up a bullshit excuse and finally disappear for good.

CHAPTER 14

SURPRISES AD INFINITUM

I wrapped up my target shooting hobby expenditures. I bought the Springfield Armory XDM 4.5" 9mm handgun. It was a thing of beauty, specifically designed for competition but at the same time regaining the classic look of the 1911 Colt. Felt great in my hand. Striker fired. Trigger felt sublime. It also turned out that it was made in Croatia! By HS Produkt. Springfield Armory just bought the license to distribute it in the US under their name. Incredible really, I couldn't believe something like that could be made back in our neck of the woods and be ranked as one of the greatest hand-guns currently in production. Although that thing being a Croatian gun and being made in Croatia in no way had anything to do with me buying it. Truly. It simply felt the best and most ergonomic in my hand, the slide was the smoothest, I liked the look and trigger of it better than any other gun I've tried. And I've tried them all.

It drove Stan nuts. First I told him I was certain I'm buying the Steyr, than I wanted the Walther Creed, then CZ P-09, then Sig P250, then Beretta, then finally this. Stan was grumpy about the whole thing. He felt I should have bought something else, something more renowned with a longer tradition, and not given those peasants back home any business. Oh well, the heart wants what it wants. Now I just needed to become a member of a local gun range, one that was actually accepting new members, and I was off to the races.

It was a Saturday, and I was getting ready to call a range out in Picton, Ontario. A couple of older guys ran it and it had both a rifle and handgun range in it. I was looking for their phone number when my cell phone rang. It was a WhatsApp call. It was my father.

In all the years since my parents have been retired and since they have moved back to Slovenia back in 2011, not once has my father called me. In any way shape or form. They always wait for my weekly calls via Facetime to my mother's iPad that Stan and I bought her a couple of years back. Before that they always waited for my Skype calls or my phone calls via calling cards. When I saw his name pop up I was scared to death. I thought my mother had another heart-attack or God forbid something worse. She had one back in 2015, right before she was supposed to come to Canada to visit Stan and Alicia and me. The whole thing set her back, she wasn't able to come until 2017. And even then my father didn't call us, he sent us messages and emails.

"Hello, hey comrade" I started, the actual word in my language we used was 'druze'. We still used the old Jugoslav partisan salutation and greeting that my grandfather, my father's old man used from his time served in WW2. "What's going on? Is everything alright?" I continued.

"Hey what's going on? Where are you at? Are you alone? Can

you talk?" said my father, sounding noticeably jittery and nervous. I also had a strong sense that my mother was nowhere around.

"Yeah, I'm by myself, Alicia is at work 9 AM - 3 PM. What's going on? Where are you? Where is mom? Is everything alright?"

"Oh everything is fine. I'm just out for a walk, your mom is having hip and sciatica issues again so she laid down for a bit. We just had dinner but she wasn't up for a walk due to the discomfort. But don't worry everything is fine. How are things with you? How is Alicia feeling with the pregnancy and all? How is work?"

"Everything is fine, same old, steady, status quo," I said. "I suppose no new news is good for us now. Alicia 's belly keeps growing, regular check-ups are fine, so I figured the baby is developing and growing according to plan. We've been through all the ultrasounds and everything seems fine. And Alicia feels pretty good, some minor heartburn, discomfort here and there but overall nothing too out of the ordinary to complain about. Otherwise, I'm fine, work is fine."

Everything I told him above I've already mentioned past Sunday, my usual day when I call my parents via Facetime every week. I was going to call them tomorrow as usual, so it was even more strange that he was calling me on a Saturday, via WhatsApp.

"And what about you?" I went on scared at what he might actually say "you are saying everything is fine, mom is fine. Are you ok? You've never called me before from Slovenia out of the blue like this, so forgive me for feeling a bit nervous in receiving this phone call. What is going on? Is everyone else ok? I hope no one died."

"Marcus," he began answering "has anyone contacted you lately?"

Oh fuck, I thought. Evidently, I wasn't going to get any calmer or rest pretty much for the rest of my life. I tore a cut into another dimension and there was no sewing it back up. Might as well face it.

"Wha.....What?? Why are you asking that?" I said.

"Well I'm just curious, have you been talking to anyone lately?

Anyone different, out of the ordinary. Not the usual people you interact with on a daily basis. Have they said anything to you? What was said? That sort of thing."

We both knew what he was hinting towards. Everything was clear almost instantaneously, a couple of well placed questions, sentences, considering the situation I was finding myself in, my father calling, and there was very little that needed to be further explained.

"That sort of thing?! I'm thinking you already know the answer." I answered dryly. But at the same time in utter disbelief.

"Marcus it was my idea for the organization, Jeff and Shauna to reach out to you and tell you about me being a member. I think you've been through enough suspense. That's why I'm calling so that you can hear this from me. I know your paranoia has been running wild and I'm sorry that I couldn't reach out to you sooner. Now is the right time, all things considered."

And there it was. We were officially living out an acid trip. My ultra conservative, little village boy Eastern European father and his son living in a fantasy. Well, I certainly crossed the point of no return. I sincerely doubted that I would ever be bored again. Hopefully not…

"Ahm" I started "I guess you just said everything pretty much. I'm speechless. Maybe we should talk some other time after I sleep on all of this for a couple of days. I'm not sure I even know where to begin. Or how to talk to you right now in all honesty…"

"You never saw this coming did you? Haha, I bet you don't think your old man is so boring anymore right?" he said.

I was in no mood for laughter. Or his self-adulation at this particular moment.

"You mean that my paranoid, don't trust anyone immigrant of a father has been a member of some secret organization for years? Yeah it's most certainly a bit of a stretch for me I won't lie. But I guess now I can explain certain things about you a bit better. You know all that weird behaviour of yours to which I used to joke around that we should ship you off to an insane asylum? Well now I know it was all because you were simply just part of a secret cult. What a relief for all of us!"

We both burst out laughing now. It took me by surprise. It was a genuine, hilarious, unbound, bottom of the soul laugh. Nothing held back. We both needed it. I was laughing pretty hard myself after I said what I said. I was shaking all over. I've been a nervous wreck for weeks and months now and it was nice to feel another emotion for once other than to just want to crawl up in a ball and cry or hide in the bathtub. This whole thing, now, felt like I uncovered some treasure, or won at a game show, or figured out a criminal case. I felt a sense of accomplishment yet I was neck deep in weird shit. Really, really weird shit. But I had to admit it to myself for the first time in however many months I did feel like I wasn't alone in all this. Like I had another soldier with me. And with all the shit and issues that I've had with my father over the years, and we've had our share I'm surprised we were still on talking terms, it was still nice that in this, out of all the possible situations in life, I had him on my side, on my team. He was in it too. And how bizarre. In all other situations this one would have been one of those that he would be lecturing me on and criticizing me to death if he knew what a mess I had gotten myself into. But instead, he already dove into this shit pile years ago before me. Again, all of this was beyond bizarre, but I couldn't help but feel reassured. I wasn't alone in this anymore. Him telling me this, finding this out about him, put a whole different dimension to my predicament. A most surely positive one. I felt my confidence start to come back and dare I say, shame on me to say it, I felt a mischievous vigor and almost arrogant swagger come over me. My father belonged to a 'thing', to a secret society, whatever you want to call it. And I was asked to join as well. This will change the relationship between him and me as well I hoped. But I was careful not to show too much enthusiasm just yet. I didn't want to come across like an overzealous little kid.

"Well, come on tell me about it. When, how, why? Why most importantly? Or where did you get the balls to do something like this? Does mom know? This is so completely and utterly out of character for you I hope you understand that. I would have been far less surprised had I found out you were actually a serial killer, hahaha." I said.

"Hahaha, well now see how your old man can still surprise you" he replied joyously. At least we broke the ice I thought and we could talk in a casual and relaxed manner, not like two frightened teenagers trying to find out a way how to hide our bloodshot eyes after a weed smoking session. And him, being almost seventy years old and all was still capable of coming across like a little boy that did something wrong. That is exactly how he sounded at the beginning of our conversation today. And I thought it great. For him to come down off of the 'grown-up' pedestal he is usually on.

"Well, I joined in 1990, just before I started the paperwork for Canada. Do you remember when you were a kid and I used to tell you stories about Erich von Däniken and his books about ancient aliens and his famous work 'Chariots of the Gods?'. The idea that Earth was visited by aliens thousands of years ago who taught early humans the arts and crafts, the modern technology, building techniques, engineering, etc.."

"Yes," I replied, "I was just thinking about that not too long ago. I was mesmerized by it, I remember I must have been like seven years old or so and some of his documentaries came on TV back in Slovenia, just after we talked about that stuff and the Universe and the rest, I was glued to the tube for hours. I remember you even let me stay up late and told mom to leave me be so I can watch after you guys went to bed. That was amazing and again, out of character for you. I felt then that I've uncovered this side of you that I never knew before. It was neat."

"Haha, so you do remember. Well I'm glad. What you and I talked about then was just the tip of the iceberg. On my own, I was doing extensive research that even your mother didn't know about. Computers and the Internet were still newish back in those days, but they helped greatly. And the way I roamed and probed I got picked up by the organization, same way you did. They reached out."

"They reached out where?" I said, "back in Slovenia?"

"Precisely" he went on, "remember that colleague of mine that I told you I knew in University but then we lost touch for decades since he moved to Canada back in the late 70s and then he miraculously showed up in Slovenia in 1990 and I ran into him in downtown Ljubljana?"

"Yes," I said.

"And then we got to talking about Canada and he said he would help me out with contacts, where to go, who to see, that I could stay with him for a while when I arrive." he continued.

"Yes, I remember that, he was a major contact and connection for you," I said.

"Well, it turned out he is part of the organization. It was the organization helping me out the whole time through him. They came with an incentive. They basically made my move to Canada possible. I had the technical skills wanted in the West, electrical engineer, over thirty years of working experience, etc...but I was 55 years old at the time. I was too old. I never would have gotten the go-ahead on the points system for the Landed Immigrant Visa and Permanent Residency because of my age. They made it happen. They even arranged for the first interviews, apartment, the works." he said.

"So they played on your incessant urge to leave Slovenia,

dangled the carrot of versatile assistance and you took the bait?" I asked.

"No, I wouldn't describe it in such a way. Well, maybe partially. But I also just felt like going for something more in life. I mean I figured since I mustered up the bravery to embark on that trip to Canada, leave my job, family, with everyone advising me against it, I suppose I just felt crazy enough and out on the limb and out of my comfort zone that I told myself fuck it, let's go for that too. Let's be a part of a society, a group of people who can finally have my back. I was in a daze of doing, moving and experimenting. I just dove in. I wanted to change most things in my life, and I wanted to try things I've wished for since my young adult years."

"You felt no fear, paranoia, remorse afterward?" I asked.

"Oh sure I did. Especially immediately after joining. Nights I would wake up not able to fall back asleep. Or not fall asleep in the first place. On top of trying to make it in a new country and society I had a new life of sorts that I committed to for the rest of my life and it was overwhelming. However, as I met with the organization, went to meetings, outings, became more involved, found out incredible information, became friends with individuals, etc...I started to calm down. I started to just live my life like anyone else. We were all normal people, like any other people, but we belonged to one another, had a duty to one another, like a military unit I suppose. None of it I felt was overwhelming or negatively impacted my life. It all made me feel enriched. Everything about the organization is like with any family really, laughs, fights, conversations, tasks, obligations. But none of it is in any way a freakish experience like those documentaries portraying other cults. Thirty years on I can still say that I in no way regret joining. I feel that I'm part of a group of people that think and reason like me. We are all forced to be part of a society every day, fulfill obligations to it, whether it's a work environment, socializing, just general living. This way at least

I feel like I'm giving my time and commitment to people I identify with. They are not just anyone. And if you look at history, not one great person existed that didn't belong to a secret society of some kind. Seeing as how disassociated I felt from the Slovenian society at that time, and what time of my life that was, it was a perfect time for me to join a world like that. Risky of course, but worth the risk."

"Ok, and how did mom take this new club membership of yours? I mean she is half scared to death of waking up in the morning, so how on Earth did you sell her this?"

As I asked this I was almost 99% sure that I already knew the answer.

"Well, she didn't know. And she still doesn't. Your brother doesn't know either. Right now it's just you who knows." he said.

Yup, I figured as much.

"Well, that doesn't surprise me. Not one bit" I said, "you've hid a million other things from her and us, obviously something like this you were not going to share."

"You know your mother Marcus, the fear would devastate her. With her high blood pressure and all for decades now and her over-reacting to everything and always having to take anxiety reducing pills for even the smallest of issues that might pop up, I simply could not bear to tell her, to worry her." Yup, he did it all with her best interests in mind. "You also could have, you know, NOT joined. Said to them that you have too much to risk, that you are in over your head trying to create a better life for us and all. Ever thought of that?" I had to put him in his place.

"You mean the way you are currently rationalizing at the moment? The way you are finding excuses why not to rock the boat and continue living in your mundane, soon to be new daddy exis-tence and not join our 'club' as you call it?" he replied back.

He had a point. Ironic, up until today I would have figured he of all the people would have congratulated me and been proud of me for rationalizing in just such a way, based on chances of risk. And for being careful. But of course everything in my life was the opposite of what I think would happen. He turned out to be a bigger risk taker than I ever would have or could have imagined. If anything, he was mocking my cautiousness?!

"Yes, had it not been for the bizarre twist of what you've told me today I'm fairly certain you would have been proud of me for thinking this way." I said.

"I am proud of you Marcus, and please don't misunderstand me. I'm not trying to poke fun at you in any condescending way."

"I know. Look I'm not trying to be a smartass" I continued, "I just never could have imagined something like this. Out of all people you. When they mentioned people I knew are members you probably would have been the last person I would think of. Although now as we are talking and you are telling me these things and knowing how mysterious and enigmatic and unorthodox you could be at times, I'm not so sure. I suppose it kind of makes sense. Maybe you are the most obvious candidate for something like this. I still don't get it though, you?! Really? But we lived so modestly, we certainly didn't see any perks whatsoever of you being a member of some secret well to do organization. Did you hog it all for yourself? Were you going to secret meetings, vacations, gateways and purposely not letting anything spill over our way?" I was noticing myself starting to get angry now as I was almost positive that this is precisely what he did. It would be something he would do.

"Not per se", he said trying to prove me wrong, "the organization has strict rules of behavior for its members. They never gave me a 'salary' so to speak. We did go on retreats, we held meetings there, there were those perks I'll be honest. And whether you believe me or not I asked if there was any way I could bring my family with me. Under the auspices of something else. They said no since they knew my wife was not a member and knew nothing about my involvement. There was simply no proper way to explain it. The risk to them would have been too great. The explanation, the ploy would have been too risky. They don't do ploys. They help their members out in times of need, this help can be financial as well. Or with their influence. But they do not encourage some lavish lifestyle of excess for all to notice."

I didn't believe him for a second. About wanting to bring mom and us along. And as far as the organization was not willing to take risks and engage in ploys I didn't buy that bullshit either. From my personal experience I knew this to be an untrue statement.

"Whatever" I went on "if you say so. It is what it is now anyways I suppose. So where do we go from now? Are you calling just to tell me about your involvement? Or are you calling to tell me your involvement in order to persuade me to join? Probably both I guess..."

"Both I suppose. Marcus all I can tell you from all of my experience with these people is that I only wished they came into my life earlier, that I would have been a part for longer. I am a very paranoid person, you, of course, know that well, I scrutinize the blazes out of everything. Mom knows that very well too. I'm not going to pretend to deny it. But these people they passed through my filter sieve. It was very hard for me to let go of my strings of control over my own life but I somehow managed. It was one of the best decisions of my life. They've made my life better for sure. So I'm asking you to trust me. And to be smart, and join earlier. People can get used to almost anything in life Marcus, it's quite remarkable. Especially mediocrity. I'm asking you not to make that mistake."

"So what you are saying is that I should join immediately and let me guess, just not worry about telling Alicia about it, right?"

"Why does she need to know Marcus? Doesn't she have enough

on her plate with your child coming and all the other responsibilities that come with that?"

"Right, well I don't know maybe I should try to include her
you know. I am aware that was not your practice with mom, Stan
and me, you didn't include your family in shit, but I'm trying to
run a slightly different course. This is a major, colossal life decision,
one that if she found out I did behind her back she would surely
divorce me over. Take the kid and never look back. And there is
another thing. You keep saying that joining this organization made
your life better, more enlightened, whatever. How exactly? You were
a pain in the ass to live with, you OCD'd on absolutely everything,
your paranoia was worse than ever and your anger was out of control. You were constantly yelling at us, took you days to calm down,
usually as Friday approached. You most certainly didn't come across
as enlightened or laid back or like you've changed for the better.
Now looking back at it I am almost certain part of the reason you
behaved this way was because you were part of this group. It was
an extra item on your plate and the stress of maintaining your
responsibilities towards them while all the while making sure we at
home never found out must have contributed greatly to you stress,
paranoia, anxiety and anger."

I tried to get all of that out there in one breath before he could
interrupt me. I succeeded. As I said what I said I noticed getting
progressively angrier at him. Typical I thought. It would have been
absolutely and totally like him to pull something like this. But at
the same time, I felt stereotypical childish pride in me that he chose
to tell me this, not mom, not Stan, only me. And no one else. And
he was trying to get me to become a part of a secret organization.
The whole thing had a James Bond flavor to it and I would be
lying if I said that I wasn't enticed. I got a kick out of knowing that
only dad and I were in on this. All the basic and trivial, ridiculous
human emotions were coming to the surface.

"Marcus you are right." he began after a few moments. I could tell he needed a second or two to pull himself together in order to come up with a diplomatic and measured response. And one that made it seem as if he wasn't pissed off at what I just said, even though I bet he was and was having visual images of beating me into a bloody pulp. "I was not an easy man to live with. I'm still not easy. And I never made myself out to be Dalai Lama. And I never meant to imply that joining the organization made me more relaxed or serene or calmed my brain down such that I embraced a hippie lifestyle or whatnot. If anything the things I've learned and knowledge that came with them engaged my brain even more. No, I am what I am Marcus and I'll die that way. The organization does not bring tranquillity and peace of mind. That stuff is still left for yoga, meditation and reading about Zen Buddhism. The organization brings knowledge and opens horizons that are completely and utterly closed off to the average man or woman on Earth. And that knowledge can feel heavy at times. And the inability to share it with people around you. The organization holds incredible pull and influence and they have your back if you are one of them. They can open up all sorts of doors for you. They did for me. I for one craved that more than anything and I would have been incapable to function for the rest of my life knowing that I missed out on an opportunity to have a glimpse into another dimension. But as I said knowledge can be a hard, heavy thing to carry with you especially when you know you can't share with anyone. And that realization adds to the anxiety and the feelings of isolation, combined with occurring moments of asking yourself 'what the hell have I done? Why have I signed up for this?? And for life too?!'. I get all of that son and this isn't for everyone. But you think about it, hard and long, and make a decision. Me, I wanted to know and to have a team behind me, whether that brought serenity or more anxiety with it."

"You mean make the right decision for me? Alicia never expressed the need and wish to go uncovering mysterious graves and looking behind the curtain. And if discovering new truths, heavy truths that I can't share with anyone, will make me more miserable and wide-eyed, than why do it?"

"You'll share them with me. And if that is the case then why does Alicia need to be taken into consideration? At least for now. I don't mean that in a cold, heartless way" even though that is exactly how it came across "I simply mean you should look at this as your own thing. Think in the now and in the near future but also think one day for your children's future. Your daughter's. And any other future children you may have. And with that in mind bring Alicia in at another time perhaps. And your children. You crave the knowledge for now. They might crave it one day. This organization is so far ahead of everything you see around you Marcus, I can only imagine where they will be 10, 20, 30 years from now. So, forget yourself even, and your curiosity that's been with you all your life, think about your kids. Lay the foundation for them now to become members one day. They will be ahead of the game. Again, ask yourself how many times we've wondered how nice it must be if someone supports you in this life. How many times did we wonder where do the people who think like us and who know more than the norm reside and if they even exist? Someone other than family, with power, with money, with knowledge, with influence to have your back. Well, now you have that opportunity. And your kids will through you."

"I'm not sure if I'm buying all of this old man, as I said before mom and Stan and I didn't get any perks because of your membership. What did we get? Did I find it easier to get accepted into University? Pass my exams? Was it easier for me to find a job? Did people in any of my previous jobs treat me better because of my father's involvement with some secret organization? Not even close, if anything I used to think my life was unnecessarily hard and I didn't quite understand why. As if I was getting punished extra unlike the rest of the population. Like I had a mark of Cain on me and every single thing no matter how trivial it was I had to put in three times the effort of an average person to make it happen." Saying all of that made me feel like a pathetic loser. Dammit I thought, what a fucking grind my existence had been.

"Also" I continued, "you remember when I told you years ago that a guy I worked with at my previous company in Toronto was a Truemason? And I could have joined through him. I decided against it. If I didn't feel comfortable with a well established, historical order and organization such as the Truemasons, mostly because of this whole 'membership for life thing', then why would I feel more comfortable joining an organization that nobody knows anything about? It's fascinatingly mysterious and I don't even know the actual name of it?! I don't know...." I finished.

"Your first observation about you and mom and Stan not having extra perks and you having to put in extra effort into everything simply to get what's rightfully yours in life are very interesting things for you to note. Think about that. That's all I can say on the matter for now. As far as the Truemasons are concerned, our organization is in a whole different league. From everything I know Truemasons are a brotherhood of men that socialize and keep each other company with mostly casual matters. They are there for each other, sure, membership is for life, but they do not endeavor into the research and do not have access to information and knowledge that we do. Not even close. No organization out there does."

"What were you trying to say there about my observations?" I tried. But got nowhere fast.

"Marcus I can't divulge anything further. All I will say is that your sacrifices and trials marked with, seemingly, unnecessary tribulations and jumps through hoops were not in vain and were not coincidental. And they were certainly not part of some curse."

"What do you mean? Are you trying to say they were all part of some test? Because of your secret association or something? Common, enough with this surreal nonsense." I kept pushing.

"I can't I'm sorry. I have to go Marcus. I'll be in Canada in a month to visit you and Stan for two weeks. Same as every year. If by then you decide to join we'll have a helluva lot more to talk about. If not, we'll talk about the same old." he said.

"Are you serious?" I was getting furious, "you drop something like this on me out of the blue from across the Atlantic, via phone (?!), during the one time you actually call me, now I have a million questions and you have to go?! Where do you have to go? You are retired for fucks sakes! What's so urgent?? News? Haven't you heard like ten news coverages today?" I was pissed beyond belief.

"Don't swear" he said, "I'm still your father. Let's not talk like we're at the same age level and from the same class in high school. Please and thank you."

He even managed to act as an offended but condescending father figure in all of this.

"Oh whatever" I came back with. "You are going to dwell on that now?! That's your last two cents??"

"I told you enough Marcus. Jeff and Shauna told you enough. Showed you what can be done, how you can improve your life. And those are just the superficial tips of the iceberg. They provided a monetary incentive to you and Alicia. It just goes to show you how the group has grown and become more capable to do more for the people it deems are worthy to become members. Your life will be richer spiritually and materially Marcus, I don't know what else to say. Take a leap of faith will ya?" The last little bit sounded almost like he was pleading with me.

"Great that makes me feel 'better'" I was littering that sentence with sarcasm. "A weird organization has become ever more powerful over time and is now able to outright coerce and bribe people into joining. Wonderful! Sure puts me at ease. And you, you still haven't answered, where do you have to go? If you or Jeff or Shauna or whoever wants me on board so badly you all sure have a tendency of disappearing the moment I have more questions to ask. That doesn't exactly instill calm and peace of mind in me you know. Have you thought about that?"

"Marcus all of your life you have needed endless reassurances. Over everything. Since you were a little boy you would ask essentially the same questions in a million different ways over whatever worry or issue you've had. No matter how many times I've tried reassuring you you would just go away and come back again later once the reserves of reassurance faded. This situation is just another example. No amount of convincing, no amount of incentive will be enough, you will want more. That is one of the reasons why you won't get more. Not from the organization and not from me. You have to be capable of showing the ability to let go. Making a decision based on all of the knowledge you have. Weigh it out and do it. Or don't do it. But either way, you must conclude it. Just don't go regretting whatever decision you made afterward, which is what you do religiously."

He had me there. I didn't know what else to add. It was a Check. Most likely a Check Mate. I had nothing to come back with. I hated this moment. He was right. He was the same by the way, capable of obsessing endlessly over whatever insane and pertinent issue or thought circled his head at a given moment, but that didn't matter now. I was on the stage, not him. Calling out his hypocrisy right now wouldn't do me any good. It would just dodge and waste time. Time I wanted wasted because I was scared and I stalled and wanted to prolong this conversation as long as I could. Scared of the decision I had to make. This sucked. Big time.

"Marcus, I will see you in a few weeks. No matter what you decide we'll spend a great time together. I can't wait to see you and pregnant Alicia ."

I wasn't ready to let go of the conversation. I felt like I wasn't ready to let go of the hand. I felt like a child. It always amazed me how many times throughout life a grown man still finds himself in a position of a scared little child. And it scared and frightened me that these moments would surely periodically come back until the end, until the last breath. They never really completely end and go away. The intervals between them were much longer than when I was a kid, but nevertheless when they came, the fear rattled the bones and I shivered with dread finding it hard to swallow, just like when I was five years old.

"Ahm, ok" I said. I didn't know what else to say. "Alright, I'll see you soon. And we'll talk on weekends via Facetime until then. On Sunday."

"Of course Marcus. Everything will be ok. If you find yourself looping in thought too much just call me, text me, whatever, ok? Anytime, any day or night. You have a lot going on at the moment. Life is hitting you like a ton of bricks. And when it rains it pours, am I right? Plus, you stumbled upon something that adds even more unique spice, haha."

"Yeah you're not kidding" I added "I'm definitely no fan of how life has to be either feast or famine always. Either famine for years or feast for a short time but intense never the less. I'd like a happy medium."

"That's why feasts are so nerve racking. They are short but over-whelmingly intense. However if the right decisions are made during feasts, feasts can then last for years too my boy. Decades. Alright so we'll talk soon, ok? And I'll see you soon too." he concluded.

"O...ok. Yeah alright talk soon. Say hi to mom." We hung up. I felt like I just got out of my two-hour Muay Thai sparring class and

I was severely beaten up and bruised. And it was a Saturday and I was feeling good about myself up until the phone call. And obviously my world got turned upside down again. How much more of this rollercoaster ride would I be able to take? Luckily Alicia was at work till 3 PM, so she didn't have to witness this. Dad called out of the blue too, how the hell did he not think that she might have been home?! And had she been now I would have to make up a story as to why he called out of the blue, as she would have been surprised by that even more than me. And it would have been extremely hard for me to come up with anything as I was pale, shivering and feeling like shit. Usually he at least announces himself via text message, no matter how pressing the news. This time a random phone call. First time ever. Strange, even for this news. And, I just realized, he never really explained why he 'had to go'. Whatever I guess, even if the world was ending he still had to keep true to his protocols and routines. It didn't matter I suppose, probably had to rush to whatever news coverage was available. Matters of the Universe, aliens, death and secret societies be damned. The oxen have to graze at pasture, come hell or high water.

I also realized that I could have asked why Stan wasn't considered for the secret organization. I'll do it next time I talk to dad I suppose. It was 10:30 AM. I decided I will go to my Muay Thai training and try to snap out of this cocooned state of mind. I mean shit what else was I going to do? Sit here and freak out or start drinking. And starting drinking at this hour was early even for me.

I was punching the bags as best as I could. Putting all my effort into it. I tried listening to the trainer's instructions diligently too. I focused hard not to show how truly distracted I was. I succeeded for the most part. The sparring went well too. Good sessions, good sparring partners. Nothing like physical torture to stabilize the impending internal, emotional collapse. I defended a ton of kicks with my legs, more than ever before. My shins felt like they've been tenderized with baseball bats afterward but regardless I was advancing in my technique. During breaks I overheard some people talking politics. Trump, Trudeau, Syria, Russia, Venezuela, Ukraine, Iran. All comments from all sides were typical, cliché tripe fed to them by mainstream media, all the while the individuals saying it tried to sound enlightened and full of themselves for having such radical and informed opinions. They were not radical nor informed nor should they have felt proud about themselves. They were regurgitating propaganda adopted as their own thought. Except they didn't know they adopted it. And that it wasn't really their own thoughts. And that was the most dangerous, fascinating part about it. You take on behavior and thought processes without ever knowing it was implanted into you. And you go forward thinking it's yours. It's been painfully too long since I've heard an original or impressive thought and I couldn't take it anymore.

Listening to them definitely sparked that fire in me again. Fire that burned to get out of the confines of the mainstream thought, way of life, norms and customs. Fire that couldn't wait to explode like a pressurized canister as it was sick and tired of being trapped, confined, chained and imprisoned. For a moment there I felt like calling Jeff or Shauna or my dad and telling them to fuck this I'm on board! Take me whenever I'll probably regret it but at least it'll be something vastly different. And that was it really, I was starting to realize that what I wanted the most, whether it turned out to be for the best or for the most horribly worse, I simply wanted change. True change, not the hypocritical bullshit kind served in the world of politics. And if there was even the slightest chance of this endeavour greatly improving the life of my family, my wife, my future children, aren't I the biggest fool if I miss out on this? But then again if it all blows up in my face, the shrapnel will fly to all around and close to me...

I came home from the training invigorated. I was beaten up but

I felt as though I found renewed inner strength. Mental strength. That's what I needed the most. And by having a good training session, although albeit a tad distracted one, I managed to strengthen my psyche as well. At that moment I felt like I was ready to grab life by the balls and do something different. To step out on a limb, out of the mould and out of the norm. But I was still going to think about it all some more, not rush, and then make a decision. I couldn't dwell on it forever though, I was risking being sucked into the downward obsession thought vortex. Like a dog chasing its tail.

The weekend went by well. Alicia was none the wiser of the insane turmoil that I've been going through, even just in the past few hours. I sounded confident, focused, brave, grown-up, the works. She complimented me several times how she's seen true growth in me, how I've matured, how she couldn't wait for me to be a father to our little girl.

In the following week I started noticing myself get even more annoyed at the day to day triviality of routine than usual. I was now overhearing political and other discussions at work of varying themes and subjects. I could feel myself cringe at every word, every laugh, every cliché question and answer. I was becoming more arrogant after that conversation with my father. The effect on me was profound and with him on the same side I simply couldn't get the fear nor humility back. With all of our differences over the years, he was still such an unmistakable rock in my life. I wish it wasn't true, but it still was. It was as if he was that anchor I needed to man up. But was I manning up?! Or was I just being an overconfident idiot who stood on glass legs? Up until yesterday I was beside myself over the hornets' nest I've disturbed and now all of a sudden I've discovered bravery and changed my opinion completely because of him?! Was I that weak and easily persuaded?? Where was my reasoning and sound judgment of just a few days ago or even during the moments when I was talking to him personally over the phone?!

I did my best to try bringing myself back to my previous frame of thought but it was a futile effort. Day by day I was slowly and surely inching towards the now new decision. I was more than likely going to join the party with Jeff, Shauna, my father and whoever else. I was almost 35 I thought, been an ant for too long but not long enough not to still have plenty of time left, if health served me well, to take a different turn in life and enjoy the rest of it. Also, to sound like a complete dick, Alicia was turning crankier by the day, I knew it was the pregnancy doing its toll but the asshole in me chose to look at it differently. I chose to look at it as a reason to do something on my own and not tell her about it. I was starting to get more and more comfortable by the day with the idea of not involving her at all with my decision of potentially joining the organization. Not telling her anything and obviously not trying to get her to join with me. If this goes through it was going to be my thing, and my thing alone. Dad and I. My family's thing. I will continue to be a doting husband and father (as much as I was ever or could be 'doting'), without a doubt, none of that will change. But I simply don't need to disclose everything to her, and this will be one of those things. I'll pretend I'm a secret agent and simply can't disclose most of my work with my spouse. And so what? No harm, no foul. I was contemplating and about to behave like a huge piece of shit, and surely this was going to bite me in the ass down the line but I was almost certain that the inevitability of what I was about to do was fast approaching.

Another week or two, more of the same old shit and I was itching. I couldn't pay attention to anything else other than my dire yearning to be different than everyone else. To belong to something else. The desire was so intense I literally felt like my sanity will be jeopardized unless I at least attempted something different. Even if it resulted in absolute failure and disaster. I was insatiable in my selfishness and ego tripping and inability to subside either of them. I couldn't put anything else before my wish to step outside of the norm. I realized that the impending birth of my daughter was not enough for me to exercise caution. I knew I was going to be swamped beyond belief caring for her and helping out Alicia but it didn't matter. This other thing was happening in parallel and I couldn't postpone it. Well in all truth maybe I could have. But I didn't want to. And postpone it for when?! Five years from now, ten? I was thirty-five now, why get older and older and still live the exact same existence? No, I couldn't, I wouldn't. I was joining. I was going all in I didn't care how overloaded my plate would inevitably be. I decided to wait exactly one more week and if nothing changed my impetus, I was going to call Jeff.

CHAPTER 15

PEAKING

A week passed and my desire got stronger, not weaker. I had to act. I gathered up some bravery like a squirrel gathers nuts and with a new found spring in my mood I decided to leap...into the unknown 'potential'. For the first time since I waltzed into his office all those months ago I was to reach out to Mr. Madison again. This time via phone. I was nervous as hell, sweaty palms and all, bathroom breaks aplenty. The night prior I barely slept. It was an arduous and disgusting thing readying for something like this while all the while Alicia didn't know anything. Nothing about the life-altering moves I was about to make. Several times throughout the night I looked at her wide awake as she was sleeping and holding on to her belly with our daughter in it and I thought to myself 'My God if she only knew what I was about to do'.

I had to snap out of whatever doubt I was having as the phone was ringing on the other side. To be honest, I prayed that he wouldn't pick up, the more rings without him answering the more I prayed. I figured it will give me more time to think things over. If the answering machine came on I would not leave a message. He would obviously have caller ID but I didn't care, if he called me back I would stall him some more. As the phone kept ringing I couldn't help but be relieved that it appeared he wouldn't pick up. And just as I was about to end the call, he picked up. I froze.

"Hello, Dr. Madison speaking." Jeff proclaimed in a clear and crisp voice, one that a man who is living and breathing fear, such as myself, does not contain.

I was silent for a couple of moments. I would be lying if I didn't admit that I actually contemplated hanging up the phone. But then I realized how insanely ridiculous that would be. I had to man up and go through with this. At least the bloody introduction.

"Hello Jeff. Ahm, Dr. Madison. It is me, Marcus. How are you?" It was almost as if I recorded myself saying this and were playing it via recorder as although I heard the words I didn't actually feel my mouth moving to utter them. It felt like an out of body experience. I felt as though I was in surgery right in the middle of the operating table and I died briefly and was now standing above my body observing myself as my own soul. The body was now being talked to by Jeff Madison.

"Marcus, well hello! I'm very well young man and how are you?" quipped Jeff.

"I'm a bit nervous." I blurted out losing whatever grown-up credibility I may have had. I'm surprised I didn't just flat out say 'I'm scared and I'm afraid I just soiled my bottoms Dr. Madison.'

"Marcus relax. There is absolutely nothing to be nervous about. What can possibly be making you so uneasy? You are talking to a friend here, we help each other out. No nervousness warranted whatsoever."

"Well," I began. Or continued, or whatever the fuck I was doing (God I wished I woke up from this dream) "I think I'm calling because I believe I have made some decisions and I'm ready to commit to them." My soul 'me' was now watching with the mouth wide agape as my body 'me' was blurting these things out. I wished my soul could return to the body so I could stop it from acting completely insane but no matter what the soul 'me' tried it was not having any success. I screamed at the 'body' to shut the hell up but it wasn't responding. The pause was too long, it was now Jeff replying, too late to go back.

"Well my dear boy if this means what I think it means than I for one am very happy indeed! I do not wish to be presumptuous however, please continue."

"I want to join." The 'body' me was blurting out as the 'soul me' was crying in fear and running for cover.

"Marcus are you sure?" said Jeff. He had no enthusiasm in that question, it was pure and serious matter of fact deadpan delivery.

"Yes" I fired.

"Did you tell your wife?" said Jeff.

I paused for a while again. And then continued. The whole thing felt a bit like strolling anxiously towards the electric chair. I'll never forget the feeling nor the vibe for as long as I live.

"No. And I haven't even contemplated talking to her about it either. I simply cannot. She has enough on her plate, our child on the way. Talking to her about it would have stressed her out irreparably, and I in no good conscience could go through with it. Like this, without her knowing at least for the time being, I choose, if possible, to join just by myself and to leave her completely out of it." I sounded a lot calmer and collected saying all that. The 'soul me' at least wasn't standing there with the mouth wide open anymore. As I said all that I realized that what I had just uttered could jeopardize my attempting to join. Maybe that's why I was calmer.

In discussing possibly joining the Truemasons years ago with a guy I worked with and who was a member he told me that all joining future members needed a witness while joining. Even though Truemasons were a fraternity and no women were allowed to join he told me his wife bore witness to him joining. Members from the Truemasons showed up at their house and laid out rules and commitments that he would be obliged to once he came on-board. And they ensured the wife was ok and aware of all of that before him joining, even though she herself could never become a member. I could not count on my wife to bear witness as I didn't want her knowing at all. I took the initiative and asked.

"Am I able to join without anyone in my immediate family witnessing?" I asked, "As I said I cannot let my wife know about this."

"Marcus, you are forgetting your father is a member. Therefore you don't need a 'witness' per se, we can initiate you just by yourself without anyone present." he said.

It made sense I suppose. At the same time my anxiety jumped instantaneously as I realized that there was no backing out of this anymore. It was going through and I was about to join. Or if not this very second then very shortly. Shit was getting real and fast.

"Marcus let's ordain you with the membership as soon as possible and as quickly as possible. We've spent enough time in suspended animation. Shauna and I will do the honors. It requires two initiated members to welcome in a new person. We only need you and a bit of your time. Let's do it at my house. When are you available?"

"Let's do it Saturday anytime around noon," I said. "Alicia will be at work, it is the best time."

"Ok how about this Saturday then?"

"This Saturday is fine, let's just get it over with." I sounded like I was about to get circumcised due to an infection of my foreskin or was going in for a TURP operation of my prostate. Inevitably he must have sensed the reluctance, dread as well as the cold feet I was experiencing. But oddly he was paying it no mind.

"Splendid Marcus, this Saturday it is. At my place. We'll have lunch and some drinks too! What is your poison? Food and drink wise?"

I could not think of my ideal choice of food or drink to have right now even if my life depended on it. I never knew how inmates could pick their favorite meals just before they got executed. The last thing I could think of was eating. So I turned it around a different way.

"As I said Alicia will be at work till about 3 PM. I have to be back home by then. I'll eat dinner with her, and it's a bit early for any drinks before that, I hope you understand. But thanks for the offer and generosity."

"Ok Marcus, I understand. We will then have a quick toast and organize something a bit more formal at another time. We'll get more people out for it. Unfortunately, as your wife cannot join us at this time, and is not aware that you are about to become a member, you will have to come up with reasons as to where you are going when you will go meet with 'us'." he said.

I figured whatever. If my father could have hidden it all this time from everyone I'm sure I'll manage.

"It's ok, I'll work around that", I wanted the conversation to be over with already. I wanted days to pass and Saturday to come and for this thing to come and go as fast as possible.

"Marcus please be at my house at 9 AM this coming Saturday." said Jeff.

"Do I need to bring anything? Is there anything specific I should be preparing for?" I asked.

"No, not at all. This will feel like a casual matter. Trust me. Just bring yourself.

This is only a formality after all."

Signing my life and soul away was only a formality.

"Alright, I will see you there." I said. He gave me the address and we said our byes.

The next few days the only thing carrying me through was the sole knowledge that my father had already been through this. That he already joined. Otherwise, I was painfully aware that had I not found out he was part of the 'organization' I never would have had the balls to take this leap. Never, not in a million years. No amount of convincing would have made me do it. I would have refused it over and over again. And had I done it in some drunken or drug-induced stupor I wouldn't have been able to live with myself, function, sleep, work, go about my daily life upon sobering up.

Even still it wasn't easy functioning the next few days in anticipation of what was to come. To be 'me' in front of everyone that knew me and not seem distracted, stressed out. All the while looking pale and see-through. I was looking at myself in the mirror unusually often in the bathrooms these days just to make sure that I didn't lose all the color in my face due to stress. No matter how smooth and easy this initiation would be, how quick, how non-chalant, trivial, casual, whatever, this was a big deal. A huge deal! And I could not forget that, no matter what. I was about to change my life forever and before I could even begin to contemplate the amazing new doors of knowledge and insight this decision might bring, I still needed to let sink the awareness that this was a tectonic change in my life. My family's life! Oh God that was the biggest dagger, I wasn't just changing my life, others will be impacted too. And I could only pray that my family would never suffer any con-sequences because of it. If it all goes to shit for some reason, I hope the 'organization' takes it all out on me. I found a loophole with this thought now to make myself feel better if you could believe it. Perversely I thought of myself as a knight in shining armour, protector of my family. I wouldn't let them join or know about me joining because I was protecting them!! Aha! There, I was being super responsible. And magnanimous really, offering to sacrifice myself if shit hit the propellers.

Back and forth and back and forth of mood and fear swings, rationalizations and internal battles, and Saturday came and went. And in all honesty, it felt very much like the scene from *The Sopranos* when Christopher Moltisanti joined Tony's New Jersey crew. It was in Jeff's basement, the swearing-in, blood from my index finger, candle vax, and all. Seriously. The only thing missing from the scene was the raven on the basement window sill. Everything else was virtually identical. Oh and there were only two other people. Jeff and Shauna, initiating my ass. Another difference I just became aware of, there were no women there to initiate Christopher, it was a bunch of dudes. I suppose one would think that Shauna being there would add a sort of a sensitive, feminine touch, something a mother might, maybe put me at ease or something, but none of that was the case. Her and Jeff standing there in their ultra-serious, stoic veneers reciting their spiels to me and asking me to repeat after them added no ease nor relief. It was all I could do not to break out crying, ask for my mommy and daddy, or run to the bathroom.

It was over. I joined. After the 'ceremony' next to Jeff's washer and dryer in the basement, Shauna and Jeff turned back into humans in a blink of an eye. With smiles, emotions and color back in their faces. They were doing their darnedest to make me feel how I've made the right decision, how this was one of the greatest things I could have done and how I should feel like one of the happiest and proudest people on Earth right about now. But I was barely listening. We were sitting around Jeff's dinner table in his big dining room by now, like old friends, brothers and sisters, like we've known each other for decades. Shauna was now doing her best to add that feminine touch and ease me into the atmosphere, to make me loosen up. She even grabbed my forearm a couple of times, as did Jeff and told me to 'relax', 'loosen up', 'it will be great', they would say. Jokes were flying about, plans, I was barely paying attention. The whole thing seemed fake and disingenuous. I kept thinking back to my father's guarantees, but it helped little with the feeling I had. I also could not forget Jeff and Shauna's robotic, cold faces and demeanor as they were initiating me. It was chilling, their expressions will forever stay with me, no matter what jolly good times we will have together. Something very serious went on here today, and I could never let myself forget it. And God only knew what would come of it.

Finally, the shenanigans of shooting the breeze like nothing significant had happened was over and I was allowed to leave. Jeff at least had the sense to say the following just before me leaving:

"Marcus let's give it a couple of weeks before we even speak again. Let you breathe, sink everything in. Your life will not change in any way but all the ways you wanted it to. You will get the improvements you've always desired. Trust me. Now go home, be with your family and get us out of your mind for a while. You reach out when you are ready. Ok?" he said. I nodded and left. I liked the sound of that. Maybe something will prevent me from contacting them again. Like sweet death for example.

When I came home I shat twice and puked once. It was 1:35 PM. I had exactly forty-five minutes to pull myself together before Alicia would come home. I was emotionally drained. I missed my Muay Thai training today to get myself initiated into God knows what. Still, I felt physically as though I dug ditches for days. I actually felt beaten up like I did after my sparring routines. Maybe Shauna and Jeff beat the shit out of me, raped me while they drugged me.....I didn't know what the hell happened today. Did I hallucinate the whole thing?! Maybe the last few months had just been one giant magic mushroom trip.

Several messages were on my phone from Alicia. As Murphy's

Law would have it she was extra needy today, since life knew I couldn't reply as I was otherwise engaged. She went on about going baby shopping, furniture, stroller, clothes, the works. Then she went on about how her work keeps pressing her to work longer and not start maternity leave as early as we wanted her to. Then about EI benefits and how and when to start that, then about me putting the soup on the stove and warming it up for her when she comes home as she was exhausted and starving. And then, of course, asking me why the hell I wasn't answering?! I replied full of shit, as was my MO these past months, about how the training went extra long, how the gym brought in a guest kickboxing trainer and how I stayed longer because of it. Then I said that I went to the local gun store just outside of Kingston to inquire about the handgun I bought. I wanted to know how to disassemble it, clean it and re-assemble it and I found no useful YouTube videos. Then I apologized. I quickly snapped out of my lunacy and managed to scrounge up some food for us prior to her coming home. She never replied to my flurry of explanatory messages so I was dreading to see what kind of mood she would be in when she came home.

I was in luck, she was normal. Which was the best I could hope for in the given circumstances. I tried my best to be normal as well, which really meant I desperately attempted not to seem completely lobotomized from the experience I just went through earlier today. And somehow I succeeded. We ate, I was surprisingly hungry and had a healthy appetite considering how stressed out I was. Then we went for a walk. The day was nice, sunny, clocks got moved forward and the winter was slowly starting to release its death grip over us. Which really meant nothing as it was more than likely going to rain now until June. I started to loosen up and relax. Afterwards, we had dinner downtown, I even bought some cigars. I was most certainly drinking and smoking tonight. Later on, we settled in and started watching Oliver Stone's *The Untold History of the United States*. It was by far the greatest and most accurate account of world events since WW2. Eye-opening and fitting with all the bullshit that was starting to surface these days.

We were both tired from the day. I from my extracurricular activities that very well have been most likely worse than outright adultery, and Alicia from being ever more pregnant and exhausted from work which never seemed to end. I pulled it off I thought. I was a world-class liar and manipulator. That night, although I was beyond exhausted, I couldn't sleep due to anxiety at the thought of what exactly would Alicia do at this very moment if she knew what I had done today. What if I were to whisper it into her ear right now? Every time I would feel myself starting to nod off that thought would pop up in my head and I would immediately jolt myself out of my sleep. It was like a never-ending punishment and torture game which I imposed upon myself because of what I've done. Soon the anxiety of what I had done had morphed into the anxiety of how my usual morning alarm time was approaching and how I am going to have to get up soon without having slept at all! And that thought alone was causing stress and me not sleeping. Once I started hearing the birds chirping and seeing the outside light of dawn starting to creep up I knew it was all over, the night had been lost.

The next day I spent at work functioning like a catatonic mental patient. I stumbled around the office, running into things, unusually spatially and interactively uncoordinated. Luckily I had a full glass of lemonade in the morning so at least I wasn't getting sick due to the stress-induced immune system activity drop. I always got sick when overly stressed out. That and when I was brutally hungover. The immune system goes down, I feel a tickle in my throat and next thing I know the fever sets in. So I was trying to fight this as best as I knew how. Everything happening to me right now was my fault, and if I ended up getting sick because of my reduced immunity due to anxiety that I've dragged into my life, and if I got Alicia sick who was now over six months pregnant, shit will surely hit the fan, that is for sure.

That night I forced myself to go to the gym, even though I was dead tired from not having slept the night before and ironically risking getting sick from being in contact with everyone there while my immunity was in the toilet. Early spring viruses were running amok. But I also knew if I could tire myself out sufficiently enough I would sleep tonight. And the gamble paid off. I didn't get sick but I passed out at 9PM, I barely lasted until then.

Over the next few days I slowly pulled myself out of my mental gutter. I got my sleeping under control, I exercised, ate properly and explained to myself that I had to be a man and stick by my decisions. There was no going back. I thought of all the great men of our day, past and present, and the hard decisions they had to make. The things they had to keep hidden from their women, families, to keep them...'safe'. This thing of mine paled in comparison. It was trivial. Also, Jeff and Shauna were indeed keeping their distance from me during this time as they had promised. So I truly had all the time in the world to come to terms with my decision and the implications thereof. I slowly started to convince myself that I did the right thing, that what I did was for the greater good. It would all work out in the end. Better life, opportunities, internal wholeness, etc...Plus my dad was in it too.

Within a week I turned my mood around completely. I started looking forward to my father coming. No matter what, he would make me feel better, and he was due to arrive in two weeks. At first we would all meet at my brother's chalet in Vermont, go skiing, socialize, him and I would not be able to talk about anything then as Stan was non the wiser about our secret. But when my father comes to visit Alicia and me, the two of us would go out for some drinks and we would talk about everything and anything. So everything would turn out alright I thought. Soon I would see him and talking about this in much greater detail now that I was part of the team and my father wouldn't have to hold anything back, would only ensconce my decision of joining. At least that's what I was hoping for. So as his arrival to Canada approached I was more and more elated and I felt better and better about the whole thing by the day. Now I couldn't sleep due to the positive anxiety of going to see my dad and brother. At least I wasn't scared to death.

CHAPTER 16

MENTAL KNOTS

The weekend of my Vermont trip finally came. The time leading up to it came and went somehow in a daze. I adopted a new coping mechanism with any worry in my life, including this one. It was a method of postponement. I told myself, and actually convinced myself, that I wouldn't worry about a certain problem until later. No matter how big I will engage the worry about it only shortly before a decision would have to be made. And that 'later' was an undetermined future date if no particular decision was necessary. As more time went by I simply kept pushing that undetermined date even further down the timeline. Essentially it was kicking the shit can down the road but it was an amazing stress reliever. So, in this case, I said to myself that I won't even think about the consequences of my actions until I spoke to my father. And, he was in the same boat anyways! So he wouldn't preach to me and stare at me wide-eyed wondering and lecturing why I did something stupid and dangerous since he was in the same predicament. For once in my life, both father and son were irresponsible goofs playing with fire. Idiots really, but no matter. Boys will be boys. That, furthered with the fact that my father was due to tell me all sorts of things that I wasn't privy to know before joining, and my 'irresponsible' actions will soon start to feel like the smartest thing I've ever done.

As I drove to Stan's (dad was already there, he arrived via plane the night before) I realized that I hadn't been at his chalet in almost half a year. I unwound the clock of everything that transpired over the last few months while driving through the serene mountain ranges. My 'undercover' work at King's University with their profs, then Military College, Jeff, then steroids and proteins from outer space. How the fuck did I get to here?!?! Will I wake up at any time? I wondered...

The weekend was our usual yearly get-together at Stan's. Drinks and skiing, and the familiar Slavic style venting and yelling over each other, over random topics, which was really just our normal way of talking. You can leave the Balkans, but the Balkans never leave you. At least we were in the middle of the woods, and no one could hear us scream and holler like Neanderthals.

Of course, I knew that the entire time I wouldn't be able to speak to father about the matter that itched the most. Our mutually shared secret. The secret doors that were there which I couldn't wait to open. I felt bad every once in a while that Stan was completely clueless about the whole thing, and wasn't part of it. It seemed rather unfair actually. I guess he didn't have what it takes. So I was paying it no mind, I was too self-absorbed to care about him at that moment.

I had to pretend like everything was the same as always, as did dad, and we had to carry on just traditional, usual conversations. That being said I had to admit I was a bit surprised at how well my father was playing the part. The part of obliviousness, the part of utter cluelessness as to there being anything else besides our normal, boring lives. I was impressed, he must have learned to play this part well over all the years he hid this from us. Nevertheless, it was eerily unnerving just how well he played it. Then again, didn't I as well? Stan sure didn't seem wise to anything, to either dad or myself behaving strangely or out of tact or character. We were both chameleons, both actors, players, liars......like father like son, more and more every day. Well at least one of the sons. Now Stan had a tendency to be clueless about many things in general so the whole obliviousness of the situation might have just been a testament to his zoned-out way rather than to my father and my acting skills.

As the weekend progressed though it began to bug me, claw at my obsessive prone mind the continuing observation of dad acting just quite so well. I mean shouldn't he had pulled me aside and said something quickly, something about hearing me joining, a wink, a stare, a coy smile, a thumbs up. There was nothing. Even at times when Stan was not in the room, he didn't break from character, from the act. He and I only spoke of nonsense subjects.

By the time Sunday rolled around and it was time for me to head back to Kingston there was a moment outside on Stan's porch when we were saying byes that I decided to test him a bit.

"Ok Marcus, so tomorrow early morning I'm driving from Stan's first thing and hopefully I should be in Kingston at your place around 2 PM, with all the stops I'll be making to eat and whatnot, how does that sound?" he said to me as Stan was grabbing something from the basement.

"Yeah, sounds good," I said "it will work out well. Alicia will make spinach with some mashed potatoes and eggs, I hope that's good right? Mom used to make that meal often."

"Oh Marcus she didn't have to make anything. The woman is almost seven months pregnant for God's sakes, we should have gone out to eat." he squinted at me like I was a little boy although his insincerity and happiness that we didn't have to go out and eat was painfully evident. Plus, he would be with us for three days, we would go out to eat one of those days, Alicia sure as hell wasn't going to cook every day.

"It was no trouble, I told Alicia the same thing. She said it was quick for her to whip this up. On your way back we were thinking we could all go out to the Mandarin buffet for lunch, our treat, what are your thoughts?"

"That is absolutely fine, thank you."

"Otherwise" I now started "you and I will have quite a lot to talk about won't we? More so than ever before in our lives right? Maybe when Alicia goes to bed we can go out for a walk and a drink somewhere, as usual, how does that sound?"

"Of course Marcus, that would be nice. Anything specific you are referring to with respect to these topics of discussion? Am I missing something? Is everything alright?"

The look on his face was unmistakable. No matter what a bull-shitter, what a manipulator, actor, con artist, whatever, I still knew my father. And without any doubt in my mind, he legitimately had no clue what I was talking about. It was as certain as the fact that I had to drive back to Kingston for three and a half hours carefully minding the location of all the toilet containing pitstops along the way.

I felt an instant freeze go down my skeleton core. Like a spell from Sub-Zero in Mortal Kombat. It was about the same feeling you get when you drink a strawberry daiquiri through a straw too fast and you get a nasal cavity and brain freeze that feels as if someone rammed an ice pick in your brain through your nose. I felt that throughout my body right about now.

"Marcus, are you alright?" he continued. His look of utter wonder now actually changed to a look of genuine concern for my well being. I could only imagine I turned pale faster than if some-one dumped a bag of flour all over me. I had to think and act fast but all I really wanted to do is run away into the woods.

"Ahm....yeah, I'm fine." It came out of me somehow. I was searching for something else that I could present him with to des-perately try and get a recognition that he knew what I was talking about just moments ago and that he was simply doing a really good job of hiding it.

"No, I'm fine." I said after a couple of deep breaths, all the while having an intensely constipated look on my face. "There is absolutely nothing wrong with me. All good. I just figured, you know, there might be other things to talk about, maybe some new developments, topics of conversation."

"Haha, oh I get it, it's a joke right? Yea yeah, I know we always talk about the same things" he went on. "But what can I tell you we are pretty simple people at the end of the day. Some family gos-sip, world politics, work, jokes, and what else is there? I mean we did talk about astronomy a bit, a bit of science, so there it is, we are expanding our topics of conversation. Plus you and Alicia are expecting a baby, there is much to discuss there. How your lives will change and all that."

Was that a hint? Astronomy? Science? I was desperate to cling onto something. We talked a bit about the calender I bought which had a different image of the Universe for each month taken from Hubble Telescope. Then we talked about Space exploration and how humans haven't really done jack shit since landing on the Moon and how everything described in the movie *2001: Space Odyssey* wasn't even close to coming true yet even though it was 2019 and that movie came out in 1969. Well most things from the movie except maybe AI was making some strides. But even that seemed a long way off despite what was being said about it. But certainly we didn't get into anything else, aliens, Erich von Daniken or anything of the sort. The discussion felt pretty general, sterile, cliché and anything my father contributed to it certainly didn't sound revolutionary like he had any different, inside knowledge.

"Yeah, haha, that's what I meant." I decided that there was nothing else I could say. For now. Stan came out too. We said our byes and I left.

The drive back was nauseating. To say the least. I couldn't even listen to any music. I was completely and utterly frightened and anxious. And this was the first time in my life that I had absolutely no one I could talk to. A major problem I had, I couldn't confide in anyone. Not my mother, not my wife, not my brother, a friend, and apparently not even my father. At least not yet. What just happened back there?! Why was he so seemingly oblivious to what I was saying?? To what I was hinting. Did he actually......not know?? What did that even mean?? He called me weeks ago, out of the blue. Told things, we spoke of the organization, of the membership. He must have known I joined. Was he waiting for the right time?

I had to calm down. I found myself gripping the steering wheel with it slipping through my sweaty palms as I was swerving over lanes on the 401 trying to avoid 18-wheeler transport trucks which seemed to vastly outnumber regular cars these days. I had to get over whatever paranoia was running wild in my head. This all had to have been a coincidence. He was just really good at hiding it, that's all. Nothing else, nothing more. The man had been a member for thirty years. None of us in the immediate family ever found out that he was a member of some secret sect. He always kept himself well camouflaged. So that must have been the case now too. He was on alert and his entire guard was up, he was acting extra carefully, in front of Stan and all. When he comes over to my place I was certain that he was going to open up like he said he would.

I slowly convinced myself and gradually calmed down. By the time I was driving through Brockville, Ontario I was almost back to normal, almost back to feeling elated about my access to a secret organization and my belonging to them, how it was going to be dad and I in it together, etc...

Talk with Alicia was brief. She asked how the weekend was, I said fine, she confirmed my father's arrival with me tomorrow, the time, the food. We quickly cleaned and vacuumed the place and went to bed.

That night however, knowing my father was arriving tomorrow, was a whole other stressed out show. I was back to paranoia. I was replaying the doubting film from hours earlier at the beginning of my drive. I was doubting everything again and my father's reactions were not making any sense. Could his acting and pretending have really been that good? Could my eyes have been fooled that much by his gestures, facial expressions? I analyzed them over and over again and there was nothing there, he genuinely looked like he didn't know what I was talking about. For fucks sakes! I couldn't wait for tomorrow to come, and for dinner and pleasantries and him complimenting Alicia's growing belly to end so him and I could go out for that drink and walk or whatever. I was itching to get the lid off of him and for him to start talking. I wanted it out in the open as soon as possible, the anticipation was killing me.

I only fell asleep at about 5 AM. I guess I exhausted myself enough by turning so much I felt like I was in a fruit blender. Waking up at 6:30 AM at my regular alarm time I felt as though someone beat and wrestled the shit out of me all night. 'Luckily', ironically, the worries of the day before quickly came rushing back in and the anxiety boost from that alone was more sobering and better wake up call than a cold shower. So I didn't feel tired at all.

I shat, showered and shaved. Dressed and ate my oatmeal quickly, then went to work. Father was supposed to be arriving at around 2 PM. I knew I wasn't going to be able to do any actual work today, so I had to do an extra good job of pretending like I'm working while all the while being distracted about some completely different issue and obsession of mine. Business as usual. Different day, different issue, same brain.

My OCD was of the obsessive thought disorder not of the obsessive habit disorder. I didn't go around locking and unlocking my car ten times or my house door like Jack Nicholson in As Good as it Gets, but obsessive thoughts were constantly attacking my mind. Endlessly. My ability to prevent them from sticking around for long was how I knew whether I was better at handling my condition. When I was younger these thoughts were exceptionally obscene and would stay with me for weeks, months and years sometimes before I finally found ways to dispel them for good. A good distraction always helped as well. Something else more tangible to worry about. Otherwise the thoughts would constantly involve the surreal, the what-ifs, the illusionary demented. I had a very weak mind that had a tendency to continually second guess itself. Mind delved about something that I hoped would never happen to me or that I would not want in my life at all costs and then obsessing well what if these things actually, somehow, happened to me!? What if?! And then a million scenarios, like 1000 ways to die, for me it was 1000 ways to turn into some kind of freak and how to prevent it.

These days the worries were real, not imaginary. Actual day to day life problems. But exacerbated due to my obsessive thought tendencies. So my worries, although real and related to real life issues such as family affairs, work, etc...had the added steroid effect of being overblown and exaggerated. It was not easy being me. But reading about this condition helped tremendously since I finally knew what the issue was as opposed to thinking that something unique and inexplicably wrong was the matter with me when I was younger. I told my father about my findings, as I thought he had the exact same condition, but he, of course, didn't want to admit to it.

As the working day progressed I couldn't exactly just stay incognito and not do anything. It didn't quite work that way. It just so happened that today a bunch of emails had to come through regarding this one project I was managing and I had to answer, figure shit out, call people, the contractor, the client, all that. I guess in a way it helped the day go by and to distract me from my issue at hand.

2 PM rolled around and I told my boss that I had to leave since my dad was coming to visit. Boss was cool about it as always, he knew I would make up the time. Plus he knew that there were countless times when I worked extra and never bothered to bank my time or charge it, I was just giving my free time to the company. In return I expected not to be scrutinized when I had appointments or had to run errands for hours either first thing in the morning or middle of the day or otherwise. And my work thus far was very flexible and reasonable. It would prove its worth even more soon once Alicia gives birth as I will have to be on stand by for our newborn. Our parents were nowhere to be found, mine lived in Europe and Alicia's lived in British Columbia, both enjoying nicer weather, and better infrastructure, amongst other things. So we were on our own. My boss told me he expected me to be all over the place with my working schedule at least for the first six months.

I left work and my anxiety although growing on my way home was ebbed by the fact that I was fully expecting to figure out a resolution to my issue and soon. First pleasantries and dinner, talk about the pregnancy and whatnots, politics and then dad and I had some serious shit to discuss. He better take that mask off or...there was pretty much nothing I could do about it. I had no contingency plans.

He parked in the same spot as usual on the road. Alicia and I had to park one of our cars in the garage so that the other car and his would fit lengthwise into the narrow driveway of our townhouse. Parking on the road was not allowed until April 1, due to winter and snow conditions.

We hugged and kissed and observed Alicia's belly. He gently touched it as he made sure he didn't cross any boundaries. He looked a bit awkward, as he usually does because he overthinks everything. Alicia got a good laugh out of it. It was a good icebreaker.

We came into the house, put his things in the guest room where he would be staying then we all went into the living room. I got us some drinks, beers, Alicia was finishing dinner. We moved the conversation into the kitchen shortly thereafter so that Alicia wouldn't feel excluded. It was the exact same replica year in and year out, gestures and conversation wise. And we've been in the same house now for three years so as the location didn't change it felt even more like a copy and paste scene. There was only one novelty, the pregnancy. But even that wore off shortly. My dad only looked at Alicia a couple of times with a big smile on his face and a crisp sparkle in his eyes as Alicia moved cautiously around the kitchen with her big belly. I jumped up a few times to help her out but she insisted I sit down and entertain my father. "Believe me Marcus with my belly there is absolutely no room in this kitchen for the both of us." Fine, I thought. I made the effort at least. Dad was positively beaming with a whiskey sparkle in his eyes that I was pouring for him at the idea of becoming a grandfather.

Dinner was good, the conversations kept flowing. Afterwards we all went out for a walk. Spring was finally in the air and it was felt all around us. The smell of the air, the birds chirping, the almost entirely melted snow. No wind either, which was rare for Kingston and a balmy 8 C degrees.

Upon return from the walk it was around 6:30 PM. Further conversation went on until about 9 PM or so. Around this time Alicia started yawning extensively and I thought time was soon approaching for me to suggest to dad to go out for a drink and finally start talking about the issue that was on my mind the entire time. It was actually Alicia who broke the ice.

"Well guys I think I'm pooped. I'll head to bed. Please don't stop talking on my behalf. Feel free to stay up as long as possible or whatever you feel like." she said.

I felt this to be a good moment to simply swoop in with: "Makes sense sweetie, you've had a long day. Hey dad how about we go out, for a bit of a car cruise or to sit down somewhere for a quick drink?"

His response surprised me. In a negative way.

"Oh I wouldn't bother with that Marcus. We've all had a long and great day of catching up, dinner was excellent, we even went out for a walk. You should go rest with your wife, I'm sure you could both use it." He said all that very nonchalantly.

What the fuck I thought?! He was rushing me off to sleep?? What the hell was going on?! Why is he brushing me off? If I go to bed now, in the morning I go off to work and he goes off to Toronto to see his tax consultant to settle up his tax return here in Canada and spend a few days catching up with his old Canadian buddies. That was the main reason why he came to Canada at this time of the year anyways, before the April 30th tax deadline. Then he would again head back towards Kingston, stay another night with us before he would proceed back to Stan's and fly back to Europe from Montreal where he landed. That means we would only have one more night upon his return from Toronto to talk about the organization and me joining. Something didn't make sense here. It was against all common logic for him to leave a topic this important for then. I had to keep pushing, I had to get the two of us alone and this had to happen today.

"Common dad, it's still light out, since we moved the clocks forward an hour a couple of weeks ago. I'm not tired yet. And remember last time you were here last year it was pouring rain we couldn't even go anywhere. The weather is nice, it might not be when you come back." I sounded a little bit like a pleading boy which was not my style ever especially with him. But truth be told I wanted to get him alone to figure out what was going on here.

"But Marcus you have to work tomorrow morning, why the insistence?" he kept up. And now Alicia gave me a swift elbow to the ribs by chiming in with "Marcus, maybe we are all tired and should just go to bed. Your dad will be back in a few days for one more visit before he goes back to Montreal, why not just wait until then? There will be less for all of us to catch up on and you guys can go out for a drink a bit earlier."

"Good thinking Alicia " my dad now seizing the opportunity to cut me off right at the legs. "When I get back we'll go for a drink. We'll start the evening a bit sooner. Tonight I'm all talked out and I'm sure you two are as well. Now go get some rest, the both of you and safeguard my little granddaughter to be, hehe."

Well that was it. There was no possible way for me to say anything to this other than to agree. Any further pursuit on my behalf would have come across noticeably strange and I knew my limits, and when to stop. This time. I agreed and we retreated to our sleeping quarters.

I didn't know how many more of these sleepless or 'sleep barely' nights I could go through before going nuts. I was just not getting the closure on things that I would have liked and the anticipation was overbearing, I was finding it hard to placate my fears and my worries. Every issue remained opened. The only thing I could conjure up tonight was the fact that my father agreed to go out for a drink with me, just the two of us, upon his return. So we will talk about the organization then, right? We had to, that must be the time. But I was paranoid now, I was certain something was going to come up to put a stop to that conversation then as well. Something in the way, a roadblock. I couldn't anticipate all the scenarios at the moment, which was a problem as I had no clue how to go about mitigating them, and the scenarios for which there was no mitigation plan were the ones that would happen, whatever they may be. All I had was worry. And dread. And hope and prayer, which rarely offset Murphy's Law constantly ruling my life.

So back to waiting I went. Another few days had to go by before my father returns from Toronto, sees his friends, takes care of his taxes and returns to Kingston on his way back to Montreal and back to Europe. The waiting game. At least I was honest with myself. I had no illusions as to why I was in the mess that I was in. I dug and I dug for something different and I kept being bored and dissatisfied with the life I had and well I uncovered not one but several bee's hives, wasp's, snake and hornet's nests, secret worlds and unusual people. So now I had to find a way to carry it with me. At the end of the day my father behaving strangely and in an incredibly weird way wasn't going to change the fact that I had become a member of a secret organization promising me insight and knowledge that living in the regular, boring world would never give me. So now I had to hope that I didn't ruin my life, and my family's life forever. Surely this would end in disaster.

The week went by as well as I could have hoped. I tried focusing on work. We won a big Light Rail Transit project. More bridge inspections were coming our way both in Spring and in the Summer. Workload and my livelihood were still intact, thank God. Jeff and Shauna were nowhere in sight just as they promised. They were giving me my 'space'. Alicia's pregnancy was going smoothly. Ob-Gyn check-ups were now by- weekly and everything looked and sounded ideal. So far so good. The only issue I had now was my father's weird behavior. Oh yeah and that 'other' thing. He must have been waiting for the right and perfect time to talk to me. He must have been playing it extra carefully, easing into it. Not blurting out a secret upon first sight of each other like school children. That must have been the case. It had to have been. All of the days dad was in Toronto we only exchanged a few, brief texts and that was it. Very casual, platonic and dry. I gave him his space. I didn't want to probe.

The day of his return arrived. It was a Thursday. He would head back to Montreal and Stan's on Friday and fly back to Europe on Sunday. It was now or never for our 'talk' to occur. And if it didn't, then something was terribly wrong, I would not be able to deny it or explain it otherwise anymore.

As predicted his second coming was more or less a lot of the same. Aside from him telling us how his time in Toronto was, meeting with some old friends and co-workers, handling taxes, etc...all the other topics have already been talked about and passé. So sure enough around 5:30 PM, after dinner, I jumped in with:

"Hey dad, how about going out for that drink?"

"Why sure. And will Alicia be joining us?" he said. God fucking dammit, I thought! What is this shit now?! Alicia?? We gotta talk on our own for fucks sakes! Why is he inviting her?? Ok, alright, maybe he was just trying to be polite. Maybe he knew that she would refuse. Hell, how many more times will I have to excuse his actions in my head?? Am I just living in denial at this point? Predictably Alicia turned the offer down.

"Oh thanks for the invite Boris, but I'll pass. I'll read a bit and watch some TV until you guys come back. You boys have fun, I'm sure you'd like to do some catching up without me always lingering around." God she was a sweetheart.

"Ok Alicia, understandable. We will miss your presence. Thanks again for everything" my father sounded a little like Jeffrey Madison. Embellishing the phrases and words like Santa Claus. It was obnoxious and nauseating. Anyways I was finally able to isolate him. Whatever I had to do or get to the bottom of now was the time. There won't be any other chances.

We got into my car and started to cruise. I drove along Highway 15 south towards downtown weaving along the previously gorgeous eastern escarpment of the Cataraqui River before they decided to sprinkle it with new popsicle stick residential subdivisions with vinyl siding. How vinyl was still legal to use as a standard for house siding I'll never know. Oh wait, I know, it's super cheap and minimalistic, like everything else in the North American society. If only these shanties cost to buy as much as they cost to construct and the value of the material they are constructed from, like $50,000 tops, I'd cash one out in a heartbeat. But I was not going to get into a mortgage over an oversized tool shed for half a million dollars or whatever ridiculous price these things were going for at the moment. And now on top of them being overpriced, oversized glorified dog houses they were obstructing my damn view from the escarpment! An asshole like me just can't catch a break. They ruined the natural feel of it. The river, the limestone cliffs and nature were breathtaking. These amateur building samples like we were still at the dawn of civilization were not. Small comments were made to this effect between dad and me as we drove. The sunset far off in the distance to the west was beautiful, you could always depend on Kingston for those especially on a nice day like this. Purple pinkish hues and haze always reminded me of fantasy books I read as a child. Or the video games I currently play, like an oversized child that I am now. Breathtaking. No room for other bitching when a sight like this was before us. People misunderstood my 'bitching' about Canada or North America anyways. I wasn't complaining about what the society and infrastructure were at the moment living here just to be a dick, my complaint and seething displeasure is the anger from witnessing this place not becoming all that it could and should become. What needs to be but isn't. That is the heartbreak and the true tragedy that more people should be talking about, since there were no objective reasons for any minimalism in any sphere of North American life.

So we kept driving. Small talk continued. "So Marcus how are you doing with all of this? Alicia's pregnancy? Work? You managing ok?" it was his usual parent chit chat. Dad checking up on his son making sure he could handle life alright. Yawn. "Good," I said, "It's all going fine and we're taking it one day at a time. How are you and mom? Health wise? Getting along? I mean we talk almost every weekend via Facetime so I suppose we already know answers to all these questions right?"

"Yeah we're fine, older but luckily not yet too much sicker, haha." he said.

As I was turning right onto Highway 2 towards downtown I was jittery to simply jump into the topic that I was dying to discuss, so I held back and exercised restraint, as I thought about a good place for us to go sit down and have a drink inside. We would talk about it then. As we wrapped around King's University, old neighborhood where the professors lived, and downtown core I thought of a nice bar up on the second floor right above this seafood restaurant opposite the City Hall.

As it was past 5 PM I could find parking practically anywhere so we parked as close as possible to the watering hole. There was an insurance company across the street and its parking lot was now abandoned for the night and the gate was up so I had no issues finding a spot.

It took us half a minute to walk across and enter the bar. It was quiet, it was a Legion of some sort, old army get-together, they had good live bands at times. But it was a Thursday night and quiet, practically abandoned of any patrons, just the TV on. It would be perfect for our talk I thought.

We sat down, looked around. The waitress or what seemed more a woman that was the proprietor of the place also playing the role of a waitress, came over and asked us if we wanted something to drink. We both got a glass of beer. I got a pint, dad got a half pint. He didn't make a fuss about the volume I ordered, he genuinely seemed to be in a good mood. He looked around, admired the place, made some complimentary observations about the old furniture, cozy feel and the stage. Grinned joyfully. I let him soak everything in. I wanted to talk badly while at the same time being impressed with myself for holding my calm, not blurting anything out. Even my father didn't pick up on my anxiety which he usually goes out of his way to comment on, even at times when I'm calm. "Are you alright Marcus? You seem nervous and anxious.", he would often say seemingly out of the blue. I swear at times he only does it to fuck with me and make me squirm and for me to go out of my way to reassure the audience that I'm not all that nervous and anxious. He loved to do it when I was in the midst of disagreeing or contradicting him over something. To see me jolted out of my element and shine a light into my eyes. But this time he wasn't on that type of roll. Maybe I somehow came across as truly relaxed and tranquil. Or it was because we weren't arguing. Or maybe he was now fucking with me as he knew what was on my mind and purposely tried to play aloof and postpone the subject...

There was nothing else to talk about or new topics to bring up. So in my most calm way possible, starting from scratch and with a proper introduction like we never even had the conversation weeks ago and without giving the effect of "Surprise!!!!" during an idiotic surprise birthday party disclosure (followed by the even more moronic off-key 'Happy Birthday' song), I started with:

"So, I joined the organization," I said. He was still looking around the place before he slowly zeroed in his eyes to make eye contact with me.

"Really neat place," he said. Not quite the response I was hoping for but I figured if I don't say anything for a couple of moments he would hone in on what I've said.

"Sorry, what was that? Organization? What kind of organization did you join Marcus? Something sports related? Or at work?"

Ahh, fuck my life...On top of the fact that it was most certainly not the type of response I was hoping for, deep down it was almost as if I knew that he would reply in this manner. That he would be clueless, completely and utterly, unabashedly oblivious. I was breaking out in cold sweats, and I was no longer in the mood to drink even a sip of the beer that was put in front of me. I didn't even recall anymore what beer I ordered. So I knew the situation was deadly serious for me. But as always in my life, I had to go to the core. Head first, eyes and mouth wide open, hands to the side. Or tied behind my back. Or down my pants. And I wasn't going to waste any more time, beat around the bush and allow the discussion to take side roads. Every word had to be precise and to the point. No more tangents.

"The organization that you told me you were part of weeks ago when you called me out of the blue on WhatsApp on the weekend. We spoke of Jeff and Shauna, of the Universe, higher knowledge and Erich von Daniken. We spoke of my incessant search over the last few months and you told me that I should join, change my life in ways never before imaginable and open my horizons like I've dreamt about for most of my life. That organization." I was surprisingly blunt, clear and deadpan considering just how unbelievably anxious I felt.

He scrunched up his face. He looked straight ahead at me and said "Marcus, what are you on about? Are you messing with me?"

His eyebrows now concaved up, from tight between the eyes to upward in the middle above the nose. Then they relaxed. He was almost doing this weird face dance, brow to cheeks to the nose, from serious to comedic, to patronizing, to condescending to worried all within a few seconds.

I was shocked and turning colder by the second. Strangely the colder I felt the more I thought I was literally melting into the chair I was sitting in. I could feel my throat tickling as my immune system was dropping faster than a flat tire.

"Am I messing with you?" I said, "tell me you are joking. Please tell me you are joking. We spoke about three weeks ago. It was a Saturday, you called out of the blue. Like, common just stop this right now, I've been stressed out for freaking weeks and months, I'm in no mood for jokes or further tests or trials. If you want to go somewhere else to talk we can, just tell me. Just stop this whatever you are doing right now." I was now pleading, which, I've learned, no matter how shitty of a situation you find yourself in, near death or a lifetime prison sentence, was never a good thing to do. It was useless.

"Well, now I can explain why you've seemed so nervous at Stan's. I thought I picked up on something. And you hinted towards 'many matters to discuss' when we see each other. What the heck is going on Marcus? What is with you?" he went on.

"Look you know very well what's 'with' me. We've talked about it three weeks ago!"

"Marcus stop yelling, relax, first of all I'm your father and second of all we are in a public place."

Again with this family hierarchy respect thing. If we were on a sinking ship he would find time to preach about social etiquette and proper conversation discourse and order. Remarkable.

"Since when the fuck did you care about being in a public or any other place when it came to raising your voice? What, you can do it whenever you want and wherever you want but I can't??" I was now screeching with seething contempt.

"Marcus, again, settle down. What the fuck is wrong with you??

I don't know what the hell you are talking about. What conversation, what issues and discussion and what organization?! I never called you weeks ago. If I'm not mistaken the weekend exactly three weeks ago I went to go see the family home in the mountains back in Slovenia, I stayed there for a couple of days. I don't have any reception or internet there, I didn't call anybody! I swear!"

"What...look I'll pull my phone out right now." I pulled my phone out and started looking at WhatsApp call history and my general iPhone's call history. I was barely operating it that's how stressed out I was. The phone call from WA would show up on both history lists.

I stared at my phone. First WA history, there was no call from dad. Then I looked at the general call history, nothing either. I felt like I was going to pass out. I looked again, and again and again, all the other phone calls before, after and around that time were there, recorded, I remembered them all, that weekend. Who, when, about what. But his calls were eerily and ostensibly missing. I even checked Viber, I figured maybe in all the commotion and confusion he called from Viber and I mistook it for WhatsApp. I even checked bloody Facebook even though he doesn't even have an account!! I turned the phone off and on again, the same thing! Nothing! I was losing it nicely. He looked at me and tapped me on the shoulder.

"Hej, what is going on??" he asked.

"I, I can't find your phone call. It's not in my fucking history! I can't find it anywhere, there is no record of it...what the fuck is going on old man?? Did you hide the call? Did you make sure it would not pop up on the history?! What is going on here???" way to lose your cool Marcus I thought helplessly as I was breaking down in a spectacular way. Even the woman behind the bar looked over towards our table. I was flailing. I was a mess. My underwear and armpits were soaked from cold sweat while the rest of me was shivering. I was having palpitations and was desperately trying to 'wake up' from this nightmare. The slow realization that more than likely I wasn't going to was causing me to go borderline insane. I couldn't grab a hold of anything as my palms were so sweaty anything would just slip right out. Thank God I wasn't in the mood to drink any beer because surely I could not operate any objects at the moment with my hands.

My dad grabbed my hand now. Both of my hands. He looked at me and said "Marcus, please settle down. Common let's get out of here." he quickly left some cash on the table and ushered us out. The woman serving us said "Is everything alright guys?" and my father in his broken English said "oh ya ya, no problem. Thank you, see you, good night."

We went out into the still cold winter air even though it was late March. I was beyond nervous, fidgety and wide eyed. He tried to calm me down, but I didn't know whether to listen to him or to punch him in the face.

"Look" I kept up, "I don't know what to tell you, unless I'm going completely nuts I spoke to you three weeks ago, over the phone. You called me. You knew what I was up to over the past few months and we spoke for about an hour. You told me that you were also a member of an organization that Jeff and Shauna are part of. You advised me to join, to change and enlighten my life, find out unimaginable information and facts not allowed for general public knowledge, how the hell do you not remember?? More importantly why won't you!! And why I can't find that conversation in my history now I have no idea. Fuck!" I wasn't even talking to him anymore, I was yelling out into the cold wind and dark night.

"Marcus, I swear to you I have no idea what you are talking about! I never called you. These things you are mentioning seem completely unfamiliar to me. Quite frankly they seem insane. Who are Jeff and Shauna?! If I didn't know any better I would think you are drunk but I know that's not the case since you've been with me all afternoon and have been acting fine up until minutes ago. Why the fuck would I lie?? And what are you talking about joining some organization?? What is this about? What is this seriously? What the hell have you gotten yourself into? Are you on drugs? Are you taking something? You have to tell me more and I hope you tell me right now."

My anger towards him was slowly starting to recede as I was, no matter how hard I tried not to, really and genuinely gradually noticing that he indeed didn't know what I was talking about. I could see it in his eyes and his face and his panic, same way how I saw the cluelessness in his eyes and face at Stan's chalet when I was probing him. Except other than just being clueless and puzzled he was now utterly worried. And frightened. There was no mistaking it. And my anger and fear now turned into pure and utter fear. Here I go again, like so many times before, finding myself in a situation that seemingly has no good end in sight. And yet I prayed that it would like all those times before when an antidote always appeared just when I thought all was hopeless. Somehow though I had a feeling that I wasn't going to get out of this situation that easily. Also in the past, especially as a child, whenever I was this scared I found comfort with my parents. Especially my father with his reassuring ways. When he wanted to be reassuring. There was no one else that could put me at ease quite so successfully and effectively. This time, I couldn't say shit. I was on the brink of spilling the beans, back and forth, should I tell him or shouldn't I, but I pulled myself back from the edge. I felt like telling him everything I've been through and what I've done over the past few months. The weight of it all was overwhelming. But I decided no matter what I wasn't going to say anything. What the hell would have been the point anyway?! I told him everything weeks ago, at least what I thought was during a conversation with 'him', and now he swears up and down that he has no recollection of our conversation. If I tell him anything now, again, will he pretend in a few weeks that it never happened?! Was he even on my side...

"No, I'm not on drugs." I felt like my immune system was so low that I was developing a fever as I was speaking. And my speaking was merely a whimpering whisper. I didn't know what else to say at this moment, I figured I'd just put out the immediate fires of assuring him that I'm in actuality not a drug addict and head towards ending this conversation.

He didn't believe it. He walked ahead of me, grabbed me by my shoulders and looked at me, right into my eyes. He was analyzing whether I was sober like he used to do back in my University days when I came home at 3 AM dead drunk and he would study my irises like an optometrist.

"Marcus, swear to me right now, on your mother's life, on your unborn daughter's life, that you are not taking anything, swear to me! That you are not hooked on anything!" he looked pretty damn pale and white from fear as well. Yup, he definitely wasn't faking this. No way.

"I swear dad, on my future child's life, mom's life, I'm not on drugs. And I'm not tripping out as we speak." I somehow squeezed out of me.

"Then what is it Marcus? Are you in trouble? What organization did you join? Did I understand that correctly? What did you mean by that?" he pressed on.

"So you seriously don't remember any conversation with me three weeks ago? No recollections, nothing whatsoever?" I tried again. Once more. Before I throw up. And if he kept holding me by my shoulders and staring into my face it would be all over his face, and not on the air conditioning units of apartments below us when I would throw up out of my bedroom window in the middle of the night back in high school. I figured it would be pointless to ask him to look at the history on his phone as I couldn't even find any record of the conversation on mine. So forget it I thought.

"Marcus, same thing you just told me about drug use, I'll tell you right back. I swear on Stan's, yours, my future granddaughter's life, I have no recollection of any such conversation and I, unfortunately son, do not know what you are talking about."

My father could be a shifty character in various situations. But this scene unfolding right here in front of me, he sure as hell wasn't faking. And this one time I really wished he was. I was hoping for a wink or a nod or a 'let's discuss later' hint, but it was not to be.

We were walking circles around the main square in Kingston downtown. I wasn't sure anymore whether either of us was aiming to attempt an actual walk, or continue the talk or were we walking back to the car or were we kind of aimlessly bouncing around like loose electrons or hallucinating lab rats under the hold of some newly synthesized drug. I figured anyone watching us would have gotten a good laugh out of this spectacle. I was getting cold now, I had to get some control back over this ordeal.

"Let's go back to the car, I'm getting cold," I said, surprisingly decisively. As I did that I marched towards the car. I sped up, the adrenalin and sporty spring in my step were helping me break up the nauseating anxiety coursing throughout my body. My dad followed as best he could in step while yelling out "Marcus did you want me to drive? I can drive you know, you don't seem yourself."

"I'll be fine" I replied. We got to the car and got in. I started to drive.

"Marcus, relax, don't drive back home yet, let's talk about this some more. You need to calm down anyway, you are in no shape to drive, you'll get us in an accident!"

"I'll cruise a bit, the driving calms me down. I couldn't walk anymore, my feet and hands were getting numb." I was very dry in my replies. I suddenly felt catatonic, void of personality, but much calmer than before. It was a new feeling for me. I was in deep shit on all fronts but the body said fuck it let's be calm about it for a change. Nothing else remained. I think psychosomatically my whole being knew that if I continued freaking out I would either stroke out, pass out or get severely and violently ill and it didn't want to put itself through that. Astonishing.

I could feel my father staring at me intensely as I drove. He was itching to talk but at the same time he was wary of riling me up as I was the one driving both of us around. I drove straight West along Lake Ontario. The night was setting in. I didn't know what other direction to take. Had his butt also have not been in potential danger of a car accident my father right now would have been interrogating me with questions and turning me towards him as his eyes would have been bulging into me. But now he kept his quiet. Also, I'm fairly certain my new developed demeanor and stoic, statuesque expression creeped him out a bit as well. He was in uncharted territory. Not in his wildest dreams would he have dreamt of this situation as he was coming back to see me on his way to Stan's. And not in my wildest nightmares just four months or so ago could I have imagined myself being in this heap of shit I was finding myself in now. So we were both wide eyed in a foreign land of life, bewildered and wondering whether this was for real.

Soon I was starting to realize that we were about to exit Kingston's city limits and start entering the countryside. The sunset was on its way down to disappear and I knew I had to start heading back. My dad wasn't going to stay quiet forever and I didn't feel like driving any longer.

"Marcus, can you talk to me?" I could sense the panic in his voice even though he was trying to talk in a balanced way. "Where are we going? It's dark, shouldn't we be turning back?"

"Fine," I said, "I will turn back at the next major road, we'll go right and up to Highway 401 and back east towards home."

"There is nothing to say really" I continued on "you don't recall a phone call with me. I can't find any history of it on my phone either. I'm guessing there is nothing of it on your phone as well. So, for all I know maybe I dreamt the whole God damned thing. Maybe it never happened. I guess I'm stressed out lately from all the things I have on my mind. Work, baby on the way. I guess I'm not as 'ok' as I indicated to you earlier. Everything is overbearing and overwhelming." I didn't know what else to say. I also started to slowly believe what I was saying. Maybe it was a dream. Maybe I never spoke to him. It is conceivable I suppose. He has no record of it, seems pretty damn sincere about the whole thing. I can't find any record of it for the life of me on my phone so what else is there? I only recall it in my head but all other indicators point to it never having happened. Maybe I was officially a schizophrenic.

I was driving back now. My dad was mulling over what I just said.

"Marcus, I suppose anything is possible. I can imagine you haven't been feeling yourself. I went through something similar just before you were born. Too much 'life' if you will. Clearly it's manifesting more than I could have imagined. I should have asked you more often how you are feeling. But during all of our conversations online for these past few months you always seemed to have everything under control. You seemed to be doing well, chipper, upbeat, optimistic. I should have known better. And again, it's understandable. That being said you mentioned some pretty specific things back there. Very particular facts. Either you have a very vivid imagination son and some wild dreams filled your nights or you are not telling me something."

As I was now driving back east on the 401 I genuinely didn't know myself anymore. Seriously. Moments like these are when one's sanity is truly put to the test. Before I could answer him with confidence I had to know with confidence myself. What else did I potentially imagine? Jeff and Shauna?? Were they real? The organization, stunts pulled at Universities. Was any of it real? I had no clue at the moment. I didn't think to check my call history to see if conversations with Jeff and Shauna actually happened as well. I would be able to check quickly though. I needed to get home. And when I was left alone with Alicia again she will be able to tell me about the daycare deal and money gift from Shauna and reassure me. At least of Shauna's existence. Or not. Who knew maybe Alicia will tell me that I'm nuts and that she has no clue who Shauna is. Maybe Shauna exists but has nothing to do with some secret society. Maybe I won't find any history on my phone of Jeff. Maybe that Saturday when I thought I joined some cult I was actually at the gym kicking and punching the bags. Maybe I could ask my trainers and they could confirm it. Or maybe they'll tell me that they saw me walking down the street naked attempting to have sex with seagulls. I could see the headline now 'Local idiot makes imbecile of himself'.

As we were approaching my house all I said was "Dad I'm sorry about the outburst. I'm not sure what got into me, the more I think about it this whole thing got concocted in my head due to a bad dream or stress or something. Or all combined. Let me get some sleep and we'll touch base on this subject again soon."

"Ok son, if you are sure I have no choice but to believe you. Let's just leave this subject matter open. I'll follow up with you whenever I can. But keep me posted on how you are doing, you promise?"

"I promise" I answered, "We'll talk. Now let's drop this for now. You are staying with us tonight again so let's have a pleasant evening with Alicia so that she doesn't suspect anything strange went on while we were out. Ok?"

"So Alicia doesn't know any of this? Everything you mentioned to me, you didn't mention any of these things to her?" he asked.

"That's right", I replied. "Nothing of the sort was ever discussed with her."

"Leave it that way Marcus. She has enough on her plate. If any of these manifestations or events you think happened come across your mind again, call me and we'll discuss them alright? I'll try to be of help as much as I can, whenever. I promise. But don't involve Alicia, your mother, Stan, any friends or anything like that."

"Yeah, don't worry. I mean if there is a chance I hallucinated the whole bloody thing, or dreamt it or whatever, if I'm stressed out to that degree, then I sure as hell don't want anyone else thinking I'm nuts." I replied sort of dazed off and looking into the distance… like a true nut job that I have become.

"Haha, hey we all have our episodes. Sometimes, and depending on the situation one finds themselves in life, it's hard to know what's real, what's wishful thinking, what is a dream. Life ain't easy a lot of the times, and we all feel as if we are stumbling around like headless chickens in a fog." he said.

Ain't that the truth I thought to myself. I've been sleep walking for the past few months that's for sure. I didn't even know where sleeping began or ended and where reality began.

Lucid dreams maybe that felt more real than life itself.

We got inside the house. Alicia was there dressed and ready to go out. I completely forgot that the plan for dad's return visit was to go out and eat. So basically she ushered us right out again as we came in through the door.

Dinner at Mandarin was a tremendous effort of mind, body, wit and gestures with dad and I going out of our ways embellishing our time together while out for a drink. We told Alicia we spent time joking and laughing and that we caught a live band. We kept making eye contact as we talked so as to sync and coordinate our thoughts and conversation and to give each other secret nods that whatever lies one of us was concocting the other one would know to play along. It reminded me of the time we walked in scot-free into Pula's ancient Roman amphitheater with a bunch of school kids as the people at the gate thought we were part of the teaching faculty. All it took then as well was simply a glance between us to know what the other one was thinking. This is how I figured it would work when I thought my father was part of the organization...

It was beyond hard for me to not think about what had transpired earlier and my appetite was essentially nonexistent but I was stuffing my face with the buffet food just so that Alicia wouldn't think something was wrong.

A couple of times I couldn't help but zone out and Alicia said "Marcus you alright? Something on your mind? Every once in a while your attention seems to drop so suddenly for a few moments."

My father looked at me in a panic.

"Oh no I'm fine, just thought of something at work, project related, that I have to deal with tomorrow. Nothing serious, client related, no big deal." Then for a few minutes after that I would be overly enthusiastic and chirpy just so she would dispel the notion that something was bothering me.

The evening ended well enough. Dinner was pleasant, as was the walk and the conversations afterward. We all went to bed at a decent time. The next morning we ate breakfast, chatted some more and made my dad some coffee and gave him snacks for the drive back to Stan's, and eventually back to Europe. He hugged me extra tight, looked at me long and hard and said "Marcus, just call whenever, I'll always pick up. Bye to both of you for now." And he left.

CHAPTER 17

SURPRISES AD NAUSEAM

In the morning I went to work and Alicia stayed home. She started her maternity leave two months before the due delivery date. For her now seven months pregnant it was imperative that she stop working and stay at home more so she could kick up her feet and rest. Apparently a woman was eligible to start her maternity leave twelve weeks prior to the delivery date. Maternity leave accounted for fifteen weeks and then parental leave would go on for another thirty-five weeks post-birth, for a total of fifty weeks. All covered by employment insurance. So we took advantage of what the system offered.

My day at work was horrible. I was obsessing, analyzing. I didn't know what to do. I couldn't think of a way forward, I had no clue how to resolve the situation I was finding myself in. Was my father lying? Was he telling the truth and I was going insane?? Both possibilities were equally terrifying. Why would he lie? Was I really that mentally unstable to start going insane?! One option was as likely as the other. And both were horrifying.

My productivity was nonexistent and there was very little of it to begin with on any given day. I sat and stared and listened to the keyboards dancing at everyone else's computers. People were proving their worth and I was wasting time and daydreaming. I had to snap out of whatever was wrong with me and figure out a way how to function as any more days like these at my company and people would start to get wise that I'm not doing jack shit. My boss for one.

I went to the gym right after I was done. I had to get some physical activity in me. I missed most of the week what with my dad coming and going and me continuously feeling as if I was on the brink of getting sick. Weight lifting and punching the bags were going to clear my mind no matter what, but whether or not a constructive thought helping me get out of this mess pops up in my head afterward was yet to be determined.

It didn't really. I felt better. But that was mainly adrenalin and blood flowing and my whole body screaming from the exercise. It was temporary, but a welcomed relief nevertheless. It's a cocktail designed to disperse fear. Thankfully it works. But as far as anything else I had nothing. My life had to continue. For starters, I had to figure out whether that whole conversation with my father weeks ago even happened. That would be the biggest challenge. The existence of Jeff and Shauna, the organization, etc, I could confirm easily. And I will as soon as I get home from the training.

Alicia was moving around the house slowly. She was getting bigger and bigger and it was harder and more awkward for her to do the basic tasks. Less than two months to go. She also tired out much more quickly than usual. Overall, she was doing great, she was a trooper and she carried the pregnancy well. There were more difficult pregnancies with far more complications than ours.

I came home, exchanged a few words with her and went to shower. I came back downstairs and ate the dinner she prepared. While I was eating I received a message from dad saying that he arrived safely at Stan's and that on Sunday, three days from now, he would be flying back to Europe.

"So how about that Shauna and that incredible gift she gave us?" I blurted out between bites as I couldn't think of anything wittier or less random to say since I was trying to satisfy my obsession that Shauna at least exists. I couldn't talk to Alicia about Jeff as she had no idea who that was.

"What made you think of her?" she replied. Touché I thought, since my question was completely out of the blue. And we haven't spoken of Shauna for some time.

"Oh I don't know, she just pops into my mind every once in a while. What an incredibly nice thing she did for us and all that. And I suppose now that you are getting closer and closer to the delivery date, I remind myself of that more and more."

"Yeah, she is something. A gift from God or someone or something looking after us for sure. It's a phenomenal boost for us. It's just weird that you all of a sudden want to speak of her especially in such a glowing light considering you were the one telling me to calm my enthusiasm about her." That was her reply. To the point, but very dry, matter of fact and with absolutely no excitement in the voice as she said it. Plus she used the opportunity nicely to call me out on my bullshit. The way she said it also sounded like she didn't want to keep talking about it. I muttered something along the lines of "Yup" like Hank in 'King of the Hill'.

I didn't say much else. I just kept eating. At least I got my confirmation that Shauna existed. I suppose soon I needed to contact Jeff and Shauna, or just Jeff and see what the next steps are in my new found 'membership'. And I was going about it alone. My father had nothing to do with them. It felt like I joined a sports team in a way except that I was fairly certain we weren't going to do a round of push-ups to warm up as the first order of business. The thought of contacting them sent shivers down my spine. I knew I would procrastinate as long as I could and what would more than likely end up happening is that they would again contact me. I could only hope that they will at least have the courtesy to call me and not barge into my office or my house or kidnap my stupid ass out of my bed in the middle of the night. Will they be angry at my delayed resurfacing? I fixated on something else now which previously popped into my mind. Maybe a woman named Shauna exists...but that doesn't make her a member of some crazy-ass organization. Maybe she is just a regular woman, a human being that reached out to help us. Literally like she described it, it was a draw, her company picked random places of business and my wife's was one of them. She has a regular job, regular life, nothing out of the ordinary. Maybe Jeff doesn't exist. Or maybe he does but he is just a regular professor at the College. And I found him on some random Internet or LinkedIn search in my quest to speak with someone else. But maybe I never spoke to anyone. Maybe I didn't speak to anyone at King's University either. Perhaps everything that happened outside of the realm of my obsessive curiosity about death and disease was pure fantasy. Could it be?? Could I have fantasized the whole...science fiction expect of it? The part about the asteroids and proteins from outer space? Hahaha, the thought of it all made me more sure that I did. The bizarre meeting with Jeff at Jim Mortons, etc.. There is no way any of that could be true and real. I didn't quite know whether to feel relieved and happy about that prospect or scared about the fact that I might be going insane. Completely insane. Because that was the only alternative to all of that being a fantasy conjured up by my brain.

I finished eating and I got up and brought my dishes to the sink. "It's ok Marcus, I'll wash the dishes", said Alicia, "you go and relax."

"Are you sure? You've been on your feet a lot. Let me do it." I said.

"I insist," she said, as she blew me a kiss. Alright I thought and went to sit down by my laptop. I was surfing the net randomly, a bit of politics (no World War 3 yet), a bit of history, civil projects, nonsense tabloid gossip. Alicia finished the dishes and came to the living room, sat down on the couch next to me. We decided against a walk outside as the weather was shit. I was expecting her to pick up her book and start reading. Or turn on the TV, or her iPad and start watching something. "Thanks for doing the dishes," I said. "No problem" she answered. I kept surfing the Internet unabated for at least good five minutes before I noticed as I randomly turned my head here and there, in the periphery of my sight, that Alicia wasn't reading anything nor was she turning on the TV. She wasn't on her iPad either. She was simply staring at me. Sometimes she did that, she knew it made me feel uncomfortable and then we would both start laughing and the more I would tell her to stop the more she would continue staring, blowing me kisses and laughing even harder. But this time it was different. She wasn't smiling or joking or blowing kisses or winking. She just stared. She didn't seem mad or sad, just very monolithic. Statuesque. Monotone. After a while I had to ask her what's up.

"Is everything ok?" I said.

"Yes," she answered. Again, very dry, automated.

"Are you sure?" I asked again.

"As I said, everything is fine." she replied. But with no intense emotion. It was just flat.

"Ok. Then how come you are not reading or on your iPad or watching TV? How come you are just sitting there and staring at me? Are you trying to see who breaks out laughing first?" As I asked I intermittently looked at her and back to the computer. Now I was fully turned towards the computer as I didn't even expect her to answer.

"So you never really fully explained what you spoke to your dad about for almost three hours when you guys were out that day he came back." she randomly began. She had a tendency to periodically bring up old topics, or start conversations based on themes already discussed which she felt weren't covered thoroughly enough prior. Sometimes when she was bored and wanted to chat with me it was a good way to start a conversation. I was not in the mood to chat however at the moment, let alone about the time spent with my dad. So I tried to brush it off quickly.

"Oh you know not much to talk about. Family, work, bashing family members with gossip, you know the usual. And then repeat it over and over again. Plus Stan just bought a new car so that was a good distraction from the usual topics. Again though, with plenty of repetitions. How he made him get the car, convinced him, otherwise Stan never would have come around to it, bla, bla. Even though I was the one who told him about the car. You know, usual dad."

Even explaining that much seemed like too much of an effort for me. And I was saying it while I was staring at the laptop. Rude. After not seeing her all day. It was an easy lie to tell her, she would obviously not think anything of it nor second guess it.

"I'm sorry that the news of your father being an already existing member of the organization and then finding out that he isn't stressed you out so much Marcus. I can only imagine what a shock that was for you and what you must have been going through inside this whole time." she said.

I can't quite describe anything anymore. Although I suppose the stress I usually feel in my chest when I'm in full-blown anxiety

I now felt in my back as well. I also felt my heartbeat in my back. Maybe the stress of what I was experiencing caused my internal organs to migrate in my chest cavity. It was a creepy feeling for sure, I felt as if I had nothing at my front anymore, including my lungs. Seconds went by and I felt that I couldn't breathe properly either. Now the heart palpitations set in and they were so intense that my heart seemed to have been jumping back and forth from the back to the front, in a constant, perpetual loop.

I suppose now would have been the right time to turn away from my computer and face Alicia, after the entirety of the verbiage that just came out of her mouth. That would have been the logical, face your problems head-on kind of thing to do.

Instead I felt her get up and walk over to sit next to me. She grabbed my forearm that was resting on the sidearm of the couch with both of her hands.

"Marcus look at me." she said. In all honesty, I was afraid to. What if I looked at her and she looked like the girl from *The Exorcist* with her head spinning hypnotically like a carousel. Now I felt her hands move up slowly towards my face as she cupped it and was beginning to turn it towards her. I faced her. She was doing her best to put on her most loving and warm, smiling face. I was desperately trying not to throw up all over her as I uttered the words:

"Alicia, what did you just say?" out of my mouth. And I did throw up a little bit, I felt it in the back of my throat but I swallowed it back down like a champ. Heartburn set in as I did that, fuck me.

"Baby, there is a lot of things we have to discuss." she said. Well, that was an understatement of the century I thought.

"Please know that I love you, I've always loved you, and I would never let anything happen to you or our family, our child." she was now going on. Wait a minute I thought, shouldn't I be the one saying these things to her after she finds out that I joined some crazy-ass cult without telling her in a spectacularly irresponsible way in one of those fantastic moments when she least expected it?!!?! Something didn't make sense here. I felt the tables were turning and the world where I was an adventurous, drunken, irresponsible prick was long gone. I was officially taking on the role of the responsible wife.

"Alicia, what the fuck are you talking about? How do you know about the organization?"

A bit more puke-up came up into my throat. Ah, delicious Pad Thai I had earlier. Not good for heartburn. I was on the verge of getting up and taking some swigs of the whiskey bottle from the liquor cabinet but she had a firm hold of my arm and face so I couldn't move. She was surprisingly strong too. Perhaps she was an assassin...

"Marcus your father isn't a member. I am a member. I have been for years. You got steered toward it all because of me."

I somehow managed to pry myself free from her grip and stand up. I couldn't sit anymore, plus my ass was sore from the little uncomfortable chair that was used to sit on at the computer desk. And my underwear was drenched in cold sweat. At the same time I was painfully aware that standing for me was probably a bad idea at the moment since there was a good chance I could pass out and collapse on the brand new carpet we bought for when the baby comes. Hopefully however, I would hit my head against the corner of the wooden cabinet and die instantly. Fingers crossed.

"Come on Marcus, please sit down. Sit next to me." she was imploring. She now stood up and was heading towards me. It was a bit of a comic scene considering how big she was getting, she looked like a big balloon gently floating in my direction. I was stepping back as I didn't want to risk collapsing on top of her and her pregnant belly. As I backed up I felt the big flat-screen TV behind me. I had nowhere else to go.

"Marcus come here. Talk to me. As shocked as you are feeling right now I assure you when you hear what I have to say you will calm down. The nightmare and the stress you've felt for months now will go away. I swear to you. And we will move on in the best possible way imaginable. You will understand everything. And you will make sense of everything. And you will see that it had to be this way, there was no other choice and you will see why. It will all work out for the best." She was staring at me with eyes bulging out while smiling at the same time. Her attempt to come across as reassuring was a tremendous failure and she was scaring the crap out of me.

"Alicia you are freaking me right the fuck out." I could feel my voice breaking as I spoke. I was a prepubescent all over again. I had no confidence left in me. It was a familiar feeling I've almost grown accustomed to over the last few months since all this shit was started, by me. Maybe my wish wasn't to discover new things interesting in life, maybe it was to become a scared toddler all over again. Mission accomplished. My heart was beating fast and all over the place. It felt as if it tried to hide in various and different cavities of my body with little success. I wish I could hide. Or turn back time. Or wake up. But the current reality I was finding myself in was persistent and stubborn in its duration and...realness, for lack of a better word. I kept pacing around the room in random sporadic patterns like a confused fly.

"I don't understand anything." I continued with that redundant and obvious statement. I didn't know what else to say.

"Come sit next to me Marcus." she kept repeating. The last thing on this Earth I wanted to do right now was to sit and be still.

"I can't sit. And I can't sit next to you. I'm having a hard time connecting the things you are saying to the body that's saying it, which is you. I mean, what the hell is going on?"

"Ok, ok, in a nutshell. And then we will go into detail. If you want, or we can discuss the details some other time if you'd like more time. I am a member of the organization Marcus. So are my parents. I joined right after University. As soon as I met you and listened to you talk about any relevant matter, whether politics, or science or science fiction or philosophy, history, whatever I knew you were the right man for me and that eventually I had to steer you to become a part of this other world I belong to. But it had to be gradual, it had to be spontaneous, you had to guide yourself, I could not make it seem in any way that I am leading you towards it. But knowing you I was sure that you would get there. And you did! Your thirst and your restlessness and relentlessness got you here, as I knew they would. My parents knew it too. You were far beyond driven and you could never let go of the notion that you need more in life. And here we are."

"You know Jeff? And Shauna? That whole show with Shauna, that was all a ploy? A theatre production?" I was at least regaining some strength in my voice now.

"Yes, and they know my parents. Old acquaintances." she answered.

"I guess you obviously know about my meeting with Jeff at the College?"

"Yes, I know it all. We had to let you take your own way and do whatever you needed to do to get to this point in time and place. I tried staying out of your way and pretended that I was oblivious to the whole thing as much as I could."

"So my research, about life and disease and all that, I guess you were all just observing me, like everyone observed Truman in *The Truman Show.*"

"Yes. We have many means and resources. Once you got as far as you did we helped you along a bit. But only because you got yourself as far as you did. And because we knew you wouldn't stop." To hear my pregnant wife use the words 'We' but not in the context of her and I was eerily traumatizing. It was downright creepy as hell.

"You sound like you are from the Twilight Zone. And as if you are an entirely different person." I said.

"Is that fair Marcus? Is it? This entire time you went on this journey thinking you were all alone on it. You purposefully didn't include me and were willing to go on like that for years. Forever. What if it had been just you the whole way and I was truly clueless and had no involvement with any of this? You would have been fine with all of that. So don't be a hypocrite."

Well, she had me there. Honestly I didn't know whether I was angry, scared or jealous that my little secret which I was going to hold onto for just myself was not a secret at all. I was no James Bond in disguise. My wife already beat me to the punch. And I was pouting. That's what I was doing. I was an experiment. She's been bullshitting me the entire time.

"Alicia you've held this from me for years. For years! The entire time we've been together. You never gave out a hint, I never suspected anything. You knew these past few months, obviously since you and your parents and everyone else 'monitored' me as you say, how much I struggled with all of this, how much I broke it all down inside. I thought about the impacts of what I was doing, and I thought about the risks. I went along with it anyways, because quite frankly I couldn't help myself, but I did this in no casual matter. I gave a fuck, regardless of what you may think. You kept this secret for a decade without giving a shit! Without blinking an eye! And you want to play tit for tat right now??"

"I know" she replied, "I know you struggled. And this is not about blaming anyone for anything. Or pointing out double standards. We have to process this and God willing move forward."

Well of course she would say this and want to squash an

argument quickly since she was the one with her hands in the cookie jar. I was just dancing around the jar like a court jester nothing more.

"I don't understand" I went back to something else now. "What about the whole situation with my father? I had that conversation with him! And then he claimed we never had it! What the fuck was all that?"

She was silent a little while. Rearranging her face and contemplating how to explain which would inevitably be some involvement of the organization with that experience as well. I was witnessing my wife of ten years trying to figure out how to 'work' me over!! Wonderful! Good trust reinforcement for the continuation of our marriage.

"The whole thing was staged. Your father's voice was computer modified and produced while an agent of ours did the talking. It was an instantaneous voice-over. We made it so he would sound like your father the whole time. The call was from us. We knew you needed a final push to make you join. We knew that had you known your father was part of it you would cross that line. It would make you feel safe and ready to take on the risk. It had to be your father, we knew it couldn't have been any other member of your family. They simply don't have the same pull with you."

Yeah, as usual, most questions asked by me come back with horrific and terrifying answers. This was just such a case. I felt like I was going through menopause at the moment with my body experiencing all sorts of rapid temperature changes. I would not have been surprised if it turned out that I was changing color during the process too. Green, red, yellow, like a fucking traffic light.

"Can you stop using the word 'We'.....it's creeping the shit out of me as I am so painfully aware who you are talking about and that it's not referring to you and me." I somehow squeezed out of my pathetic shell of a body, squealing like somebody stepped on me.

"Ok, I won't use the word 'we'. It sort of became a force of habit before I even met you. I'm sorry."

"It became a force of habit? But you've been with me for ten years Alicia, didn't the phrase 'we' become synonymous to us? How quickly you managed to attach it back to the organization and yourself is indicative and shocking." I was in full-blown argument mode now, it was a much better state than the one where I was shitting myself senseless with anxiety. And I was also more familiar with it. Oh who am I kidding I was familiar with all states of human condition related to misery.

"Again, I'm sorry, ok? Now that I had to come clean with you I reverted back to a different frame of mind. Just to explain everything. Quite frankly Marcus, it doesn't matter anymore, 'we' refers to all of us now. You, me, one day our little girl. 'We' is us. You are part of 'we'. You know you will always mean more to me than any organization, don't you? Please don't get hung up on technicalities and phrases, we have so much to discuss."

I was smelling bullshit and it wasn't the one filling my underwear.

"Alicia, you can stare at me all you want like Hare freaking Krishna. If anything you are making me more paranoid. I find you barely recognizable. The bottom line is after years of lying to me, or fine, not telling me the whole truth about yourself, you've decided to deceive me so I can join some fucking cult!" I was yelling now, another one of my familiar postures. "You faked my father's involvement!"

"You wanted to join Marcus, you joined all by yourself. You found Jeff, you did the research, the leg work, you've felt the hunger and thirst for something different and the utter boredom of everyday life! That was all you. The organization, myself included, knew that you would never stop digging for a way to satisfy your needs and join eventually, we just didn't know when. We needed to stimulate you as big things are happening and we don't have time to wait. Sorry for using the word 'we' again, I meant the organization. You'll see why we had to move this thing along."

"How the hell do you think I'm feeling right now Alicia?? Let's say I attempt to hear you out. If you thought that me knowing that a member of my immediate family was a member, my father especially, would help me join, and you know me so well and my paranoia, how in the fuck did you think I would feel once I joined and found out that it was a lie and that none of my family are members?? Eh?? You 'knew' I would join eventually anyway?! That's bullshit! What you knew was that concocting a lie such as that my father was already inside would make me join. I was manipulated into this!" I was now standing with eyeballs bulging and veins popping.

"Marcus can you please not yell? Our neighbors have enough trauma from our Balkan way of speaking and arguing as is."

She even found an opportunity to lecture during this surreal convo like my father did with his 'I'm still your father' and respect bullshit.

"Are you seriously going to fucking focus on my yelling at a moment like this???"

"Just please don't yell, that's all I ask. You have the right to be mad, I understand where you are coming from but just don't yell. For numerous reasons."

I chose not to dignify that with a response. I sort of threw up my arms at her to give her an indication of 'fine, continue speaking'.

"I just figured after everything you've been through you would want to put all this to rest. Quite frankly I thought and hoped that once you found out I was a member that would be as good as you knowing anyone else from your family was inside. I am your family Marcus, aren't I? Don't you trust me? Isn't knowing that I'm already on the inside even better than finding out your father is?"

It was a bullshit thing she was now pulling. Turning this on me and issues of my mistrust of anyone under the Sun, including her. What a time to throw that in. She was a clever manipulator.

"Alicia, this is nonsense. Don't pull this crap now. Not now! I am way too fucked up to be listening to this. If anything you are making me trust you way less! And as I said my paranoia is at record levels at the moment. You know me so well. You thought me finding out now it was you and not dad who was a member would help me along even more. So why didn't you come out at least a couple of weeks ago when I was debating to join and told me then you were a member? And never involved my father?! Well? If you wanted to see if me knowing you were in would get me to join. I would have respected and trusted you way more that way. No, instead you manipulated me and lied knowing full well someone like my father would have more weight with me only now to come and say oh hell Marcus just flip a switch, it was me all along, and show your trust in me by jumping up and down with joy! You are full of shit girl."

She seemed to catch on that her trick didn't fly. So she retreated.

"Ok, alright. You are right. It was a stupid theory I went on. I wanted to be sure that you joined. So involving your family I felt would be a sure way. But then once you did I thought you could handle the fact that it was a ploy and that you would be happy that you found out I was a member instead. Ok? Common, I was wrong. I couldn't wait to tell you Marcus! To have this conversation. I didn't handle this the best way. But again I only did it because I know how much better our lives will be because of this. And you pretty much thought the same thing after talking to Jeff, you know you did. You were just hesitating. I helped you stop stalling. Am I not speaking the truth? Step back for a minute. When you thought your father was with the organization you felt you made the greatest decision in the world. Up until today. What's different now?"

I didn't like where this conversation was going, or how it was going. I had nothing to come back with. And everything I was saying to her she could say right back to me. It was one of those circle jerk arguments. I lied to her, I wasn't going to tell her anything maybe ever, I felt special and unique and it was going to be my little secret. And now, more than anything else, I was spazzing out because Alicia already beat me to the punch. I was livid with a child-like temper tantrum. And my wife, unlike her husband, couldn't wait for me to join so this would be something we could do together. I would have done it alone reveling in the fact that no one else would have known. Well, only dad and me.

"I...Alicia , look" I started. I had nothing.

"Marcus, I couldn't wait for us to be in this thing together. You would have done it all alone and not tell me anything about it. You had no clue what you were getting yourself into and what potential danger this could have brought on to us, our kids. I know exactly what I'm in. And I will bring you up to speed on all of it every step of the way. And I'm sure and certain about all of it."

I felt like a woman in distress being desperately comforted. I felt emasculated, manipulated, humiliated. My man ego was shedding in the wind like dandelion seeds.

Moments of silence went by. I told her I needed some time to think. She said fine. I drank lots of beer and went out for a cigar. She watched old episodes of Friends and kept periodically staring at me. The feelings in my head were so intertwined and mangled that I had no clue what to make out of any of it. I hated myself, I hated her, then I hated myself even more for hating her. I doubted 'us', our marriage. Then I hated my life and ever being born. Then I spent about an hour thinking of what in the world my parents would say if they knew what a pile of shit I was in. Now I understood my father's bewilderment at my ranting. Of course he would never have joined a thing like this, cult, organization, brotherhood, whatever, any more than he would have joined the mob. What would they think of Alicia if they knew of her involvement? Of her whole family? I can't believe I fell for that. And what do I make of Alicia 's lying and hiding this 'truth' all these years? Do I just let it all slide because hey I would have done the same to her or do I dwell deeper, do I doubt her entirely? Do I believe when she says she couldn't wait for me to join along? How did she hide this so well? When did she go to meetings?? What else has she been hiding? What else is she involved with? Is our entire marriage based on lies? Is it all a sham? I lie, she lies? And now we have a kid on the way...good Lord.

I couldn't keep going on this way. Same old modus operandi for 35 fucking years now. Constantly freaking out about something, constantly analyzing and splitting hairs. Second-guessing. Immediately regretting the decisions I just made. Believing that the only way shit works out in life in a non-disastrous way is if I obsess about it first for months and come up with every possible worst-case scenario I can think of. If I live it in my head as if it was actually happening to me. The toll on my mind, body and soul must have been tremendous. I had to snap out of it. Otherwise, I was going to stroke out at the age of fucking 40. And it did no good, it was a failed theory, clearly, evidently, life was full of unpredictable twists and turns that I could not prepare for. Now, had I thought of the possibility that Alicia might have been a member ahead, then she probably wouldn't have been...yeah right.

This whole thing with this 'organization' or whatever, got started because I was trying to break out of the mold I was in for most of my life. I had to keep reminding myself of that. It started because I decided to chase what at first seemed an imaginary carrot down an even more imaginary rabbit hole. And it turned into a tangible and real discovery. Discovery I've been praying for my entire life. And now that it's here I'm going to do what?? Pray again and this time that it never happened!?!? Obsess about Alicia's white lies (big ass white lies but still)? And go back to the same MO as before, and spend another 35 years in the same way?!?! How long did I fucking think I was going to live for?? Till I was 300??? No, I had to keep marching on this path.

"Alicia" I began, decently drunk and stinking of a Nicaraguan cigar, several hours after we last spoke. Clearly she was nervous about what I would come back with and couldn't go to bed at her usual bedtime. She waited up for me. It was 2AM. She was always an early sleeper, since she'd been pregnant even more so, but tonight she was wide-eyed and awake like an owl. And maybe I enjoyed making her squirm. I continued: "I am a liar. And you knew it. They were all white lies, sure, but nevertheless they were still lies. And I was willing to keep them up. About this, about that, maybe it gave me thrills that I needed to give me that extra bit of zest in life. Now it turns out, you are a liar too. And a good one. A remarkable one. A much more seasoned and accomplished one. Much more intricate, involved. Oscar-winning one. And this is news to me. A discovery. And, as hypocritical as I may sound, not a good discovery no matter how many ways you can throw it back at me. But fuck all of that aside for now. Fuck us, our marriage and our family. Fucking everything regular and traditional and safe in our life right now in the sense let's just put it away and not even think about it for the time being. Let's focus on the irregular. The irregular that I've dug up through my incessant boredom and shit disturbing and that which you have apparently been a part of for years. The irregular that's in the long term supposed to enlighten me and give me answers to questions I've been asking since I can recall myself. Let's go for it, and let's make the best of it. You and I will deal with...'you and I' later, and step by step. We'll see what the future has in store."

The entire spiel came out a bit slurred. I was righteously inebriated. On any other given day Alicia would call me a drunken moron and a buffoon but today she was quiet. I was getting away with it due to the situation at hand. It was a small satisfaction considering the gravity of the situation I was finding myself in.

"So" I continued, "I suppose we best call Jeff and Shauna or whoever else you'd like to contact and let's set up a meeting. Let me finally see what I have gotten myself into and what new world I've stumbled upon."

She stared at me. Her eyes gradually became glossy with tears. Then she ever so carefully and lightly approached and came in for a hug. She was noticeably tired and exhausted. She should not have been up this late. I was trying to keep my stoic veneer but pretty soon the smell of her hair, the softness of her clothes and the feeling of her pregnant belly on mine made me start to loosen my guard. I couldn't help it. And quite frankly I suppose there was nothing really there for me to pout about. She lied, I lied. One day I'll probably dwell more into her and what else potentially she is hiding, but today was not one of those days. We had shit to do. I wanted to finally see what I've signed up for. Me, me, me, looking into myself more one day and what a self-centred piece of shit I am should also probably go on the to-do list.

We stayed like that for what seemed like an eternity. By the end I kissed her and completely lost my attitude. I've spent 99.9% of my entire life in two seemingly perpetual states, anger and fear. As if life spared me any trials because of this. The other 0.1% I spent bored. I couldn't take it anymore. So I decided to make a drastic change. And here I was adamant about tackling...the boredom part. Yup, priorities in order as always. I wasn't even going to attempt tackling anger and fear. Probably never. Now was time for something different in my life. And as I said before sometimes a change even for the worse is better than no change at all.

We broke up the hug but still held each other's hands. After a few more moments Alicia spoke.

"Let's call my parents. Before anyone else."

That sounded like an annoying thing to do. But it made me feel safer for some reason. This is my extended family I suppose, I trusted these people...once upon a time. They could put a sense of familiarity to this whole thing. But then wait a minute, haven't they been lying to me as well all this time too.....Whatever, let's talk to them I thought.

"Ok," I said.

"Ok," she answered.

We sat down on the couch and dialed their number. When they picked up it was evident they already knew the purpose of the call.

"Eyyy, you finally popped your cherry!!" quipped my father-in-law. It came across as reassuring, like we were buddies in high school. We were all on speaker. I thought I would be outrageously angry but somehow the whole experience was soothing. What would be the point of me being angry anymore anyways? These were the same people I've known for years, talked about everything under the Sun, but now with an added dimension. They still meant me well right? It turned out my in-laws were members for decades, since their days of living in Europe. They got tremendous help from the organization when they emigrated to Canada apparently, running away from the Communist regime in the Soviet Union back in the eighties. Now I knew where the inspiration of the 'help the poor immigrant' came from when they spun the whole my father was a member story. The entire conversation was overwhelming reassurances from them. My life will change for the better, new horizons will open and my mind will be more satisfied than ever before in my life, don't be afraid or second guess. Got it, sure.

It was eerily calm in the house after the conversation with Alicia's parents. Apparently back to business as usual. She was peeling her nightly orange as she did every night since becoming pregnant (better than craving chocolate fudge) and I was sitting around doing nothing. It was now 3 AM. All those discoveries and all those months and we sat around like it was any other weeknight. Hey we are expecting a baby, hey we uncovered a secret sect and are all now members, hey World War 3 just broke out. Oh well, after a while, the routine goes on, the most adamant and resilient of life's components. Dogs are barking, the caravan goes on.

"Marcus you need to contact Jeff. You are most comfortable with him and essentially he has reared you into this organization. I hope at least now that you are becoming more comfortable with the fact that my family and I have been a part of it for a big part of our lives, I hope you can use that as reassurance, not as a reason to mistrust. Still, I feel as though you should officially get introduced to it through Jeff." Alicia said as we were turning off the lights and going to bed. Like she was listing off items to buy at the grocery store. I was utterly hangover. I also felt as though I was coming down with something, cold, sore throat, something. I was trying to play along cool as best as I could, although now I was yet again drifting back into the whole...WHAT IN THE FUCK WAS GOING ON HERE mode. It would be so nice to wake up right now.

"Yeah, I'll do it tomorrow, I'll set up a meeting. I can't think anymore right now, and I can't analyze or dissect anything else other than what's in front of me. And that's the organization. I've heard that word so many times it's lost all meaning. I need to see now what I'm part of."

We kissed and hugged and held each other again. We were both dead tired. I could tell that she was exhausted. I felt bad about yelling seeing as how she was pregnant and all but it was what it was. The hug was too long. I was internally squirming. I wanted to just go to sleep, wake up and get this shit going. Jeff, me, unicorns, show me places, the subjects, the themes, the rituals, the sacrifice altars, I don't care. Just let's get on with it already.

I could not sleep for the life of me. Tonight I was staring at

Alicia wondering who the hell she actually was as opposed to asking myself what she would do if she found out about my side project. How quickly life turns around completely. At least I went to bed knowing full well that I wasn't going to sleep so I didn't even attempt to. The constant revelations and developments in my life these days were condensed events that certain people don't experience in their entire lifetimes. The twists. The surreal. The walks along the edge of the precipice of normal and accepted. The life of a shit disturber. This is what I was now officially living. My motto was to bend until yield. And everything in life was already too easy to destroy while arduously difficult to build and compose. Hell, I felt I was so deep into manure I was finding myself being envious of average criminals. Even they weren't this deep into the rabbit hole. Moments later I dispersed that notion, these people were awaiting unknown fates and hiding for their lives. I was still out and about and functioning without the arm of the law being after me. But how much more could I take? And how many more twists and turns? How many more surprises? I suppose if I told myself to expect a new and drastic development every day then maybe they wouldn't happen so often and I would be pleasantly surprised that they didn't. Maybe I could tell myself to expect a sudden development three times a day then if it doesn't happen at all that day or maybe only once then I would actually be.....ecstatic! And not feel dread any longer.

It was a night of rewinding and forwarding the camera film back and forth, and back and forth and then back again. Again. How it all started for me with that one drive back from Ottawa. When I decided to take my obsessive-compulsive nature that I've been living with since birth not in the direction of attempting to cure it, to turn my life away from such tendencies, but instead I decided to put it into overdrive, to empty the entire brand new canister of oil onto the barbecue and see how big the flames can get.

And now I had a forest fire. Forest fire the size of Canada. This was a classic example of what happens when you have an itching tick, you scratch your skin so hard till it bleeds. No turning back now.

It took a while of lying in that bed before I finally got to thinking about my parents. It was only a matter of time before I would. What on Earth would they say if they found out about my transgressions of the past months? What the hell am I going to say to my father after accusing him of having a phone conversation with me and lying about it? I had to follow up with him and soon. If I don't he would follow up with me for sure. I will be lucky if he didn't say anything to my mother. She would freak out and her blood pressure would go through the roof. She would conjure up infinite scenarios about the trouble I'm in, and for the first time ever, she wouldn't even be that far off. If anything, her imagination wouldn't even do justice to the actual truth. Maybe I should have asked freaking Alicia how she would advise breaking something like this to my parents or how to at least placate my father after that showdown about the phone conversation seeing as how this whole mess and involving him was her brilliant idea. I was again livid at her for alchemying that whole thing up. Angry at her about holding that secret from me all these years, even though I guess I didn't have the right...Or did I?

And that's how my night was spent. In fear, then some in-between state of mind between fear and anger, then anger. And they spun and rotated, budding in ahead of each other. Like day and night cycles. Dawn was coming up now, the morning light was starting earlier and earlier, summer was approaching. The birds started to chirp. It was morning. And as I completely gave up and came to terms that the entire night was wasted, coming to peace with that combined with being so utterly exhausted from thinking and booze, I passed out for fifteen minutes before my alarm went off. Like with everything in life, it's only when you let go that things that you actually want happen.

The touch of sleep was enough for me. I was grateful. It was plenty, as I already came to terms that I wasn't going to sleep at all and I would have functioned regardless. So this was an added bonus. I jumped out of the bed ready for...something. Alicia was in a peculiarly lovey-dovey mood expressing elaborate acts of affection and making it seem that everything I said that morning was incredibly interesting, funny and she was overly thankful for everything I did, even though I did nothing other than move out of her way a couple of times. She made breakfast and my lunch for work. And I was off.

CHAPTER 18

ACQUIRED DAWN

I could barely wait until the first coffee break at work to call Jeff. We were allowed to take brakes, coffee or otherwise whenever we felt like I just purposely made myself wait until 10 AM. I tested myself in such ways every so often, discipline and patience in times of utmost anxiety. It worked wonders for my character, not so much for my arteries and blood pressure. Mr. Madison must be pretty antsy at this point I thought, I was supposed to check in weeks ago. That was the agreement after my momentous initiation into their society. Well, there was no particular consensus on a timeframe they simply told me to take some time, think, get comfortable and get back to them. I started using the word 'society' in my head instead of 'organization', the repetition of which made me nauseous. It might as well have been a drinking and orgy frat club at this point since I had no clue what I was getting myself into. Although considering that Alicia of all people was a member, I figured it probably wasn't. And Jeff most likely knew of the tribulations I was undergoing since my initiation so he was patient somewhere waiting for me to contact him. And I was right.

"Hello Jeff, I hope you've been well" every word sounded idiotic but I had no clue what else to say.

"Marcus, I'm glad you've finally come up for air. I am fine. And how are you feeling now after all is said and done? Lots of novelty for you I'm sure. And a lot has been said, and found out."

He sounded like he could care less how I was doing, he was just fake courteois. It was evident he didn't wish to get into any specifics of my soap opera life over the past few weeks, private affairs, conversations with my wife even though he obviously was aware, it simply didn't interest him. He sounded like he wanted to get on with business or whatever agenda he had. Enough fucking around. I felt the same way.

"I am as well as I can or ever will be", I replied.

"That's good enough for me young man. I hope you agree that we should get on with letting you know exactly and precisely how you got our attention and what's in store for you, what do you think?" short and sweet like pulling back foreskin. Painful but necessary. One day I should really write my own book of analogies.

"Let's get on with it Jeff. Come whatever may. At the end of the day I wanted this, be it potentially for better or worse. Like with everything in life, diversity is the art of stimulation." Oh bravo Marcus. "So let's cut to the chase." I said that like I was James Cagney. Indeed, I was aware of how feverishly overzealous I was in my need to stop being bored with life's routines.

So, I just pulled the mother of all attempts to end my boredom with life once and for all. I joined a cult. Let's call it for what it fucking was. And may God help me.

"Marcus have you ever heard of the Bradbury Neutrino

Observatory?" began my matter of fact buddy Jeff. As it just so freaking happened I have heard of it.

"Yes, I have. The previous company I worked for, my manager's father was one of the scientists that worked there and won a Nobel Prize in Physics for research with neutrinos. Very impressive. The whole office knew about it. It's a deep, underground laboratory. A couple of kilometers beneath the surface I believe. That's how I know about it." I answered.

"Hahaha, well informed young man" quipped Jeff.

"Well, not really. Even though I like to read about a bunch of random things on the Internet on any given day I have to admit this one was a fluke of a revelation for me. I only read a bit more about the lab after my office told me about this story about my manager's father. Pretty random. But still incredible and fascinating."

"Incredible is one way of describing it. Well, I'll get deeper into it then. Hahaha, 'deeper', get it?" Jeff was amusing himself with his fantastic cheesy puns. I think it's been a few months for me since I laughed.

"So anyways, the Bradbury Neutrino Observatory or BNO began operating exclusively as a neutrino observatory. Since its inception several older experiments have since ended and several new ones have since begun. There are about five major research experiments currently ongoing, mainly to do with the Universe, collectively under the umbrella of BNOLAB or Bradbury Neutrino Observatory Laboratory, even though research has since expanded beyond neutrinos. The facility has been extensively expanded. Several impressive civil engineering feats of innovation have been accomplished to successfully enlarge the cavity 2km underground, essentially carve it out more, and not having the whole thing cave in on itself. I'm sure you will appreciate it since you are a civil engineer. Anyways, upon enlargement, and based on reasoning I will further explain, a new laboratory branched off and has since been constructed. Funded entirely by our organization. The program is called NTLab. Short for Non-Terrestrial Laboratory."

"UFO research? Looking for signs of extraterrestrial life forms I assume?" I blurted out.

"Amongst other things yes, but not your everyday UFO research. This is not like SETI or Breakthrough Initiatives. We are not on the surface, literally or metaphorically, in any way. Everything we do is underground. And our research is very specific to certain things, we don't do broad, we narrow in."

"So I guess we are now free to openly talk about the matters you mentioned all those weeks ago at Jim Mortons coffee shop?" I asked.

"Yes, we are. But only this much I will share over this secure phone line for the time being. The rest in person. And on location. In Bradbury. We've disclosed enough over the phone."

"If that's the case haven't you already disclosed too much over the phone? You just mentioned a bunch of details in just so many sentences." I could notice myself sounding rude and condescending. I didn't care, I've earned it over the last few months of stress and mental anguish.

"Marcus what weekend works for you?" he ignored my insolence and motored on.

"What is the plan?" I asked.

"I want you to come to Bradbury. I'm taking you on a tour of the Observatory. Costs will be born by us. I need you to be here for the entire weekend."

I figured I was free any weekend. Pending there are no complications with Alicia and the pregnancy. I kept him waiting long enough while I was meditating, debating and ruminating all these months so I didn't want to prolong this any longer.

"Any weekend is fine. Alicia and I don't need to do any more shopping for the baby, we have everything we need so now is just sit and wait game. So, I'm free whenever. Pick a weekend. Hopefully she doesn't go into premature labor, I suppose from that perspective it would be good to do it earlier rather than later."

"Alicia is due at the beginning of June correct?" he asked.

"Apparently, if all goes according to plan. Around there, give or take a week."

"Alright drive up in the last weekend of April. Friday night after work. Either take your car or get a rental. We will cover the expenses as I said. Plan to return Sunday night. Don't worry about Alicia, anything unexpected happens with her and we will take care of her.

Neat I thought. All of a sudden I was beginning to like the word 'we'. I also realized that I didn't have to lie to Alicia about where I would be going as she was already a card-carrying member of the 'Communist' party. I smiled, for the first time in a long time at that thought. It felt really good.

"Alright," I said. Jeff proceeded to give me directions to the hotel where I would be staying. He would be there too. Holiday Inn. I had no way of knowing yet what part of town that would be and how infested with prostitutes that particular location is. I've never been to Bradbury, and from what I heard it was nothing to write home about on any front.

"So that's in a week and a half. Anything else we need to discuss until then? Do we need to meet prior?" I asked.

"No, you know everything you need to know until then. I'm looking forward to seeing you Marcus."

We said our farewells. That was about it for now. The conversation was also really nothing to write home about. Neither were the accommodations in Bradbury. I could also say goodbye to a fancy limo picking me up and taking me there. Oh well. I felt a sudden void. Like...'that's it?' sort of thing. I wasn't very impressed I suppose, although I haven't really seen anything yet nor been informed about a whole lot. Bits and pieces of bait here and there. I allowed the chains of my fears and doubts of the past few months to slowly detach and fall off of me and I started to think back to actual tangible information that Jeff told me about. I tried not to focus on the secrecy and the opaqueness of the 'organization', or the 'society', or the whatever. On the nebulous details. I needed to think about other things. Things that were of interest to me. Jeff mentioned Tredarious Corporation which sent rockets and probes to go drilling on an asteroid named Ryugu. As I got off the phone with Jeff I put the term into Google. 162173 Ryugu, near-Earth object, a potentially hazardous asteroid of the Apollo group measuring approximately 1 km in diameter. Wikipedia breakdown was readily available as with most things such as my research about death and cancer. Looking at images the object looked almost like a perfect diamond. Even the description said so. 'Almost spherical' and 'diamond-shaped body'. I felt geeky and utterly interested in this stuff reading about it. Apparently in June 2018 a spacecraft Hayabusa 2 arrived at the asteroid and with the use of four rovers was supposed to return samples from the asteroid by December 2020. The asteroid was deemed a 'rubble pile' with about 50% of its volume being empty space. The thing was like Swiss cheese, fairly hollow with a low density.

There was not much else on Wikipedia. Or in any other articles I could find. Certainly nothing about drilling for minerals. I wondered if Hayabusa 2 was a front for another Tredarious expedition or something completely unrelated. One last thing rang in my head from that conversation with Jeff a while ago. He ended our pow wow by saying that apparently 'they' determined that Ryugu was not an asteroid at all. That was the punch line. An object similar to an asteroid would be a comet, and reading further about it the only difference between the two was their physical composition. Asteroids were usually composed of rock or metal. Comets were made up of ice, rock and dust. Meteors were something else entirely. It seemed conceivable that Tredarious and 'the organization' could have designated this rock wrongly, gotten mislead by indicators and research and assumed it was an asteroid containing metals but instead it turned out to be a comet containing none. It would have cost them billions and the entire mission would have been wasted. But what would be such a significance of this misdiagnosis other than financials? Why would that be a big deal? Maybe it was the opposite, maybe they found out the asteroid is not hollow, perhaps is made up of rock-solid gold or something. Or maybe the whole thing really was one big giant diamond. And how did the new established NTLab fit in all this? It would be nice to finally get some answers.

I have noticed myself get progressively calmer as the days went by. I was in this new reality but I figured as long as no new shocks to my system come up I would be able to find a method of coping with my new lifestyle. It was still awfully weird knowing that my wife was in on the whole thing, that we could openly talk about this entirely new dimension, this new almost magical world. It would take a while for the weird to merge into comfortable and reassuring. I was simply not feeling that way yet. It was strange telling Alicia about my upcoming trip to Bradbury and her saying:

"You will find it enlightening Marcus, it will blow your mind."

"Can you tell me anything before my trip? Are you allowed to disclose anything? I'm not going to get probed and experimented upon once I get there am I? You are not selling me into body parts for organ transplants are you?" I asked like a little boy.

"Haha, no, you won't. I promise. And you've grown quite dear to me over the years plus you are the father of our child so I'm quite content with keeping you around."

Yet more evidence that getting her pregnant was the smart thing to do.

"Well, I suppose I wouldn't know about it even if that's what ended up happening. I imagine sophisticated drugs and surgical methods would be used to make me not remember or notice any-thing at all. I would just come home and not even realize that I'm missing a kidney or part of my liver."

"Enough with the absurd Marcus. I could tell you everything, but I want you to find out when you are up there. You will appreciate the element of surprise and I guarantee you that you won't...shit your pants from it as you say, hahaha. We will talk about everything when you get home."

Enough with the absurd eh? That was rich. It became clear and evident to me as she said that that all of the organization obviously knew me psychologically inside and out. My fears, OCDs and all the pathetic, childish nonsense that came with it complete with the frequent bathroom breaks. I felt completely naked. Oh God, what if they watched me in some utter state of debauchery late at night somewhere in the dark shadows of my house?! I guess since Alicia hasn't murdered me yet I suppose they couldn't have witnessed any-thing too despicable.

"Alright, I won't press you anymore. Just as long as you promise me that I won't be getting any heart attacks while I'm up there. We all know I've induced myself a few these last few months."

"I promise you won't damage your body, or your mind or your nerves. Although your heart will be racing, that much I know."

"So my heart will be racing but it won't be damaging and I won't shit my pants...really? Somehow I doubt that I will be grinning with joy and childish excitement the entire time I'm up there." I said.

"Haha, it won't be that kind of happy go lucky excitement. You will be in awe, and a bit of shock, but not in the sense that your world is crashing. It will be more in the sense that your world is being opened up to you in a way that you never thought possible. You'll become convinced how small the world you knew is and how much bigger the world you entered is about to become. I'll be here for you if you need anything. I mean you should be happier by now that you and I are in this together instead of you and your father, right?"

I said yes. Was I sincere? Debatable.

I sort of felt like a child at Christmas about to visit Santa, and concurrently as a person about to get screwed over by everybody and end up in some dungeon in Ivory Coast with my body being used as a machete sharpening cadaver all at the same time. Whatever, change is good. I suppose all these emotions on either spectrum were equally strong so I, at the end of it all, felt just about neutral. Calm with a normal heartbeat. It was as if I was shooting up heroin and sticking a 20cm long steel adrenaline needle into my heart at the same time. I'm fairly certain my analogy was correct, I have seen Pulp Fiction several times after all...

"Just don't worry. The worst stresses, the ones that induce grey hair, boldness and high blood pressure are behind you." she said as she held my face with both hands fully stretched out...her belly was huge by now.

"If you say so. I've made it this far. No looking back. I asked for this." As I was saying these short sentences my confidence was not exactly sky high, if anything I felt like there should be question marks at the end of each and not periods. I was not making statements I was questioning everything again while trying to sound confident. It felt like losing my virginity all over again. Which is what sex will probably feel like next time it happens since Alicia and I haven't done it in months due to her pregnancy.

CHAPTER 19

COME WHATEVER MAY

The last Friday of April arrived. With sweaty palms and in a daze, me and my freshly rented Dodge Charger set off for Bradbury. Alicia packed together a banana, two oranges and some grapes, and gave me a trail-mix of nuts to snack on while driving. We exchanged overcaring platitudes about amazing new life, and sounded nauseatingly cheesy in the process. I felt like I was going camping with my public school music class. I was again reminded that nothing and no one turned out the way I imagined as a child. I brought my giant Swiss Army knife with me, as a form of self-protection, just in case something sinister went down. It wasn't much, but that was as good as it was going to get, and probably as useless as bringing a Q-tip. But it gave me a piece of mind. I had no intention of illegally carrying my handgun and I couldn't get a permit since I clearly wasn't heading to a shooting range. I was lucky, the weather finally started to look decent, snow was long gone, the wind was almost non-existent and the Sun was still up. I should have daylight till about 7:30 PM and since I usually got off work at noon on Fridays (while working an extra hour Monday through Thursday) I gave myself a good head start. It was a long ass drive, 6.5 hours by Google Maps. One would think the 'organization' could have paid for my flight up there, or had teleportation machines, I mean both Kingston and Bradbury had childish airports that operated toy planes to get back and forth with. But it was not to be. So my tiny ass was going to sit for a while and get better acquainted with cruise control, which I only really started using recently after almost 20 years of having a driving license. I picked the route that went straight North from Kingston and along the Ottawa river, instead of going to Toronto then going North via Hwy 400. I've never taken this route before in my life so at least I would see something new out of it. Hopefully it was worth it.

As I left our house in the morning, I registered, only as I drove off, that Alicia's car wasn't in the driveway. Weird, but I had other things to preoccupy my mind with than to dwell on that small detail.

It was a nice route, different. The drive along the Ottawa river was unusually calming. Ontario was mostly flat everywhere but it managed to have its moments of rolling hills, beautiful greenery, lakes and rivers in this section. The hills were quite significant around Calabogie Lake and for moments I felt like I was in a different country altogether. Like I was in the hills of Vermont, or Triglav National Park in Slovenia. Once the hills subsided Ottawa river opened up and that kept me mesmerized pretty much all the way to Bradbury. The weather held up the entire way and I reminisced when I saw the area and the nature surrounding Lake Nipissing. I was up here many Moons ago for a dam inspection on the French river with a previous company. I lived in Toronto at that time.

The nature did a wondrous act of keeping me distracted and relaxed. At times when I delved back into deep thought the main worry that kept me preoccupied was how in the world I was going to handle my father. And my parents in general. I worried him half to death and I haven't explained anything since. I've had one conversation via Facetime with them since then upon his return back from Canada, and exchanged a few text messages with just him. From what I could tell my mother was none the wiser about anything that went down. And I was about 50/50 sure he was going to tell her simply to worry her, which is what he loved and enjoyed doing. So before he left I actually begged him, to my own disgust of myself, not to tell her what transpired over that drink we had. He said he wouldn't. So every couple of days I would be getting "Are you ok? Are you handling everything alright? You are not drinking are you?" messages from him which although painfully annoying, I had no choice but to humor him and answer as me ignoring him or answering in a half-ass way would for sure cause a shitstorm. Every once in a while I wondered about whether the messages were really coming from him or was it another ploy by the organization, but then I realized that there would no longer be any point in them pulling something like that. Thankfully he didn't tell mom anything. I think he was pretty freaked out by the whole experience himself and was actually afraid telling her this might indeed kill her. And as long as I kept reassuringly answering his questions and telling him that I'm getting plenty of sleep, working hard and seemed to have gotten my bearings back on track maybe he would eventually let the whole thing slide and not mention it again. One could only hope, but knowing him, another in-depth sit down was almost certainly an inevitability and he would keep bringing this up for years to come. "Use your intelligence son to overcome life's problems, not substances." he would repeat. Even though I stressed numerous times I only drank because I was bored with sobriety and not to drink my sorrows away. Intelligence. What a concept anyways I thought. A very relative concept assigned to ourselves in the human race...by ourselves. Lately, I firmly believed that human 'intelligence' as we adorned ourselves with is only good for and enables two things. One is overcompensation for the lack of numerous physical abilities that humans lack compared to animals. And two...fueling and strengthening greedy and selfish, lust for power tendencies. The second thing was a purely parasitic trait. It served no one and nothing any good ultimately. Anyways, I digress...

I arrived at the hotel in Bradbury at exactly 8 PM. The traces of sunset were still visible. I felt fine. Fresh. Jeff was sitting in the front lobby bar with a whiskey on the rocks drink in his hand. Well, it was at least reassuring to know that I did not join a club of teetotallers. Because that would have surely been a disaster. As I came in with my stuff he put his drink down and approached me.

"Good to see you Marcus. Can I help you with your bags?" he was beaming as he asked.

"Hey Jeff. No, I'll be fine, I only have the one luggage bag and just one shoulder bag with my laptop. Thanks though."

"How was your drive up here?"

"Good, long, but interesting. The weather held up. I came up and along the Ottawa river, beautiful scenery, I like going through the Calabogie area, I ski there in the Winter, closest decent ski hill to Kingston."

"I taught both my boys to ski up there. It's a little hidden gem. Too bad it's not closer to Kingston. Taller vertical drop than Blue Mountain north of Toronto, did you know? It's a shame they don't invest more money into it."

Little peculiar things like these and attention to detail made me think that Jeff and I would get along well. These were the kinds of similarities I was looking to have more with people in my life.

"Oh yes, I researched all the ski resorts in Ontario back when I still lived in Toronto. Calabogie stood out. Kingston is a good little place to live in, in the middle of everywhere as I'd like to think of it. Quebec, New York State and Vermont all decently close for some spectacular skiing. Plus Toronto, Montreal, Boston, New York City orbiting around if one wants to go get some big city feel."

"Precisely! So I take it you are a big ski junkie too?" asked Jeff.

"Yup, dad, brother and me, been skiing for around a century combined between the three of us, haha."

"Hahaha, that's an interesting way to put it. And please tell me that you are not contemplating to learn snowboarding."

"Jeff, not if it was the last thing to do in this world. I don't understand people who after years of perfecting skiing have to try snowboarding because they are bored with skiing. I don't get bored with endlessly perfecting what I already know." we both laughed out loud for a while. Well what do you know, I guess I don't get bored with everything.

"I know exactly what you mean. Alright Marcus, why don't you check-in, drop off your bags and come meet me down here for a drink."

"You got it Jeff."

I was really looking forward to that drink. I could taste it already. I was tired, weirded out and strung out by my life of the past few months and living in a dream state as of late, and I could not have been more sick and tired of being sober and analyzing any more shit I was finding myself in. So I made the check-in quick. I went into my room, dropped off the bags, washed my face and went downstairs to sit down with Jeff. The room was nice, king size bed, modern bathroom, tables and armchairs and a huge flat-screen TV. I didn't pay too much attention to it, I was that thirsty for some alcoholic poison to start coursing down my veins. I ran downstairs to the bar. When I got there I saw a scotch on the rocks already waiting for me, courtesy of Jeff. Or the 'organization'.

"Thanks Jeff. I won't lie to you I need it." I took a couple of sips and I hoped that I didn't come off as an overzealous drunkard.

"No kidding. This is my third one, I'm buzzing like a beehive, hahaha." I could tell that he wasn't lying. His cheeks were rosy, and his eyes nice and glossed over. He was a man who liked his drink and that was fine with me. Happy Santa, like he seemed to me all those months ago when I first met him at his school.

"I feel excited. That's all I feel right now. No fear, no doubt, no regret, at least not at this moment in time. I just want to see what this is all about." I said. And I was sincere, maybe it was the alcohol talking, most certainly actually, but at that moment I felt great. The booze was hitting me quick, I didn't have anything to eat since the morning.

"Good Marcus, I'm happy to hear it. It's going to be an eye-opening weekend for you, I guarantee it. And it's only the tip of the iceberg. It will be considerably more exciting for you than back when I joined. There is remarkably more going on right now, stuff movies are made of. I still...can't really believe it myself." He looked off into the distance as he said that. It was a bit eerie.

"Can we talk about any of it right now?" I asked.

"No, let's wait till tomorrow. We get picked up at 7 AM. Once we get in the car you can ask whatever your heart desires and I will answer. I promise."

Crap I thought. Another sleepless night ahead of me. I hoped that I would get the gist of whatever he was about to show me this weekend all this evening while I had the alcohol to help me stay brave and him talking. To break the ice. I felt my mood drop but I quickly made it claw its way up again as I couldn't sit there sulking.

"Fair enough," I said. Man was there any way that I could sneak some booze tomorrow into the underground laboratory....probably not. Somehow I doubted this was going to be an experience where Jeff and I go down there shitfaced or even partially sauced up. Whatever went on there and whatever Jeff wanted to show me was going to have to be experienced sober as an arrow.

We stayed up until about 11:30 PM. Considering what an early start we had tomorrow we kept drinking till the end. I was down 4 glasses of scotch and Jeff at least 7 counting the ones he had before I even came. We talked about completely random things, politics, some sports, military capabilities of the world's best armies, some movies. It was fun. Completely bizarre how regular and every day that conversation was all things considered. I decided not to continue to pester him about the matters at hand this weekend. For entire moments I managed to completely disconnect from it myself. Every once in a while a ping of dread came creeping up in my stomach at the thought of what unknown awaited, but the booze was doing its job of pushing it right back down again.

I came into my hotel room nicely juiced, took off my clothes in one of the sloppiest ways possible, brushed my teeth and flossed in a half-ass way and went straight to bed. I passed out right away with a steady melodic static of the alcohol in my head.

The alarm went off at 5:30 AM and scared the shit out of me. First I thought I had to go to the office, then I thought I had to go to an early site meeting, then for a couple of seconds I thought I had to go catch a plane. Then finally it came to me that I was actually acting in a science fiction movie, in Bradbury, Ontario and was about to enter an underground laboratory 2km beneath the Earth's surface. No cameras involved. At least I wasn't hungover, no headache or anything, I was just in a haze.

I scrambled clothes on and before I gathered myself up Jeff was calling me from reception.

"I'll be right down." I said and hurried out.

When I arrived downstairs Jeff was already at the revolving front door to the hotel. He was waving me over.

"Morning Marcus. Come, the car is waiting for us."

Outside a black Yukon Denali was parked with the engine idling.

"We figured we will steer clear of the Chevrolet Tahoe so people don't think we are CIA, hahaha" said Jeff slapping me on the shoulder as we entered the massive cave of the car. I almost barfed as he did that. Inside Shauna was sitting diagonally opposite the door. A driver and a passenger were sitting in the front.

"Hello Marcus, it is nice to see you again. Welcome aboard finally." she extended her hand as she said that and I shook it.

"It is nice to see you too." I replied like a little boy saying hi to his family doctor with a vaccination syringe in his hand.

"Marcus the driver is Vince and the gentleman riding shotgun is Shane."

"Hello Marcus", they both turned around and shook my hand with genuine, non-creepy smiles on their faces. They looked like guys my age, fit, like they could hold their own. They must have played some kind of security role.

"Alright everyone, let's get going." said Jeff and the car went off. It wasn't any kind of peeling off on the road like in the books, but nice and easy. For a second I thought what if the SUV turned into a space ship and we disappeared through a warp tear, but then again THAT would have been a bit too far fetched. Good, I thought. I wasn't going to get a stroke just yet. I was a delicate flower, no sudden drastic actions please.

Jeff turned to me.

"Marcus we have about 25 minutes till we get to the Lab. You are officially allowed to start going nuts with the questions." He was looking at Shauna as he said that. She grinned. He kept looking straight and Shauna looked at me in a forced friendly way. Or maybe I was just analyzing her facial expressions too much. Either way I felt very uncomfortable and put on the spot. Like I got parachuted into the middle of a circus performance and was expected to know how to handle all the wild animals waiting for my instructions. I didn't feel like asking anything when someone was shining a light in my eyes as if I was in a circus. Jeff sensed my discomfort.

"Sorry to put you on the spot Marcus. And I'm sorry to have prevented our conversations from going any further all those times you tried asking spontaneously. It simply wasn't the time to talk yet but I am aware that blunting spontaneous discussion while trying to push forced ones is awkward. Well, let me start. The other day on the phone you asked basically what was the point of me stopping our conversation from going any further considering I already told some details about the NTLab. I said I was going to explain further. We can control the lines of communication from being overheard or intercepted for about a good ten minutes or so. That is how much we are confident about. Anything past the ten-minute mark is open season for any hacker, government agency or whoever else might want to cross our lines of communication. That is why I was comfortable with divulging what I did in those initial ten minutes and why I somewhat abruptly stopped us from going any further after that. I do apologize. I should have mentioned our ten-minute line block right at the start of our conversation. It would have made a lot more sense to you at the end once we ended talking."

That made sense I thought. Protected lines of communication. But I couldn't help but ask more.

"How come you can't protect the entire call? Why only ten minutes?" I suppose out of all the things I could have asked this was one of the most useless ones. I almost immediately regretted it. I wanted to tell him to forget it.

"The jamming measures we use to protect the lines are signals strong enough for about ten minutes. Afterward, our signals start losing strength the longer the call goes on for. Too many radiowaves out there bouncing of and intercepting each other. Electromagnetic interference. Can't tell you much more, you'd have to talk to one of our tech guys. I majored in Chemistry, all this radio and phone frequency stuff is black voodoo magic to me, haha."

We both laughed out loud. Both my father and my brother were electrical engineers and I felt the exact same way about their professions. And Jeff's answer was good enough for me not to want to go any further with it nor with any other stupid and irrelevant questions or topics.

"Alright, well I suppose you could tell me what this organization is called. I keep hearing the word organization, corporation, company, cult, club. What are....'we' exactly?" Now there was a non-useless question if there ever was one, I wished I could pat myself on the back.

"Marcus we are the Tredarious Corporation. Tredarious is not part of the organization, Tredarious is the organization. Mining just happens to be our largest business front." said Jeff.

Ok. I did extensive research on Tredarious. Website, Wikipedia, numerous articles on sub-Earth mining, practices, equipment. Established in1947, post-war. Doing well for itself.

"So I have been initiated into the Tredarious Corporation?" I asked. I had to, I felt genuinely confused.

"In essence yes. You are now part of a family Marcus. It is not a gender-exclusive organization. In that regard, it is neither a specific club per se that has meetings and rituals with no one really understanding from the outside what the club does, if anything. We are a business, a society, a small nation if you will, all in one."

"So is there a designation for us? What do we call ourselves?" I asked like a naive first grader.

"You mean like the Truemasons? Do we call ourselves Tredarians or something like that?" Jeff came back with.

"Yeah, I guess something like that." I answered.

"No, we do not have a designation. And unlike the Truemasons or the rest, we are not allowed to discuss our membership or 'belonging' so to speak to anyone outside of Tredarious. Not to try and sound medieval, but bottom line it is forbidden. You are not permitted to tell anyone that you are part of the society that is the Tredarious Corporation. A person actually working for Tredarious Corporation, making a living from the business side of it, is obviously allowed to say that he or she works there, but never to indicate that Tredarious is anything more than a place of work and business."

It was a different concept, something I've never heard of before. I immediately thought about how many other organizations operated this way. Behind the scenes. But still technically out front. There could literally be thousands of them, millions. Nations within nations, within nations...

Then I started thinking back to the day when I joined. Have I told anyone that I am a part of an organization? No, I did not, I have been too scared to barely breathe let alone make a peep about this.

"One thing confuses me. Is every employee of the company that is Tredarious Corporation also a member of its....secret society?"

"No Marcus. There is three branches of the Tredarious Corporation. Kind of like with Bombardier Inc. Although they only have two branches, Bombardier Transportation and Bombardier Aerospace all under Bombardier Inc. We are similar. But we are split into three segments. Tredarious Mining, Tredarious Mechanics, which deals with mining equipment design and manufacturing mainly and Tredarious Geodetics, all under the umbrella of Tredarious Corporation. Tredarious Mining is the company and the society we are speaking of Marcus, and your new extended family. People working for Tredarious Mechanics and Tredarious Geodetics have no knowledge of a secret society, they are simply there to do their jobs, get paid and go home to their families."

"Isn't this sort of unfair towards the other two-thirds of the company?" I asked, and immediately regretted it. I was barely through the door and already I am managing to sound like a condescending smartass and a self-righteous boy scout.

"Not at all, people working for our other two-thirds are perfectly wonderful human beings who contribute greatly to our company as a whole. They are well educated, hard-working, resourceful, committed. They work and make a living like millions of other people out there working for different companies. They simply didn't have certain parameters and attributes that a person is screened for when they get considered for admission in the society portion. There is nothing wrong with that, it's just the way it is. That being said, you also have to understand that people are screened almost on an ongoing basis. If through time one of our employees from the 'business' portion does something or 'clicks' if you will, of particular significance, we are more than happy to consider them and admit them into the 'society'. It's been known to happen a few times."

I was happy about his speedy answer. It's almost as if he knew that if he hesitated it would cause my anxiety to go through the roof. He knew me well. They all knew me well. And it wasn't surprising. 'La Familia' did their research. I had no clue how to feel about this just yet.

With my new found confidence I couldn't help but brave up again to ask another smartass question.

"So let's say you need to fill a position in the Mining part of the company. And an individual sends in their resume and technically he is a perfect fit. But otherwise, you know you could never admit that person into the 'society'. What do you do then? Does that person get rejected even though they happen to be a specialist in mining but not a match....personality-wise for the society?"

"Tredarious Corporation is roughly equally divided across its three segments. The individuals in the Mining sector that comprise the 'society' make their living in all sorts of different walks of life. They are engineers, lawyers, doctors, professors, teachers, some are mining experts as well, well you get the point. The bulk of our actual 'mining experts' are scattered across the Mechanics and Geodetics divisions, they just don't know it. They think they are part of the 'Mining' segment. So if we need a mining specialist, one we feel doesn't belong or shouldn't be part of the 'society' according to our criteria, we put them in the other two segments. And the business model rolls on. We do know however where everyone fits at the end of the day." Sounded convoluted. But I tried to keep up. "Why did you decide to make the 'Mining' part the 'society'? Why not call it something else?" I kept up with questions. I was on a roll of not getting slapped across the face or getting told to shut the fuck up so I figured that I'll see how far I get with it.

"The company started as a mining company back in 1947. In Pittsburgh, Pennsylvania. I'm vague on the details of how the name Tredarious came to be, but the business was formed by two Russian brothers who immigrated to the US after World War 2 after having fought in the war on the Eastern Front. I think they were both involved with the army units that liberated Stalingrad. Impressive stuff. Over the years those individuals decided that they wanted to expand their horizons into many different venues. So, they came up with the idea that the 'Mining' segment would become a front for miscellaneous business ventures and research while keeping the designation of Mining, it simply became an organizational matter. They always wanted to keep the mining sector but decided to lump it into other categories. But only the people from the 'society' know that. The actual mining experts in the other two sectors have no clue that they are not technically within 'Mining'. So they can go around telling their friends and family that they work for Tredarious

Mining, but meanwhile, they are not part of the 'society'. The Mining part is kind of like mining for knowledge outside the parameters of the norm. That's why Mining got associated with the 'society'. As corny as that sounds, haha."

The whole thing sounded interwoven as all hell and I only truly understood portions of it. No further questions were advisable from my end as they would simply reveal just how little comprehension I produced to the answers Jeff provided. The car pulled up to an impressive looking red building with dark glass windows. It looked modern, but nice modern, new and aesthetically pleasing to the eyes. Unlike most other 'new' huts in North America with aluminum or vinyl siding. There was a sign out front of the parking lot 'BNOLAB Mining for Knowledge'. Figures, I thought. Clever.

We exited the Denali and walked across the narrow parking lot into the front entrance. Nothing unusual yet. The reception was polite and breezy, they gave us Visitor cards to hang around our necks and told us to sign in. One security guard sat behind a divider, grinning. Ok, we were in. So far there was nothing more security involved about this place than there was about say the office of the Bureau of Transportation where I tend to go frequently enough for civil engineering project meetings.

"Welcome to BNOLAB Marcus." Jeff smiled and kept walking. Shauna followed suit. The two guys from the front of the car were behind me. It was a well thought out military-style formation. Everyone walked fast. I usually walked fast but I was finding it difficult to keep up with this pace. Shauna was kicking my ass. The hallways were clean and sparkling, windows everywhere. We took many turns, right then left then right then left again. It was like pacing through the White House at a time of some conjured up fake emergency in the world.

Eventually, we got to an elevator. We got in and went five stories down. The elevator had two doors, at the front and back. When we stopped we went out of the back opening up into a long hallway. There were no more windows. But the hallway was well lit up. Better than most of Kingston at night during Christmas time. Towards the end the hallway went into 90 degree turns to the left and right. We went right. Another elevator. This one went ten stories down. It opened up into a working space not unlike most modern offices. It was spacious, I estimated 50 by 50 meters footprint. Huge. Like a cattle feedlot. It was filled with people. The difference being the people were not divided and split up by cubicles but by glass walls that went all the way from the floor to the ceiling. Too bad they couldn't do this with toilet stalls elsewhere. Towards the back, there was a much larger space cordoned off on its own with several people inside working on what appeared to be a massive turbine shaft, either made up of titanium or stainless steel. Or maybe aluminum.

"Marcus, go to the end of the room. Sam over there, tall guy, glasses, in a long white coat, he will give you a suit to change into once you have a thorough shower in our facilities just around the corner."

Ah the cold sweat breaking out in my armpits, how I've missed you. I froze. Has the moment of realization that I'm about to be experimented on started to finally and miraculously appear before me?? Am I just now discovering that all this thing was was me signing up to an experiment where I handed off my body to be used for lab rat purposes for biological and medical advancement?? Were they about to throw me into that turbine looking thing stark naked?? Jeff quickly noticed my catatonic and pale disposition and chimed in.

"Get a hold of yourself Marcus, haha. That contraption you are staring at is not a meat grinder and we do not intend to make sausages out of you. We are all going to go through the same thing. The underground where we are going is an area with highly sensitive instrumentation and some radiation. NTLab especially is quarantined, both to protect the highly sensitive machinery present and the samples stored from human contamination as well as to protect the humans working there. This whole procedure is to protect the laboratory from us, and us from the laboratory. So please go ahead, we are all following suit."

I gradually started to break out of my plaster cast disposition and skin color and move towards where I was directed, albeit slowly. The rest of the party seemed unfazed. Shauna stepped in one of the glass offices and was discussing something on the computer screen with the person working inside. The two guys from the front of the car, whose names I completely forgot and had no intention of asking for again at least not on this trip, were already taking their coats off and heading towards what I could only assume were changing rooms. We all headed down the room corridor, I picked up my pace one step at a time. I had to keep my paranoia in check. It was becoming ridiculous. How quickly I lose faith in everything was remarkable. The whole society, my wife, this facility, what, it was all so that they could rape me and run medical experiments on me?! I had to calm down before I ended up making a complete ass of myself.

As we walked towards the end of the room none of the people inside the glass offices seemed to notice or care that we were there. They were preoccupied with their own ongoings. Some were on the phone, some on the computer, some juggling both, it seemed like a regular office environment. I didn't feel like asking, but I assumed the glass walls that went from floor to ceiling were there so that sound wouldn't travel too much around the office while at the same time ensuring that the people working there could be watched at all times.

As we got to the end of the room we found ourselves standing in front of the see-through lab that contained the glitzy turbine-like cylinder. Standing this close to it I could hear that it was emanating a low humming sound.

"More on that later Marcus, we got other things to discuss this weekend. Let's get ready so we can keep moving along."

We all went through the doors around the corner. Inside, as I thought, were numerous lockers, toilets and showers. I counted five showers. The facilities were spacious, clean, overall immaculate. I picked out a location around an empty locker, got undressed and went in the shower. So far no one tried inappropriately touching me or groping me. The showers were great, better than the one I had at home, superior water pressure with numerous settings. Fifteen stories underground, better living setup than above surface. And I could tell that the entire underground facility was built of solid reinforced concrete. I wondered if it was too soon to ask Jeff if I could move in here.

I finished up, dried myself off and put my underwear on. Jeff and the other two guys were already standing there in their drawers.

"The suits are in the closet on the sidewall." said Jeff.

I turned and looked. There was another row of locker style cabinets along the wall. They were solid metal. We all walked towards them and opened four of them. Behind each door, there were three suits. Dark green, but not odd looking. Nice cloth material, kind of like a full mechanic style suit but nicer. As I said, all in one piece. I put it on legs first. I picked the one that had 'L/G' on the back of it. The rest of the guys were ready before I was.

"Alright let's keep going shall we?" said Jeff and we kept moving. We got out of the locker rooms, and into the main room again. Shauna was outside waiting. We all seemed to be following her now. She took a turn to the right down the hallway. There was a door that looked like an elevator door but once it opened inside was a tunnel, like a subway shaft. We stepped on a platform. Towards the end of the shaft were four pods, about two meters wide each. They looked like massive safes but oval not rectangular. On a bench on the side and in front of the pods were five helmets. They looked unusual. Sharp edges, thick glass or plastic on the back, clear in the front. The bottom of all the helmets had a zipper all around. Side edges had grooves, shoulder spaces carved out. The zipper was towards the interior rim of the helmet and I realized the inside of my collar on my suit had a zipper all around the neck hole as well. It was becoming clearer how they fit together.

"Well let's put them on." said Shauna. We all did. The helmets were surprisingly snug and comfortable. They didn't feel heavy or as awkward as they looked.

"Elevator No. 3," said one of the two dudes this time whose name I wanted to say was David. But I'd be damned before I blurted that out as I had no confidence that I was correct. Probably wasn't.

As the pod door opened up I could see that the elevator was spacious and it had seats fastened to its sides around the perimeter. The seats had backrests and looked new and comfortable. They looked like something a pilot in a fighter jet would have. Seat belts were present as well as shoulder straps. We all went in and buckled up. I felt like I was buckled up into a rollercoaster ride at a theme park. Shauna worked the console which was located on its own independent pedestal in the middle of the pod floor.

"Is everyone strapped into their seats?" she asked as she worked the buttons. The console looked very similar to a console of a movable swing bridge. Except she was operating a pod that was about to go 2km underground. We all said yes.

"The ride will last about an hour. If you notice any dizziness or discomfort, I'm specifically referring to you Marcus as these guys have already been down there, let me know. I will help you adjust the controls on your helmet for better oxygen intake and acclimatization."

I started getting queasy. Am I going to pass out in the middle of this ride and make a complete ass out of myself? Or worse still am I actually going to need medical attention? I had to stop panicking. As Shauna got the elevator moving she sat down opposite me and buckled up. Her looking at me managed to calm me down. I was slowly starting to get a hold of myself.

After about fifteen minutes or so it didn't seem like we were moving anymore. The elevator or machine or whatever it was called was so smooth moving that after a while I felt nothing. The lights inside didn't flicker, falter, there were no hiccups in the movement whatsoever. And there were no windows to look out at the shaft walls we were moving down in. Jeff and Shauna had a few technical exchanges about 'parameters' and 'sodium voids', the other two guys were both sitting there with their eyes shut, trying to nap. I had a million questions of course but I did not feel like starting to ask them at this particular moment. Not to mention that with the helmet on the sound was a bit muffled, as well as I thought that I was going to fog up the helmet the more I talked. So, kind of like a pregnant woman, I conserved my strength and controlled my breathing because my main concern at the moment was trying to make it to the center of the Earth without passing out like a little bitch.

Half hour into the parachute ride down I started feeling the effects of sinking. Mainly in my gut. I started to feel nauseous, my legs, specifically knees, started twitching more. I hoped I wouldn't puke inside my helmet. I looked around. Everything seemed still. Jeff and Shauna were on their phones now, I did not dare ask what they were doing nor how they were getting any reception down here, if they were...The other two guys were still sitting there with their eyes closed. I tried closing mine. Big mistake. Now I was starting to get the feeling of spins like when I was trying to fall asleep hammered drunk. I quickly opened them up again. There was a digital time clock on the control console, I could see it easily from where I was sitting. According to my estimate we still had 20 minutes to go. I didn't specifically register the time when the ride began. I wondered if I was going to make it. Shauna was taking notice.

"Take a long, slow breath in through your nose Marcus, first filling your lower lungs, then your upper lungs. Hold your breath to the count of three. Exhale slowly. Repeat. It's a basic anti-anxiety breathing tip, but I always found it worked well in this descending rocket until you get used to it, haha."

I did as she told me. And slowly my body started to relax. The problem with that, as so often before, was that now I had the feeling like I needed to take a shit. We had ten more minutes to go according to Shauna. I prayed to God that she was right.

I felt a slight pressure along the back of my calves. I looked around and saw the rest of the party starting to unbuckle their seatbelts. It would appear that we had finally arrived. It was going to take all the effort in the world for me to try and not run to the bathroom as soon as that door opened. Luckily for me, Jeff threw me a lifeline.

"Welcome to Sub Tier Level 1. If anyone needs to use the bathroom it's straight ahead."

We all went to the bathroom. It was a team effort. We grinned at each other awkwardly without saying anything as we did so. I went straight into the stall as did Jeff and one of the younger guys, the other just did some washing up at the sink. I was hoping everyone else would make it quick so I could make unseemly noises in peace, but unfortunately it wasn't meant to be. Turns out the other two didn't get blessed with the gift of privacy either in this situation, so the three of us sounded like an orchestra in there. I could only hope that this subterranean facility was built in a structurally sound way and wasn't sensitive to loud sounds causing it to collapse like an avalanche.

Upon re-emerging into the main hallway it became evident that the area we were in was just another waiting subway type station. We still haven't arrived at our final destination. Now we were waiting for an actual train. I could see the train tracks beyond the ledge of the platform edge.

"The labs' facilities are about 500 meters horizontally in that direction. More solid rock strata in that region of the underground so the engineers recommended it as the safest location for the laboratory." Shauna said that as she was predominantly turned to me even without addressing me by name. The others present were already in the know.

Looking at the one end of the tunnel shaft I could see a dead-end about 20 meters to the left with a buffer stopper and a rock formation wall behind. There was only one way to go and that was to the right. Within minutes I was proven right as a shuttle, similar to the ones used at airports came from that direction. Two sets of doors opened and we all boarded. Seconds later the shuttle departed back towards the same direction that it came from. There was no driver, and no one from our group worked any console or remote control so I assumed that the shuttle was remotely operated from somewhere else, probably from an area within the laboratory facilities deeper within. The tunnel was spacious, well lit up and I could tell that there was ample room around it. There were two sidewalks one on each side, presumably for maintenance purposes. The ride was smooth and easy, steady and melodic due to the wheel contact on the rails and seemed decently fast. I was considerably more relaxed than in the vertical pod. And about two kilograms lighter which undoubtedly helped. I was so relaxed in fact that I even closed my eyes and started to nod off for a bit.

I did not pay attention to the time at all and before I knew it we had arrived at what I could only assume was our final destination. If I had to estimate I would have guessed that we traveled for only about five to ten minutes. But I was spaced out and distracted so I could have been wrong. The docking station was massive. It was the size of Grand Central Station in New York City, only underground. All of it for just this one shuttle. There were no murals on the walls but the lighting on the ceiling seemed to have been placed in a certain artistic pattern. No particular shape of an animal or scenery but neat and symmetrical nevertheless. Almost hypnotic. And the light that emanated was pleasant, warm and easy on the eyes, perfect intensity, not cold and intense. The massive room was a hollowed-out cave, it was as if the Flinstones created a lab underground. Carved out rock protruded visibly in places despite the decorative effort. As we got off onto the platform I realized that the terminal wasn't quite like a usual train terminal. There were no stores and kiosks and magazine stands all around, people soliciting crap such as cab drivers. Instead, there were gates to different branching tunnels littered all around the perimeter of the massive hall. The place was nothing short of lively. Numerous individuals in white lab coats were coming in and out of random hallways. Our group exchanged nods and polite waves with a lot of them.

"This way gentlemen," said Shauna as she headed towards one of the holes in the wall which upon closer inspection had a Roman numeral 3 above it. The gate opened and we entered in. This hallway looked gouged out as well, I supposed there was no sense in trying to make the hallways into perfect arch shapes and spend the money on all that concrete. As we walked again numerous scientific-looking individuals were walking by us. The place was a humming underground city of science. The lighting and air quality were pleasant throughout. I had to keep reminding myself that I was underground as I breathed better than in most hotels I've been to.

"Keep your helmets on," said Jeff. It was at that moment that I realized that only our group had the helmets on the entire time, everyone else encountered didn't have any headgear. Strange. But I decided to follow suit and not ask any questions, for now.

After about a good ten minutes of walking there was a gate angled slightly to the left from the main hallway. As we came upon it both

Jeff and Shauna took out keys and put them in the key lock in the door simultaneously. As they did that they each entered a code. The door opened. We entered another hallway. As we did, the door closed behind us and Jeff and Shauna used their keys to now lock the gate, and entered codes again. It appeared that we were now hermetically sealed inside this chamber. I heard air pressure change as we walked along it. There was some kind of air current exchange. This hallway was a perfect concrete arch shape, not a randomly carved out cave tunnel. We kept walking and came upon another door. The door at the end opened automatically, like an eyelid, we ventured in, it shut itself right after. We were now in a seemingly perfectly spherical room that contained a sphere itself which I assumed measured about 20m in diameter suspended in the center. Like a giant disco ball in the middle of the ceiling. We were all standing around a perimeter with a railing in front of it and a massive hole filled with water right in the middle below the sphere. The water seemed crisp clear, the light from above penetrated at least three meters down but there was still no sight of the bottom. I looked around. There was lab equipment, sensors, lights flashing, massive computer screens all around. A few individuals sat in front of them, some stood, and some looked up at the sphere and took down measurements and recordings apparently seeming to know what they were doing. They were all wearing see-through helmets as well and full bodysuits. The perimeter platform was at least 5 meters wide all around, so there was ample space for chairs, tables, writing and measuring platforms and equipment, etc... Everything seemed surreal, cool, scary and scientifically wonderful all at the same time. As I stopped gazing around I looked back at my group and realized that they were all looking at me with subtle smiles on their faces. They were waiting for me to stop my wondrous amazement.

CHAPTER 20

NEW HORIZON, SAME OLD CHEMISTRY

"Welcome to NTLab Marcus. The most isolated, ziplock sealed and classified chamber of the BNOLAB. This fine sphere of a chandelier hanging above us all in the middle is what's called the detector. This one, in particular, is a modified and specialized version of the BNO Neutrino Detector, which is a water Cherenkov detector dedicated to investigating elementary particles called neutrinos. I'll let you read about who Pavel Cherenkov was in your own free time. The short version is that this type of detector was designed to provide revolutionary insight about the production of neutrinos in the core of the Sun and to extend previous results by measuring three reactions of solar neutrinos. BNO was designed to determine whether the currently observed solar neutrino deficit is a result of neutrino oscillations. The detector is unique in its use of heavy water as a detection medium, permitting it to make a so-called solar model-independent test of the neutrino oscillation hypothesis by comparison of the charged and neutral current interaction rates. Hence the massive pool of water beneath. The neutrino experiments are still ongoing in other chambers of this underground cave and five of these spheres are scattered all around. The detector above has been modified and put to a different use, to study something else that we are about to elaborate upon."

"How deep is the pool?" I asked. I really wanted to go for a swim in it.

"50 meters." said Jeff. "Now I'm sure you have plenty of other questions as well don't you Marcus?"

At one point I had all the questions, there were tens of them. At the time I swore to myself that I would write them all down so I didn't forget them when the right time came. Then I figured, driven primarily by my laziness, that there is no need to write anything down since the things unfolding in my life were so monumentally Earth-shattering and trailblazing that I would surely remember everything in the given moment, my mind was that sharp and interested. Having four people staring at me and putting me on the spot as they had like I was being forced to perform in an x-rated adult production I was beginning to realize that I was dead wrong. All of a sudden I didn't know what I wanted to say or inquire about. I was having a stress brain freeze right then and there and the more I focused the more the ice in my head hardened.

"What is all this? And how did I get randomly selected to join Tredarious? What's so special about me that you thought would make me a good fit in your society?" finally came out of me like squeezing dried up glue from a tube.

"For a second there we thought you actually needed to jump into the pool of water behind you to clear your head, hahaha." said

Shauna and we all broke out laughing. I laughed, long and uncontrollably and it felt good. After several moments the laughter wound down and Jeff started speaking.

"Well Marcus, in all honesty, I don't know about how 'purely' randomly it happened seeing as how your wife and her family have been a part of us for years." Yeah, no shit Sherlock I thought. "But still, how did we officially decide to bring you onboard right? After all a lot of the members are married and have families with people that never get initiated and are none the wiser about their partner's membership."

"Right, that was the angle that you played when you made me believe my father was a member. And my mother was apparently clueless, and had been for years. Knowing my father, I fell for it."

"Precisely. We have cases like that which are real Marcus." replied Shauna.

"All except mine." I replied. And as I did I felt a ping of that entire episode with Alicia sear its way through my gut. Slowly inching its way up like a bad case of heartburn. They all lied to me, manipulated me. Alicia, Jeff, Shauna, all of them. I really felt like having a cigarette, and becoming the smoke produced escaping and blending into the surrounding air.

"We will more than make up to you that whole unpleasant experience." said Jeff as he gently leaned into me. Right, the whole 'you will not regret this' propaganda. Whatever. They lied, and I should never forget it. I kept thinking of what my parents would say right now if they could see me. I was suddenly missing my mommy.

"Anyways, your wife had great hope and faith in you Marcus." Jeff now continued "She would bring you up often in conversations, much more so than our other members who have wives and husbands outside of our society. She would insist sometimes almost eerily that one of these days, weeks, months, years, you would do something to show that you are worthy of joining us. That your inquisitive nature and perpetual boredom of all things 'regular' would make us recognize you as one of us. And you did. It took all of us by quite a surprise actually how correct she was. And we know you did it all on your own, she didn't steer you in any way. Well…for the most part."

"How exactly?" Let's get the fuck right to it already I thought. I was sick and tired of the bullshit listening to roundabout fairy tales of yore and fantasy.

"Your research on death. And why we die. And how you researched it. And what you…stumbled upon."

"Ok. And what was so special about it? Are you telling me that no one else out there in your sea of screening for people to potentially join your society never did similar research? Human beings are generally obsessed with death and why we die, no? I'm sure countless people are reading about it, especially the ones that have a terminal illness." I replied.

"Similar type research yes, but in details and angles of approach, conclusions, vastly different. Your whole research theme Marcus was basically centered around one theme. A theme that nobody else even came close to singling out. See people can research and talk and write emails about any topic out there. And we'll listen in. And 99 out of a 100, sorry, more like 999 out of a 1000 times this will all be trivial curiosity research. Very superficial. Nothing to write home about if you will. But in your case, it wasn't the topic so much as was the theme and realizations on that topic that made you stand out. Made you relate to us."

"And what was that theme?" As I asked that for a second I thought that they would look at me like an idiot, recognize that I'm actually clueless as a doorknob, that what they thought about me was untrue and that I should be kicked out of this society immediately and catapulted out of this mine shaft in earnest. Again and luckily for me, Jeff was quick to answer before I got too excited and made a run for the bathroom.

"The theme you uncovered Marcus, or were suspecting so to speak, is that it makes no sense, really, for humans to die. Any living species. For the body to age, to break down, to stop repairing itself and to cease all function and to start disintegrating. Biologically speaking that is. Actually, it makes about as much sense as a human body to randomly decide to not heal a simple scratch or to never heal a sore or achy muscle or piece of tissue. Which is only a case with certain diseases, not with otherwise healthy tissue. That is the theme you uncovered. You see anything in known existence, live or dead matter as classified by humans, needs two things to essentially continue existing or functioning more or less forever. Fuel and ability to repair itself. The reason why a star starts to die is that it runs out of fuel which powers its fusion processes. The reason why a car becomes junk is that eventually enough of its parts can't be repaired and it becomes garbage, even though we can keep putting fuel into it. It can't repair itself unless we change all of its parts. A human body, or any 'living' species on Earth, can find endless fuel supply in terms of food and sustenance, and every part of a living being's body has the inherent capability of repairing itself. So the eventual random cessation of the ability to repair makes no sense. You see my point?"

When you conclude that the previously branded 'farfetched' and 'implausible' was the actual reality and that the world based on sound logic and strong common sense is a farce. I was slowly starting to realize that the biggest hindrance in life was one's sanity. If one is insane than the horizons for thinking outside of the box are limitless and you can't get fazed by anything at all.

"It makes no sense?" I asked, squinting like a little boy being told for the first time that Santa doesn't exist.

"Well, no it doesn't. And you know it doesn't Marcus, you think so yourself. And that brings us here. When we first landed on asteroid Ryugu and started analyzing some of the samples brought back, we began to realize, coincidentally, that there is a high probability that the concept and act of 'death' of all living species on Earth might be by technological design. That what 'death' itself really is, meaning the process of aging, gradual biological breakdown and so forth is in actuality just the ultimate terminal disease, not an inevitability."

"But hang on", I interjected. "Things do fall apart in nature, living or dead matter. Don't molecules, even atoms, disintegrate in certain circumstances?" I asked with a clever glee in my eye like my mother when she felt she made a good point. The only thing missing was me getting on my toes and yelling "Aha!".

"Right Marcus", replied Jeff. "But those circumstances are calamitous and destructive in nature. Earth has not had a 'hostile' environment, overall on its surface, for millions of years. That is how 'life' here was able to begin in the first place, otherwise it probably wouldn't have. And once life begins, there is no seemingly catastrophic event in Earth's day to day existence to suddenly cause death. It's not like meteors keep hitting our planet, or deadly pathogens emerge regularly that wipe out millions, or nuclear war. Therefore since the environment on Earth has clearly been 'friendly' for eons here on Earth for life to begin, develop, prosper and expand, it makes no sense, in this continuously 'friendly' environment and nothing out of the ordinary on the regular basis, for life to end. You see what I'm saying?"

"I see", I replied with, putting my best talk show host face on, all the while going through unimaginable clueless wonder unfolding between my ears.

I could hear the water in the pool beneath the giant Christmas ornament detector move and sway, that's how silent everything around us was.

"Let me explain further Marcus. Originally we landed spacecraft, some of which were designed specifically for Tredarious by the world's preeminent space agencies, to mine for minerals that we were led to believe were there after we obtained the rights to the asteroid through years of substantial and vigorous lobbying. We believed that it was a well worth investment and that the minerals we bring back we could then sell to all sorts of industries and customers out there and through these sales finance and fund our various clandestine research. When we landed on Ryugu and started drilling we uncovered that the asteroid is in actuality what's termed a rubble pile with about 50% of its volume being empty space. So we of course looked at this as a big slap in the face. We believed that our sensory equipment was malfunctioning, that our sophisticated detection equipment was infected by a software virus, or broken down. You have to understand we spent millions on this expedition."

"So it turned out that the rock was half empty and the other half was just plain old dirt and rubble? Nothing valuable?" I asked. I remember reading about the 'rubble pile' designation of Ryugu on the Internet. I could see why that would make them pissed off after spending millions on it hoping it would make them money.

"Well, the 50% 'empty' part you are absolutely right about Marcus. But you are not quite right about the other half. You see as we began to realize that we just blew a fortune for an expedition that was supposed to help with our finances we were so disillusioned that we simply couldn't just give up. We couldn't just leave with our tails between our legs, so we had our machines keep digging. Why the hell not we thought since we were already up there. We had to find something of value. Or worst case we would just tear the whole thing up. All our equipment had built-in cameras recording everything as we specifically wanted to take some shots of the hollow voids comprising the spongy rock. And well we found and recorded something quite different than we bargained for."

Sound of a rim shot would be fitting right about now. Otherwise, all we had was the orchestra of my guts rumbling away.

"What did you find?" how clever of me to ask I thought.

"We found chambers. Walls, rooms, some large theatre sized,

some football field-sized, some house-sized, we found equipment, hallways, the works. Going on for hundreds of meters. The voids in Ryugu as it turned out were, by all scientific accounts and common logic, compartments and chambers that could have only been conceptualized and constructed by some sort of intelligent design. A functional contraption if you will."

It was strange how practically completely normal and eerily calming hearing something like this was. I was stupendously overjoyed. I wanted to jump up and down and twirl and jump into the heavy water chamber next to me but I did not want to make a complete juvenile fool out of myself. And it was surely incredibly unsafe and harmful, radioactive perhaps.

"Are you telling me what I think you are telling me?" I asked practically completely giddy. They all smiled, but then retracted it as if not to make all this into some parody style situation.

"Yeah, we are fairly certain that what our astronomical journals identify as an asteroid named Ryugu is, by all objective and scientific accounts, a space ship. Of sorts. A spherical, large spaceship."

"My God, this is freaking unbelievable!" I screeched. "I mean holy shit, don't you think so? You're not shitting me are you, this is not some kind of a joke, for initiation purposes or something like that? Like 'haha' I bet you were hoping for something like this but tough luck we are full of shit." I was failing in keeping my restraint. I was a wet-nosed child.

"No, we are not kidding. And your excitement is warranted and most certainly not without just cause but please understand Marcus that we must tread with caution here. There is a lot more to this story and ultimately we are yet to determine how this will impact our present and future, and by 'our' I mean this planet's, although we may have already, possibly, broached the subject of how this discovery has impacted our long distant past." Jeff slowed down his words towards the end of that last spiel. I was listening but I still failed to realize why I should or would dim down my enthusiasm. Yes, yes, alien species, how will humans react, bla bla bla. Fuck it all I thought I was ready for a finding like this my entire life! I have been living for a revelation just like this! And on so many levels I always thought that I would end up getting it one day. And here it was. And I didn't care if the end of the world as we know it was approaching, this here alone was enough for me, something 'different'. True change in the present reality.

"So you have photographs of the interior? Chambers and all?" I asked like a kid in a toy store.

"Yes, thousands of them." replied Shauna. I guessed that the other two guys were most likely not allowed to speak at all, ever. Oh well.

"Can I see them?" I noticed I was actually rubbing my hands together like Mr. Burns as I asked that.

"In due time Marcus." said Jeff and continued. "As I was saying. Upon the discovery, shocking and awe-inspiring as it was, that the 'asteroid' was highly likely designed and built by intentional design we immediately began exploring with a different purpose in mind and taking samples. We used machinery to cut off pieces of the walls and brought them back for analysis. We have been analyzing them ever since. The pieces that we...could cut off that is. Some parts our 'tools' couldn't even make a scratch in. Other samples we got lucky were detached pieces our equipment could simply collect. A lot of them weighed tremendously for their size. The only materials that we could recognize were the ones of the most value here on Earth. Diamond, gold, platinum, silver, all sorts of traces of ruby, emerald. Everything else is unknown to us. You see there are numerous, and by that I mean hundreds of examples of elements, materials and com-pounds that we have never encountered nor recognize here on Earth. But the properties, in terms of robustness and complicated nature of the structure, atomic lattice, links, far exceed that of diamond for most of them. We've been analyzing them for years, trying to come up with names, figuring out the exact attributes, susceptibilities, and so forth. So far thirteen of the elements we found are irresistible to absolutely every and all possible laboratory torture tests we've put them through, using acids, exceptionally excessive temperatures, etc. And we are still attempting to break them."

Pause. I was processing and the rest of them kept looking at me and each other.

"At the risk of asking the obvious but is the ship empty? Meaning there is no one in it?"

"Yes, completely. No traces of anyone alive, or dead. The most common thing we saw throughout the chambers is what can only be described as massive laboratories."

"Laboratories?" I asked.

"Yes, laboratories. Chemical, mixing chambers, monitoring and measurement equipment. Endless pipes and massive vials made of same materials mentioned above. The most astounding thing is, the lab seems to be operating as we speak. It is completely self-reliant and it is...functional. Also, there are no levers, buttons, handles, knobs, you know the usual aids for a human hand to use to do...anything. This thing seems almost to know what it's doing on a molecular level. It's functioning from inside out."

"So Ryugu is a massive spherical shaped space laboratory? That's...alive in a way??"

"Yes, a Non-Terrestrial Laboratory. Hence the name NTLab. This entire section of BNOLAB underground here in Bradbury is dedicated to studying it. Therefore the name NTLab, after that object in the sky, that we are observing." explained Shauna.

"So the name is for the...lab in the sky?"

"Yeah, we are studying the lab in the sky." said Jeff.

Cool, I thought. Super cool. I forgot all about my fears. I had absolutely no qualms about joining Tredarious at this moment in time. I thought of myself over the past few months and recalled all the times I felt doubtfull and I wanted to laugh at myself. These people are my friends, like-minded brothers and sisters, I belonged here. The world as I knew it was officially over. And good riddance. Concurrently I thought to myself of how clueless and oblivious most people in the world are in this very moment in time of the discoveries that I'm privy to be informed of. The feeling of 'above the rest' was unparallel. I was practically licking my lips.

"What else do you know?" I was antsy to find out more.

"Further to what we just mentioned throughout the ship there is no indication whatsoever that the craft was ever supposed to house anyone. There is nothing resembling sleeping or habiting quarters, bathrooms, private quarters, chairs, desks, kitchens, no traces of food or sustenance, preparatory chambers. Nothing. The entire thing is kind of like an unmanned lighthouse, programmed to be perfectly independently functional without any living thing working it. We can't find any doors whatsoever. So there doesn't appear to be any compartments for engines, fuel cells, machines, nothing. And we found none of those things. That's why we concluded that it seems to function on a sub-molecular level."

"Unbelievable" I muttered. Jeff continued.

"As I was saying the pieces, segments, materials and components we brought back, biopsied, broke down into elements. There are several samples that we can't even break down yet. They seem...solid to the core if you will. No matter how far down to basic element size we attempt to reach there doesn't seem to be any structure of atoms or molecules, only monolithic and uniform matter. Another thing, peculiar as all the rest I suppose. Radiometric dating used to determine the age of this structure determined that based on materials up there that exist here on Earth, the precious metals we did discover and the ones we recognize, the object is at least one million years old. However, the unidentified materials and elements that the object is made of gave no conclusive results. There were no radioactive impurities, no radioactive isotopes, no indication of decay at all, and most of them we couldn't break down with any method here on Earth. Those materials could essentially, based on their completely monolithic structure as far down as we go and no emittance of any radiation, no breakdown, nothing to give us any hint or clue about them, be as old as the Universe itself I suppose. Or...immortal. In existence since eternity. Infinitely old."

Probably for the first time in my entire life I was paying perfect, uninterrupted attention to every single word, nuance, comma, that I was being told. No ADHD whatsoever. Had I paid this kind of attention to my engineering profession both while in school and during work I would have aced all of my exams and have opened up my own engineering consulting company by now.

"Do you have any indication of how long this object has been up there for? Orbiting Earth." I asked.

"Well, it was discovered in 1999 by astronomers with the Lincoln Near-Earth Asteroid Research at the Lincoln Lab's Experimental Test Site near Socorro, New Mexico, US. Its orbit around the Sun varies anywhere between 0.96 and 1.41 astronomical units, or distances from Earth to the Sun. It has a minimum orbital intersection distance with Earth of 95,400 km. That much we know for sure. Based on the properties we've mentioned, we have no way of determining how old the object itself truly is or how long it has been next to Earth. Some of its properties and materials seem immortal, others, ones we recognize, at least a million years old, as I mentioned. It is possible that the object in its original form was only comprised of properties and materials which we don't recognize and that the ones we do have only been later additions to the object. Perhaps they were brought on-board from Earth, as constructional add-ons. So maybe the whole reason the object has any compounds we recognize was due to this fact. It has morphed, been transformed from its original state. By whom, we don't know, or whether that stipulation is correct. Otherwise, the object behaves perfectly like so many of the other asteroids circling Earth in irregular orbits. It has camouflaged itself well."

"How is it possible that only by going in did you determine that it is in reality not an asteroid? The satellites couldn't see that from the outside?"

"No, as it turns out the entire exterior is perfectly covered by layer several meters thick of space dirt, rocks, random comet debris, dust, same as on any other asteroid. The assumption is that it picked up these things due to its gravity and traveling through the Universe for God knows how long. So from the exterior, from its movements and behavior it fits perfectly into our neighborhood asteroid family."

They all looked at each other and then Jeff kept speaking.

"As I mentioned there are no traces anywhere on Ryugu that it has ever been navigated, operated or accessed by any living entity onboard. It seems to be a completely self-reliant machine since times immemorial. However, there are a couple of other things that we observed which are fascinating if not unsettling to say the list."

Silence.

"No need for pause Jeff, I'm fairly certain that all things considered I'll handle anything else you throw my way." I grinned coyly as I said that. We grimaced like commandos wanting to look all tough.

"I have no doubt Marcus. So, our observations indicate that although the object is seemingly self-reliant, it is receiving a steady and strong radio signal. We are unsure as of yet how this signal influences the object. Maybe it is remote controlling it. Perhaps remote power supply as well. Unless the object somehow harnesses the energy of our Sun, or something else unorthodox. Our studies thus far are inconclusive. The signal itself is coming from a highly unlikely location and region of the observable Universe. It is not from another Star system or another galaxy which we suspected initially, and which most Earth-based Universe observations focus on. Instead, it is coming from a region of Universe about 10 billion light-years away which contains very little if any galaxies. However, this region does contain large amounts of dark matter and dark energy, the rest of it is simply...nothing at all. Empty space. A giant void. This region is known to astronomers as the Eridanus Supervoid. This structure was discovered in 2005, is roughly 1 billion light-years in diameter and is quite possibly the largest known single 'object' in the observable Universe as we know it."

In that very moment I had to admit to myself that I had no idea what a Universal supervoid is. But as Jeff said it and as he accompanied it with an explanation it made sense that something like that would exist in the Universe. I knew of dark energy, dark matter, I knew most of the Universe was comprised of it. So I imagined these supervoids he was mentioning, entire regions of barely any galaxies at all in them, were probably numerous. I literally had no follow-up question to ask, as what he was saying was self-explanatory.

"Interestingly enough the supervoid was discovered shortly after discovering Ryugu."

"Why do you find that strange?" I asked.

"Well, I'm not entirely sure if that's what I'm trying to say. It could be random enough I suppose and not particularly coincidental. On the other hand, we have been observing the night sky with thousands of telescopes both Earth-based and orbiting ones for decades, we thought we had all the orbiting asteroids and meteors mapped out as well as the map of the observable Universe. Especially the map of the observable Universe. And then within five years, we discover a major asteroid as well as a humongous empty hole in the night sky which were apparently there all along."

No words in the modern dictionary can describe properly the magnitude of anything in the Universe. I always thought that during all my amateur hobby reading about astronomy. The numerical value of light-years I've just been provided with more or less had no proper meaning. 1 billion light-years across. You listen but you don't properly hear or grasp. Whatever...the...fuck that all meant.

"Unreal," I said just to add something.

"So what are the thoughts here? Have you guys come up with any conclusions or we are just swimming in speculation and wonder?" I went on.

"Speculation and wonder. Aside from the factual observations we've told you about." said Shauna.

And then I asked one more thing.

"You said the object appears as though it is a non-terrestrial laboratory. What did you mean by that?"

"Glad you asked. That's the cherry on top. Marcus, have you ever seen the Frankenstein movies? Any of the iterations?" asked Shauna.

"I've seen the one with Raul Julia and the one with Robert DeNiro. In that order." I answered.

"Well remember Victor Frankenstein's lab in either movie? The lab was geared towards creating life correct? All sorts of contraptions, potions, electrodes, for the sole purpose of bringing Victor's monster to life." Shauna kept talking now.

"Correct." I added, redundantly for some reason.

"Well, this lab is the opposite of that and on a vastly larger scale. It is seemingly organized to bring about death."

"What? Are you saying this thing is getting ready to destroy us?? Destroy Earth??? It's like a Death Star or something? Well if that's the case why the hell are we just sitting here? Why don't we nuke it and be done with it?" I came back forcefully. And foolishly.

"Haha, sorry Marcus. I'm not trying to make fun of you it's just that your reaction is more or less the same across the board from anyone who was told the exact same information."

A slight pause, then Jeff went on, as I stared at them with my eyes bulging out.

"You see, it's not geared towards wiping us off the Earth or destroying the Earth itself. By studying it over the past twenty years we've come to determine that it is geared towards initiating the processes of ending individual human and biological life on Earth… eventually. It's not in the business of creating random accidents, disasters or events which can also cause death or species to go extinct. Meaning it initiates and aids tissue and organ degradation, gradual incapability of organic tissue to repair itself and of its eventual death, complete breakdown. It in no way impacts any living species' on Earth from procreating, there is nothing up there indicating that it's trying to sterilize the whole planet, but it would appear to be there to ensure that any living, individual entity on Earth…ages and dies. It's a life circuit breaker. Remember our discussion from before. The same protein and enzyme and gene in the family of Clk1 which is one of the most important catalysts of aging, the inability of cells to repair themselves and of eventual cell death? This chemical compound is produced, through intricate chemical processes on Ryugu. And not just it. Other proteins and chemical compounds all of which we know for certain cause the process of death are also manufactured, on an industrial scale on that 'asteroid'. Remember your Internet searches Marcus? Remember how many times you've used the word 'programmed', how you could never quite get to the bottom of why these processes all of a sudden kick into high gear, prevent further cell repair, etc…and lead to death? You could never make sense of it? Well, the path and pattern of your searching lead you to us, our society and that road leads to that thing up in the sky. That is why you are here. This is what all your research, talking to professors, myself included, was all about. To get this answer. Even though you didn't even know it existed. That was the link between us and why you joined. That is why you were finally picked. You hit the nail right on the head Marcus. And the bafflement that has troubled biologists for ages as it turns out is a carefully programmed sequence."

"So, what exactly are you saying? And please explain it to me like you're explaining it to a dog" I said as I stood there mouth wide agape and slightly drooling, so my analogy was not far off.

"What we are saying is that after studying this object for twenty years, in-depth, with a team of hundreds of scientists, analyzing its behavior, materials, mode of operation, age, mechanics of movement we are beginning to conclude that; a) the object is unimaginably ancient. Or at least the core components of it. And b) one of its main purposes is to control life spans of all living things on Earth. The object appears to be the reason why anything on Earth dies. You more or less asked the question yourself Marcus. Why die? Why do we die? Is there a need for it? Is it inevitable? Is it random? The answer is more than likely no. We die because we are programmed to die. By the Ryugu death lab. And all the chemicals and chain reactions cooked up up there are, essentially, the cocktail for death. Why and by whom and for what purpose we are no closer to figuring out twenty years on."

My head was spinning like a merry-go-round. It seemed evident that Jeff was antsy to just spill out the rest of the spiel he wanted to tell me, to get it all out in the open and for me to start tumbling the information in my head like a dryer. And that is exactly what I was trying to do. I had a hard time sifting through it all, information laundry was all tangled up in my head.

"Well, how exactly is the lab making us die? I mean maybe it just contains similar chemicals that are involved in biological processes here on Earth, but maybe its a coincidence, maybe it's doing something else up there with those chemicals. Is it not possible?" I asked, trying to put on my most intellectual of all faces and tones of voice. Like when I'm dead drunk.

"We thought that as well in the beginning. But, things sort of converged throughout the years. Almost anything biological here on Earth, or anything a body contains, whether a human body, or an animal body, or a plant body, cell body, bacteria body, we can't really get to the bottom where its comprising components came from. All we can ascertain with confidence is that life forms evolved over eons. Chemicals kind of came together and started forming more and more complex biological organisms. But, no one has a clue where the 'spark' of life comes from. To this day. For example, if you and I put together the same mix in a lab that comprises an amoeba, that compound would sit there doing nothing. It would never start resembling life or acting 'alive'. Yet mother nature puts all these elements together and adds a bit of seasoning called...spark of life, for the lack of better words, and a dog's breakfast of chemicals, fluid and plasma becomes a living organism. However, we can conclude, with fair confidence, that elements involved in the process of dying and in this case, all the catalysts of death of a living organism that we are aware of, 'aging' being one of them, are being synthesized on that ball up in the sky masquerading as an asteroid. More than likely there is no one terminal bullet, all of them work together as a Molotov cocktail to bring end to life on Earth to any given species. We've studied it for twenty years now. Chances that those compounds do anything else is minimal to none. There is seemingly no other purpose for them within the biological realm. There is one more thing that is helping us connect the dots of Ryugu's influence on our biological demise. We've, quite accidentally actually, picked up traces of all of the compounds we are discussing on Ryugu up in our atmosphere. One of our shuttles coming down from Ryugu collected samples by pure chance in its vents upon descent. We were analyzing the air intake in the combustion chambers of the ship, regular maintenance. And we found those compounds. We were dumbfounded. Therefore it is more than likely that Ryugu is dispersing the chemical compounds created by it through our atmosphere down to Earth. Depending on what age you or anyone wishes to bestow upon Ryugu, then Ryugu has been doing this since any life on Earth began."

Wow. I wish I was drunk.

"So, without asking a million sub-questions" everyone laughed at me when I said that, "with everything you've mentioned and considering its age is it possible that Ryugu also created life on Earth as well? Provided the 'spark' as you would say? To this petri dish of an experiment called life on Earth."

"Nothing we've found on Ryugu gives any indication of it possessing any building blocks of life. Only of biological death. We keep doing extensive research on the object as we speak, and will continue for years to come, but in the twenty years thus far, nothing to do with any creation is present on that thing. At least anything humans have ever considered related to foundations of life. Unless we are missing something. Or have been severely in the wrong thus far regarding our understanding of conception, genesis, and the rest. Thus far, Ryugu only appears to be the kryptonite to all biological life on Earth, nothing more. Also, we have no clue how it regulates why some species on Earth live to a certain age while others live to a vastly different age. One would think anything living on Earth would have the same life span. But it doesn't. Like so many other things, that is another mystery. It's probably likely that different organisms on Earth simply react towards eventual death with different timeframes to the chemicals produced on Ryugu. You see it's all about the concentration of Clk1 and other molecules which it produces, not the immediate exposure to them that causes death. New life needs years, decades to build up the quantity of these elements to eventually stop the ability to continue functioning and existing. So likely, different organisms cease function at different quantities, hence the different lifespans of various species on Earth, but we are far from certain."

Mystery like human emotions and behaviour I thought to myself. And why humans always do the opposite of what is needed. When you are strong they come to you with compassion. When you are weak they come to you with a sword. Maybe I should have researched that fucking phenomenon and what is up with that bullshit instead of this death business. Oh well, that can be my obsession next time, if I get out of this hole in one piece.

"It is quite possible that in the same manner we've discovered the true nature of Ryugu that we will do the same with other objects orbiting Earth in the near vicinity. Or on Earth. Or beneath Earth. Objects and contraptions that serve unusual and extraordinary purposes that were made by intelligent design and efforts. This discovery opened up a sea of possibilities."

"Who else is aware of this discovery? Worldwide?" I asked.

"So far the US and the Russian governments know. Something like this was completely impossible to hide from them. They basically contacted us shortly after our discoveries and all they said was that they want to be informed as we progress with our research. They knew everything we discovered literally within days as we discovered it, without our organization saying anything to anyone. It is anyone's guess what information access methods they possess, or whether there are moles within our organization, but it is clearly evident that they are very much in the know. Have been from the start. The casual manner of their approach towards us makes us think that they could potentially know more, and have known for years before our expedition, about this object in particular, and other related matters. However, all of our attempts to work jointly with them and for them to disclose more about what they know and have known have failed. They made it perfectly clear that they do not wish to be a partner, but simply overseers who demand progress reports. Tredarious has security and military assets, but nowhere near that of the US and Russian governments. So, as we wish to continue research unimpeded, we are deciding to comply. By doing so we have experienced no hindrance from either country. They simply let us do our thing. As long as we report back."

Figures I thought.

"So...the only true terminal disease is death itself? Aging as a programmed disease? Not as a random biological inevitability?"

"It would appear to be that way Marcus. Most other diseases and illnesses can and will be able to get cured. With time anyways. And more advanced means. Pretty much all of the most severe terminal illnesses we are currently aware of will not forever be terminal. Except death itself."

"So is there a plan for curing... aging and cell death? Couldn't we simply destroy this thing up there and live forever?" I asked.

"We have very specific instructions thus far from our 'overseers' that the object up there stays intact and functional. Many entities here on Earth want to learn a helluva lot more about it before any further action is taken. Especially any action destructive in nature. If humans could even do it any damage with the means we currently have available. And knowing how 'benevolent' world powers are they probably want to endlessly explore its destructive potential and power. Whatever the reason, we do not seek to contribute any intransigence. No, we have been working on something else instead. Plan is to get to know the intricate mechanisms and workings of cancer in much greater detail."

"What? You are going to try to figure out the machinations of that sphere up there in the orbit by attempting to...cure cancer?"

"Nobody is talking about curing it. You see cancer's properties all contradict and defy every and all mechanisms of aging and death that 'normal' cells, as we call them, go through as they degrade and cease function. Cancerous cells appear immune, completely, to the terminal intentions and processes of that object up there in the orbit. They have evolved, we don't know exactly when and how long ago, to resist aging and death. They have figured out how to live, multiply and repair themselves endlessly."

"Come again? They are evolved?? Cancer is a freaking plague! What are you talking about?" I said.

Smirks all around.

"People die of cancer no? And you are trying to tell me cancer is some kind of advanced version of living tissue? It seems completely counterintuitive and quite frankly insane." I said.

"Nothing living on planet Earth dies due to cancerous cells per se. The only reason why 'cancerous' cells cause death, aggressive and fast demise in most cases of cancer-related deaths, is because they react in a very rapidly accelerating chemical reaction with the non-cancerous cells around them. The two types are highly incompatible. Cancerous cells appear to destroy non-cancerous cells because cancerous cells deem the non-cancerous cells as the diseased tissue. Diseased with the side effects and chemicals of 'death' produced on Ryugu. Diseased in the sense that non-cancerous cells degrade and die and cannot continually repair themselves. So cancerous cells treat non-cancerous cells as infected tissue. Capiche Marcus?" said one of the two dudes whom I just heard speak for the very first time. It was like hearing a dog suddenly gain the ability to converse.

I stared a bit in amazement in the same wide-eyed, mouth agape way that infant babies in loaded diapers do moments before they are about to puke.

"So...help me out here. Cancer cells are actually the good cells and non-cancerous cells are in actuality bad cells since they stop repairing, degrade and die? They are like a flawed product? Rejects? So seemingly healthy living species that don't have...cancer are actually made up of flawed tissue?! Tissue infected by bi-products created on Ryugu?"

No one said anything. For a second I thought that maybe I was naked or had noticeably peed myself and that was distracting them.

"Well, you might be oversimplifying a bit Marcus. 'Good' and 'bad' are trivially exaggerated terms. Cancerous cells seem more valuable based on their traits. It's like platinum versus bronze analogy or nuclear fusion versus burning fossil fuels for energy production comparison. All methods work, albeit with varying degrees of efficiency and longevity based on their methodology and product traits.

Platinum will outlast bronze due to its higher quality attributes. Here, the difference is immortality versus demise."

"Hang on a second. Now we are comparing cancer cells to fucking platinum??" I just realized I swore for the first time in front of these people. They could shoot my ass and boil me in the pool of heavy water next to me and no one would know a thing about it. Wait, Alicia would be suspicious. Alicia, what the hell was she up to right about now? I could have sworn I saw her car in the parking lot when we first arrived above. Anyways, I kept ranting.

"You know, from what I know cancer cells don't know when to stop dividing. Endless cell divisions. So how can that be termed 'perfect' or high quality? That is why they destroy all other healthy tissue around it! And isn't their cellular nucleus different or altered or something??"

"Cancer cells only keep dividing seemingly 'endlessly' as you say Marcus because they recognize that they are surrounded by vastly higher numbers of non-cancerous cells that they deem need to be destroyed due to their 'terminal' attributes. Therefore they divide into eternity, as they are severely outnumbered. So they alter their cell structure, become more resilient to destruction in the process and continually divide, and fast, to overwhelm the much higher numbers of 'enemy' cells around them they need to destroy."

"But how did you figure out that.." I began. Stopped. Blurted out: "So, what you are trying to tell me is…cancer as a cure for death?? The cancerous tissue is evolution? Or, the original and intended way to be? 'Right' way to be? It will help us fight this thing up in the orbit?" I was frantically trying to catch up, firing off questions in a seizure style and intensity.

"More on that later. First Marcus, our immediate directive is to land a first human being up on Ryugu." interrupted Jeff as he grabbed me by the shoulder.

The notion that a sudden jolt of fear might actually end my

life became instantaneously overwhelming. It was an unmistakable feeling that the continuously stretched umbilical tether holding me to my mothership of sanity over the past few months had officially snapped.

INTERMISSION